Histo▮

for the IB Diploma

Political Developments in the Americas after the Second World War 1945–79

Nick Fellows and Mike Wells
Series editor: Allan Todd

Cambridge University Press's mission is to advance learning, knowledge and research worldwide.

Our IB Diploma resources aim to:
- encourage learners to explore concepts, ideas and topics that have local and global significance
- help students develop a positive attitude to learning in preparation for higher education
- assist students in approaching complex questions, applying critical-thinking skills and forming reasoned answers.

CAMBRIDGE
UNIVERSITY PRESS

CAMBRIDGE UNIVERSITY PRESS
Cambridge, New York, Melbourne, Madrid, Cape Town,
Singapore, São Paulo, Delhi, Mexico City

Cambridge University Press
The Edinburgh Building, Cambridge CB2 8RU, UK

www.cambridge.org
Information on this title: www.cambridge.org/9781107659957

First published 2013

Printed in the United Kingdom by Latimer Trend

A catalogue record for this publication is available from the British Library

ISBN 978-1-107-65995-7 Paperback

Contents

1 Introduction

This book is designed to prepare students taking the Paper 3, Section 9 topic, *Political Developments in the Americas after the Second World War 1945–79* (in HL Option 3, Aspects of the History of the Americas) in the IB History examination. It introduces the main political developments of the period, and examines a selection of the political systems that characterised the Americas at the time. This book also explains some key political terms and concepts.

Between 1945 and 1979, most countries in the Americas faced social, economic and political challenges. This book investigates how the USA dealt with these challenges immediately after the Second World War and beyond. It also examines the survival of democracy and unity in Canada, with specific consideration of the situation in Quebec. The different responses to the political, social and economic issues facing states in Latin America – many of which were not democracies – are investigated. The book discusses the causes and consequences of the Cuban Revolution and populist rule in Argentina under Juan Perón. Finally, it examines the effects of military rule in much of the Americas, with case studies focusing on El Salvador, Paraguay and Argentina.

Activity

Democracy was the form of government in North America in the period 1945–79. It is therefore important that you have a clear understanding of the characteristics of democracy and how it functions. Using the internet and any other resources available to you, research the different types of democracy. What are the main characteristics of this form of government? What circumstances can cause the success or failure of a democracy?

Themes

To help you prepare for your IB History exams, this book will cover the main themes and aspects relating to *Political Developments in the Americas after the Second World War 1945–79*, as set out in the IB *History Guide*. In particular, it will consider the following key areas:

- **The domestic policies of Truman and Eisenhower in the USA.** How far did their policies meet the needs of a changing society in the USA? How effectively did they cope with the transition from war to peace? How successful were their policies in dealing with anti-communism and civil rights?
- **Kennedy, Johnson and the Great Society in the USA.** How successfully did these presidents maintain the living standards of the American people? How far were the policies of the New Deal continued and developed? Why did the powers of the president and federal government increase?
- **Domestic policies in Canada from Diefenbaker to Clark, and the causes and effects of the Quiet Revolution.** To what extent did domestic policies transform Canada? Why was the Liberal Party so dominant in Canadian politics during the period under study? What was the Quiet Revolution? What impact did this have on Quebec? Why did Trudeau dominate Canadian politics for so long?
- **Perón's rise to power and rule in Argentina.** How did Perón achieve political dominance? How successfully did he modernise Argentina? Why did he fall from power?
- **The political, social and economic causes of the Cuban Revolution and its impact on the region.** Why was Castro able to rise to power in Cuba? What was the impact of the Cuban Revolution on the Americas?
- **Castro's political, economic, social and cultural policies in Cuba.** How successful were Castro's domestic policies? How were minorities treated in Cuba? How effective was Castro's rule?
- **Military regimes in Latin America.** Why were military governments established in much of Latin America from the 1950s to the 1970s? Why and how did the military dominate El Salvador and Paraguay? How did military rulers in these countries remain in power for so long? How effectively did the military regimes in Argentina maintain power?

Theory of knowledge

In addition to the broad key themes, the chapters contain Theory of knowledge (ToK) links, to get you thinking about aspects that relate to history, which is a Group 3 subject in the IB Diploma. The *Political Developments* topic has several clear links to ideas about knowledge and history.

Political historians still debate why democracy survived in some parts of the Americas – notably in Canada and the USA – and not in others. They also question why some Latin American states experienced revolution, why populist or military regimes were installed in others, and why some of these regimes survived significantly longer than others. In addition, the period 1945–79 witnessed an increased role for governments in domestic affairs. This can be seen particularly in social welfare policies such as Lyndon Johnson's 'Great Society' in the USA, and in Lester Pearson's welfare programme in Canada. Such policies also have links to ideas about knowledge and history.

When trying to explain the policies implemented by leaders, the motives of those leaders, and the success or failure of the policies themselves, historians must decide which evidence to select and use to make their case and which evidence to leave out. But to what extent do the historians' personal political views influence them when selecting what they consider to be the most important or relevant sources, and when they make judgements about the value and limitations of specific sources or sets of sources? Is there such a thing as objective 'historical truth'? Or is there just a range of subjective historical opinions and interpretations about the past, which vary according to the political interests of individual historians?

You are therefore strongly advised to read a range of publications giving different interpretations of the theory and practice of the various policies attempted by the states discussed in this book. This will help you gain a clear understanding of the relevant historiographies (see Further reading, page 235).

IB History and Paper 3 questions

In IB History, Paper 3 is taken only by Higher-level students. For this paper, it specifies that three sections of an Option should be selected for in-depth study. The examination paper will set two questions on each section – and you have to answer three questions in total.

Unlike Paper 2, where there were regional restrictions, in Paper 3 you will be able to answer *both* questions from one section, with a third chosen from one of the other sections. These questions are essentially in-depth analytical essays. This is reflected in the time available, which is 2 hours 30 minutes. It is therefore important to study *all* the bullet points set out in the IB *History Guide*, in order to give yourself the widest possible choice of questions.

Exam skills

Throughout the main chapters of this book, there are activities and questions to help you develop the understanding and the exam skills necessary for success in Paper 3. Your exam answers should demonstrate:

- factual knowledge and understanding
- awareness and understanding of historical interpretations
- structured, analytical and *balanced* argument.

Before attempting the specific exam practice questions that come at the end of each main chapter, you might find it useful to refer *first* to Chapter 9, the final exam practice chapter. This suggestion is based on the idea that if you know where you are supposed to be going (in this instance, gaining a good grade), and how to get there, you stand a better chance of reaching your destination!

Questions and markschemes

To ensure that you develop the necessary skills and understanding, each chapter contains comprehension questions and examination tips. For success in Paper 3, you need to produce essays that combine a number of features. In many ways, these require the same skills as the essays in Paper 2. However, for the Higher-level Paper 3, examiners will be looking for greater evidence of *sustained* analysis and argument, linked closely to the demands of the question. They will also be seeking more depth and precision with regard to supporting knowledge. Finally, they will be expecting a clear and well-organised answer, so it is vital to do a rough plan *before* you start to answer a question. Your plan will show straight away whether or not you know enough about the topic to answer the question. It will also provide a good structure for your answer.

It is particularly important to start by focusing *closely* on the wording of the question, so that you can identify its demands. If you simply assume that a question is *generally about this period/leader*, you will probably produce an answer that is essentially a narrative or story, with only vague links to the question. Even if your knowledge is detailed and accurate, it will only be broadly relevant. If you do this, you will get half-marks at most.

Another important point is to make sure you present a *well-structured* and *analytical argument* that is clearly linked to *all the demands of the question*. Each aspect of your argument/analysis/explanation then needs to be supported by carefully selected, precise and relevant own knowledge.

In addition, showing awareness and understanding of relevant historical debates and interpretations will help you to access the highest bands and marks. This does not mean simply repeating, in your own words, what different historians have said. Instead, try to *critically evaluate* particular interpretations. For example, are there any weaknesses in some arguments put forward by certain historians? What strengths does a particular interpretation have?

Examiner's tips

To help you develop these skills, all chapters contain sample questions, with examiner's tips about what to do (and what *not* to do) in order to achieve high marks. Each chapter will focus on a specific skill, as follows:

- Skill 1 (Chapter 2) – understanding the wording of a question
- Skill 2 (Chapter 3) – planning an essay
- Skill 3 (Chapter 4) – writing an introductory paragraph
- Skill 4 (Chapter 5) – avoiding irrelevance
- Skill 5 (Chapter 6) – avoiding a narrative-based answer
- Skill 6 (Chapter 7) – using your own knowledge analytically and combining it with awareness of historical debate
- Skill 7 (Chapter 8) – writing a conclusion to your essay.

Some of these tips will contain parts of a student's answer to a particular question, with examiner's comments, to help you understand what examiners are looking for.

This guidance is developed further in Chapter 9, the exam practice chapter, where examiner's tips and comments will enable you to focus on the important aspects of questions and their answers. These examples will also help you avoid simple mistakes and oversights which, every year, result in some otherwise good students failing to gain the highest marks.

For additional help, a simplified Paper 3 markscheme is provided on page 223. This should make it easier to understand what examiners are looking for in your answers. The actual Paper 3 IB History markscheme can be found on the IB website.

This book will provide you with the historical knowledge and understanding to help you answer all the specific content bullet points set out in the IB *History Guide*. Also, by the time you have worked through the various exercises, you should have the skills necessary to construct relevant, clear, well-argued and well-supported essays.

Background to the period

The United States

Throughout the 1930s, there was an unparalleled expansion of the role of the federal (central) government in the USA. To deal with the effects of the Great Depression, President Franklin D. Roosevelt introduced a wide-ranging programme of reforms known as the New Deal. This included extending subsidies to farmers, financing large-scale public works, reforming banks, giving money to the arts, passing trade union reforms and generally making the government responsible for 'relief, recovery and reform'. Such efforts challenged traditional beliefs in free enterprise and economic *laissez faire* ('let it be'), and Roosevelt was accused of becoming a dictator by his political opponents and those who disliked government intervention in the economy.

In 1939, the Second World War broke out in Europe. Up to this time, the USA had adopted a largely isolationist attitude towards European affairs, although this policy did not extend to Latin America or the Caribbean – or to the Pacific, in which region the USA was competing with Japan. However, it soon became clear that this would be a global conflict. Even before the USA officially entered the war in 1941, Roosevelt signed the Atlantic Charter – a document outlining the Allied vision of the post-war world. The Japanese attack on the US naval base at Pearl Harbor in December 1941 brought the conflict to the Pacific. Shortly afterwards Germany declared war on the USA, allowing a full-scale US commitment to the Allies' fight against Hitler.

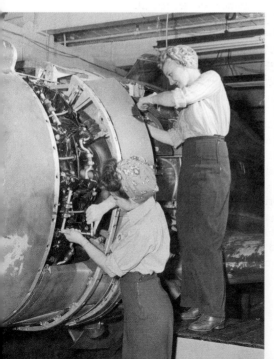

The Second World War transformed the US economy and had a profound effect on US society. Unlike many European countries, the US escaped direct damage from bombing raids. The need to produce war material resolved the problem of overcapacity in US industrial production that had characterised the Depression years. Total production (GNP) rose from $101 billion in 1940 to $215 billion in 1945. Unemployment – which had not dropped below 1.5 million in the New Deal years – virtually ended.

Female workers in a wartime aircraft factory in the USA in 1942

By 1945, the federal government directly or indirectly employed half the US workforce. The federal budget had risen from $8.5 billion in 1940 to over $100 billion. Goods were rationed, prices were controlled, rents and wages were regulated, and federal bureaucracy had broadened to previously unknown levels. The USA's position on the world stage had also expanded. Throughout 1945, the US occupied large parts of central Europe and, later, Japan. As a result of this, the US was responsible for feeding millions of people across Europe and Asia. It was a leading power in the United Nations and had global responsibilities.

In the space of about 15 years, therefore, the USA underwent dramatic changes in both domestic and foreign policy, and there were many who welcomed the changes. However, not all Americans were enthusiastic about these developments.

- Traditionally, the power of the federal government was limited in comparison with that of individual state governments, but this had now changed. Many Americans wanted a greater balance between federal and state control.
- Many people felt that the taxes and controls on economic activity were essentially un-American, and some even claimed that they were communist in nature.
- As the US economy boomed in the post-war years, cities grew. Some people felt that this had caused an erosion of traditional small-town values.
- The role of women and African-Americans began to change, and many groups regarded this as an unwelcome development.
- Membership of labour organisations rose dramatically during and immediately after the war, as people hoped there would be improvements in working conditions and wages. Between 1945 and 1947, there were a great many strikes.
- More generally, there was a feeling that people wanted life to return to 'normal' after the difficult years of the Depression and the Second World War.

Canada

In the early years of the 20th century, the Canadian economy relied heavily on the export of agricultural goods. As a result, the country was severely affected by the Great Depression, when the price of these goods declined dramatically. Recovery was slow, and the economic situation in Canada began to improve only when the Second World War broke out.

Canada emerged from the war a prosperous nation. By 1945, GNP had more than doubled from its pre-war levels. In addition, Canada had the third largest navy in the world and the fourth largest air force. The war strengthened the political and economic ties between Canada and the USA, and the countries signed two key defence agreements: the Ogdensburg Agreement (1940), which established a Joint Board to integrate defence, and the Hyde Park Declaration (1941), which co-ordinated the two nations' war efforts. Critics such as Donald Creighton have argued that the Second World War brought Canada too far into the USA's sphere of influence, particularly economically. The links between the two countries continued in the immediate post-war period, as Canada courted US investors.

Ultimately, it was this close relationship that brought Canada into the Cold War, which developed almost as soon as the Second World War was over. William Mackenzie King, the Canadian prime minister from 1935 to 1948, preferred an isolationist policy. However, it was clear that staying out of a conflict in which the US was so deeply involved was not an option for Canada. Therefore, although this book focuses on domestic policies, an awareness of Canada's key role in the 40-year Cold War is necessary in order to gain a clear understanding of domestic decision-making.

Domestically, Canada experienced both turbulence and prosperity in the post-war years. Union membership and the number of strikes increased, but prices were low and incomes rose. The war had provided employment opportunities for women, but as men returned from the conflict women were expected to go back to their traditional roles in the home. Canada's population boomed, increasing by 50% between 1946 and 1961. The social changes caused by this population growth were most noticeable in the development of a new, suburban commuter lifestyle, as Canada shifted from being a producer to a consumer society.

Central and South America

Although the Great Depression badly affected the economies of most states in Latin America, the effects were not as sudden or as devastating as they were in the USA or Europe (especially Germany). The Depression did not lead to the immediate collapse of democracy in Latin America – where it existed – nor did it destroy capitalism.

Like Canada, many nations in the region were dependent on agricultural exports, and their markets shrank as the Depression took hold. This put great pressure on existing political systems, and many governments were overthrown in military coups as the failure of an import–export model of growth discredited the ruling political élites.

However, many Latin American regimes were under pressure even before the Depression. The economic downturn simply reinforced existing trends of nationalism and authoritarianism, and accelerated the decline of liberalism. Although some of the regimes that emerged seemed at first to be democratic, many of them soon switched to more authoritarian methods of rule.

The Depression caused many states in Latin America to consider alternative economic models, including fascism, corporatism, Soviet-style planning and the US-style New Deal. Some countries attempted to forge closer links with European nations in order to safeguard their export market, but others embarked upon – or accelerated – a policy of import substitution industrialisation (ISI, see page 16). This gave them greater economic independence and made them less reliant on either the USA or Europe. This change often affected a country's social structure, as agricultural exporters lost their dominance to urban labour, which grew in influence as more jobs were created for the expanding working classes.

When the Second World War broke out, the USA began to seek more military and political allies in the wider Americas, turning away from the ruling élites on which it had traditionally relied. Even before the US joined the war, it sought military bases in the Caribbean and on the Atlantic coast of South America, which guaranteed accessibility to raw materials such as rubber. The USA also hoped to win promises from other countries in the region to join the US if it entered the war – or at least to maintain their neutrality in the conflict, to prevent Germany and its allies gaining a foothold on the continent. The USA was largely successful in these aims, and most nations – with the exception of Argentina – supported the Allies during the Second World War.

After the war, as the Cold War developed, the USA tried to persuade Latin American states to cut ties with the Soviet Union, and many did so. However, some countries felt a respect for the USSR – a former ally – not only because of the huge human cost it had endured as a result of the Second World War, but also because of the apparent effectiveness of its communist system. As poverty grew more widespread in Latin America, and the gap between rich and poor widened, many nations were drawn towards communism, most notably Cuba.

State governments played an increasing role in post-war economic development in the Americas. At the same time, agriculture declined, with the result that more people moved to the cities. The ISI policies caused a GDP growth rate of 5–6% in the 1950s, but they also had political consequences. Increasingly, the working classes were seen as a threat to public order or were exploited by populist politicians such as Juan Perón in Argentina and Manuel Odría in Peru.

However, these developments did not mean that one type of regime dominated Latin America. There was a tendency towards authoritarianism, but democratic movements prevailed in countries such as Venezuela after 1958, and Costa Rica and Chile until 1973. In contrast, the military regime in Paraguay lasted for nearly 40 years under Alfredo Stroessner and his successors. Change was the most common pattern. In Bolivia, Brazil, Chile and Uruguay, democracy was replaced by military regimes, while Argentina frequently switched between the two.

Activity

Before you begin to work your way through this book, try to find out a bit more about the Americas in the 1930s and 1940s. Were the experiences of the Great Depression the same in all nations in the Americas, or did they vary? What involvement did each country have in the Second World War?

Terminology and definitions

In order to understand the political developments that took place in the Americas after the Second World War, you will need to be familiar with a few basic terms – both technical terms and those relating to political ideologies.

Cold War

This term is used to describe the conflict between the capitalist USA and the communist USSR, which began soon after the end of the Second World War and lasted until 1991. During this time, these two superpowers tried to extend their influence and spread their ideologies throughout the world. Although there was no actual fighting between the two countries, both powers became involved in conflicts elsewhere in the world, most notably in Korea and Vietnam. In Europe, there were disputes over the communist takeover of much of Eastern Europe, but Berlin became the centre of the conflict. The Cold War spread to the Americas with the Cuban Missile Crisis of 1962, and the US often supported dictatorial regimes in other parts of Latin America in the hope of preventing the spread of communism.

Communism

In theory, communism is a social and economic system in which all significant aspects of a country's economy are socially owned and managed. This means that they are run by the state or by local communities or co-operatives, rather than by the wealthy classes.

Such social ownership is intended to create a classless society, in which wealth is shared out equally among the people. These ideas came to prominence with the writings of Karl Marx and Friedrich Engels. However, as practised in the Soviet Union, communism became a form of state socialism in which political power lay with the Communist Party and the economy was organised on the basis of central planning and collectivisation.

Democracy

There are a number of types of democracy, but the most common form – and the one seen in practice in the Americas – is representative democracy, whereby the people elect representatives to rule on their behalf. In this system, the participation of the people is limited to the election, and it should be noted that in several Latin American states, 'the people' were only a small minority. The most common form of representative democracy is liberal democracy. In this form, there are checks on the power of the state so that the freedom and rights of individuals are preserved. There are regular, free elections and society is organised along capitalist lines.

Democrats

The Democratic Party is one of the two main political parties in the USA. Democrats are usually in favour of some measure of welfare reform and support government intervention in the management of the economy.

Executive

This is the branch of government that makes policy. In the USA, the Executive branch is made up of the president, the Cabinet and departments headed by secretaries. In Canada, the Executive comprises the prime minister and the Cabinet.

Federal

In the context of North America, 'federal' refers to the national government based in Washington (USA) or Ottawa (Canada). This is where the main government departments are situated. However, both nations have a federal structure, which means that power is shared between the central government and the government of each state (USA) or province (Canada). These state or provincial governments have substantial powers, and they can often be an obstacle to federal legislation. States in the US are run by a governor; provinces in Canada are headed by a premier.

The House of Representatives and the Senate

The legislative body in the USA – Congress – is made up of two chambers. The House of Representatives is the lower chamber. Each state elects a number of representatives depending upon the size of its population. One-third of members are elected every two years. The Senate is the upper chamber. Each state elects two representatives (senators), who serve six-year terms.

Import substitution industrialisation

Import substitution industrialisation (ISI) is the term given to the economic policies pursued by a number of countries in the post-war period. It involved the state-led replacement of foreign imports by domestic production, thus reducing foreign dependency. In order to protect the new local industries, countries introduced a protectionist policy to reduce imports. The state controlled economic development through the nationalisation and subsidisation of industries.

Junta

This term is used to describe the situation in which a group of military officers, rather than an individual, rules a country.

Populism

Populism is a system of government in which the wishes of the people are the main influence on the actions and policies pursued by the government. Populist regimes claim to support the needs of the ordinary or working people against the corrupt rule of the élites. Under such regimes, populist leaders make direct appeals to the people, and claim that they can solve their problems.

Republicans

The Republicans are the other major political party in the USA. Republicans are usually more conservative than Democrats, and lie on the right wing of the political spectrum. They tend to believe in low taxes and minimal government intervention. The word republican is also used to refer to a system in which a president, rather than a hereditary monarch, is the head of state.

Supreme Court

The Supreme Court is the highest court in both the USA and Canada. It safeguards the country's constitution and decides whether laws are constitutional or not. In the 1930s, both the governments of the USA and Canada had legislation rejected by their Supreme Courts.

Summary

By the time you have worked through this book, you should be able to:

- understand how effectively governments in the Americas dealt with the social, economic and political challenges they faced in the period after the Second World War
- explain the reasons for the expansion of social provision in many countries in the Americas
- understand how effectively the governments of the USA and Canada dealt with the challenges to unity and society
- show a broad understanding of why the period 1945–79 saw an increased role for the state in many American nations
- understand why different countries adopted a variety of responses to the political, social and economic challenges they faced
- explain the appeal of Juan Perón's populist regime and the dangers it posed to the élites in Argentina
- understand why communism was able to spread to the Americas and how it influenced the policies of countries in the region
- understand why the military played such a significant role in the politics of many Latin American nations, and why military influence lasted so long.

2 The USA: the domestic policies of Truman and Eisenhower

Key questions

- What did Truman achieve during his presidency?
- Why did Eisenhower win the 1952 presidential election?
- To what extent did the Republicans pursue a distinctive domestic policy?

This chapter deals with how the administrations of Truman and Eisenhower responded to the needs of US society after the Second World War. The Great Depression, the New Deal and the war itself all resulted in profound changes in US government and society. During the 1930s, Roosevelt's New Deal attempted to tackle the effects of the Depression, but it was really the massive rearmament programme brought about by the Second World War that returned the US to full employment. The war also caused considerable economic and social change, and afterwards the US public expected its leaders to maintain the prosperity their country had enjoyed during the war years. On the international stage, the USA became a world power with global responsibilities. This affected domestic policy, as US leaders had to find the resources to maintain military forces as well as continuing the economic and social reforms begun before the war. This chapter considers the personalities and backgrounds of Truman and Eisenhower. Their main domestic policies are outlined, as well as how they dealt with the transition from war to peace. This section also discusses the economic and social issues that arose in the post-war years, including the wave of anti-communist feeling and the development of the civil rights movement.

Overview

- As Roosevelt's vice-president, Truman assumed the leadership when the president died in office in April 1945. In doing so, he stepped into the shoes of one of the USA's most popular leaders. Roosevelt had introduced radical domestic changes in the 1930s, and brought the US into a foreign war that had made the country a global superpower.
- To begin with, Truman's domestic policy remained faithful to the ideals of Roosevelt's New Deal, and the new president maintained high levels of government control to ease the transition from war to peace.
- A surprise victory in the 1948 presidential election kept Truman in office. After this, he introduced the ambitious Fair Deal programme, but many of these domestic reforms could not be put into practice.
- Attempts at further reform were hindered by the USA's involvement in the Korean War, which began in 1950. By 1952, Truman's popularity was declining and the USA was in the grip of anti-communist hysteria.
- The Republican Eisenhower was elected president in 1952, but he did not pursue conservative domestic policies to the extent that some in his party wished. He presided over the period known as the 'Red Scare', but he did not openly condemn extremism.
- Like Truman, Eisenhower found himself distracted from domestic issues by foreign affairs as the Cold War developed. Despite this, Eisenhower managed to maintain and even extend certain social policies throughout the 1950s.

- Civil rights emerged as a main issue in US political and social life from 1954, and in 1957 Eisenhower pushed through the first Civil Rights Act in over 80 years.
- Eisenhower did not run for re-election in 1960, and the Democrat John F. Kennedy defeated Eisenhower's vice-president, Richard Nixon, by a small majority.

What did Truman achieve during his presidency?

Truman's succession

Franklin D. Roosevelt died in office on 12 April 1945, while the USA was still at war. He was succeeded by his vice-president, Harry S. Truman.

Franklin D. Roosevelt (1882–1945) Born into a wealthy New York family, Roosevelt rose in Democratic politics and became governor of New York. He was elected president in 1932 and soon introduced his New Deal programme of reforms, a large-scale plan to use federal government resources to combat the effects of the Depression and bring about reform in US society. Roosevelt led the USA in the Second World War, but died in April 1945, shortly after beginning his fourth term in office.

Truman came from a family of farmers, and worked as a bank clerk as well as on the family farm. He joined the army and fought in France in the First World War, rising to the rank of captain. After the war, Truman used his army connections to get into politics, and he became a judge in Jackson County, Missouri, in 1926. This was an administrative rather than a legal post, and one of his major achievements was to build new roads in the county.

The Democratic Party in Missouri was dominated by a career politician – 'Boss' Tom Prendergast. In 1934, Prendergast backed Truman's campaign for the Senate, although at the time he won little attention from President Roosevelt. As a senator, Truman quickly earned a reputation for efficiency, and he got approval for a Senate committee on the National Defense Program to investigate poor performance by defence contractors. This role became a key part of the war effort after the US joined the Second World War in December 1941.

Truman was a loyal supporter of Roosevelt's New Deal policies, and his energy and honesty made him the Democrats' choice for vice-president in the 1944 election campaign. He had a reputation as a straight-talking, typical American and a good family man. In fact, Truman had not wanted the nomination and had little desire to be president.

The transition from war to peace

On taking power, Truman was aware that the unprecedented militarisation of the USA and the increase in government control of everyday life had become unpopular. Prices, rents, wages, the supply of food and raw materials, and the drafting of civilians into war service all contradicted US traditions of freedom and limited government power. Half the working population was employed directly or indirectly by the government, and 16 million US citizens had been drafted to fight for their country. Truman knew that the American people now wanted life to return to normal.

The Republicans began calling for an end to government economic controls as soon as the war was over. However, Truman feared that a sudden withdrawal of government contracts, subsidies and controls might result in inflation and widespread unemployment across the USA. Above all else, he wanted to avoid another economic depression like that of the 1930s.

Harry Truman holds up the Japanese surrender document, which marked the end of fighting in the Pacific, and the end of the Second World War

Influenced by New Deal policies, and anxious to avoid social and political unrest, Truman was careful to maintain government controls. In his 'hold the line' Executive Order of August 1945, he extended wartime federal powers to peacetime – particularly those of the Office of Price Administration (OPA), which set price controls and rents. In September 1945, Truman also proposed a programme to maintain full employment. This included a house-building programme and a rise in the minimum wage. The government provided loans for ex-servicemen to buy homes, and offered grants for both training and education.

Despite the wishes of the Republicans, therefore, there was no sudden end to federal economic controls, and the transition from a wartime to a peacetime economy was successful. Towards the end of 1946, prices began to rise significantly, but by this time economic activity was enough to ensure that wages and employment increased to keep pace with the price rises.

In the early post-war years, Truman also faced several foreign policy issues. He was more suspicious of Soviet leader Joseph Stalin than Roosevelt had been, and disliked the spread of Soviet power throughout Eastern Europe. Despite the rapidly developing Cold War, Truman's administration came under pressure to demobilise US forces and reduce the military budget. In the first year after the war, Truman reduced the armed forces from 12 million to 3 million. Eisenhower – supreme commander of the Allied forces in Europe during the war – famously claimed that the US had 'run out of army' by 1946.

Labour unrest

The Second World War led to an increase in the membership and status of labour organisations in the USA. These groups were determined that the gains they had made in wages and working conditions during the war should not be lost. By the beginning of 1946, as peacetime brought wage reductions and less favourable working conditions, major strikes began to take place in key defence industries such as coal, iron and steel, railways and electricity. At a time when the USA claimed to be facing a threat from the Soviet Union, such action was felt to be intolerable, and in May 1946 the government took control of the railroads. Truman then went even further, and asked Congress for powers to draft railroad workers into the army. The Senate blocked the proposal, believing it was a threat to the liberty of US citizens.

Truman also took control of the coal mines. Coal was essential to US power supplies and rail transport. When the United Mine Workers of America (UMWA), under its leader **John L. Lewis**, refused to honour an agreement negotiated by the government, Truman took Lewis to court and the union was fined for breach of contract.

John L. Lewis (1880–1969) Lewis was a major figure in US labour history and founded the Congress of Industrial Organizations (CIO), a federation of trade unions, in 1938. He was president of the United Mine Workers of America from 1920 to 1960. A major supporter of the New Deal, Lewis helped to get Roosevelt elected, but his popularity declined after he organised coal strikes during the Second World War.

Truman believed that the strikes threatened national security, and he took extreme measures to end this threat. Although the war was over Truman maintained a wartime mentality, believing that the USA continued to face a national emergency and that the government had a right to take whatever steps were necessary to deal with this. However, his actions cost him the considerable support of the unions, which had previously been allies of the Democratic Party.

In fact, Truman was not as anti-union as the Republicans – or even some members of his own party. However, he opposed the Taft–Hartley Act, which ended the closed shop policy (by which all employees in a business or factory had to belong to a trade union), banned political payments by unions and strikes by government employees, and made it illegal for union officials to be communists. The Taft–Hartley Act was made law in 1947, despite the president's opposition.

The midterm elections 1946

Despite his early successes, by 1946 Truman was becoming increasingly unpopular. Unions disliked his hard line; prices were rising and those soldiers still waiting to be demobilised were growing restless and resentful. The Republicans once more urged economic freedom. Under the slogan 'Had Enough?' they demanded a reduction in taxes and greater limits on government control. In the 1946 midterm elections the Republicans won control of Congress, and government now became a struggle between the Executive (the president) and the Legislature (Congress). The fact that Truman had not been elected president weakened him – there were even some Democrats who felt that he was ill-equipped to lead the country.

Truman tried to boost his popularity by proposing a series of social reforms in the New Deal tradition. In truth, the country could not afford to implement these reforms – and Truman knew it. However, he also knew that the conservative-dominated Congress would not approve the proposals, so he could portray himself as a reforming president working in the interests of the people, without having to follow through on the changes. He put forward plans for health and education reforms, and suggested more subsidies for farmers and a repeal of hostile labour legislation. As expected, Congress rejected all these proposals.

Civil rights

The increasing participation of African-Americans in vital industries and in the armed forces raised questions about their status in the post-war USA, and the National Association for the Advancement of Colored People (NAACP) experienced a dramatic increase in membership. The USA claimed to be the champion of freedom, and had fought a war against racist regimes, yet discrimination against African-Americans continued and laws dating from the 1890s still restricted their civil rights. African-Americans who had served in the armed forces had witnessed the greater racial tolerance in other countries, so when they returned from war service they found discrimination at home harder to bear. This resulted in an increase in incidents of racial violence.

As racial tension grew in the South, Truman established the Civil Rights Committee to investigate the issue. The committee's report recommended changes to end abuses, and in 1948 Truman proposed measures to end restrictions on black voting in the South and to make lynching a federal offence. This would prevent local police and judges allowing race crimes to go unpunished.

Southern Democrats were furious, and in 1948 a group of them set up their own party – the States' Rights Democratic Party, or 'Dixiecrats'. In the past, reforming Democratic presidents had often had to deal with an uneasy alliance of northern progressives and southern white supremacists, but Truman was determined not to be controlled by this faction of his own party. Instead, he pursued his agenda of reform in several ways:

- He ordered desegregation to begin in the armed forces.
- He banned discrimination in federal employment and in hotels in Washington, DC.
- He refused to give government contracts to firms that discriminated against African-American employees.
- He appointed the first African-American federal judge.

These measures lay within Truman's existing powers as commander-in-chief and head of the federal government. However, more general legislation depended on congressional approval, so further progress in civil rights was limited.

SOURCE A

We have reached a turning point in the long history of our country's efforts to guarantee freedom and equality to all our citizens. Recent events in the United States and abroad have made us realize that it is more important today than ever before to insure that all Americans enjoy these rights ...

When I say all Americans I mean all Americans ...

We must keep moving forward, with new concepts of civil rights to safeguard our heritage. The extension of civil rights today means, not protection of the people against the Government, but protection of the people by the Government.

We must make the Federal Government a friendly, vigilant defender of the rights and equalities of all Americans. And again I mean all Americans ...

Each man must be guaranteed equality of opportunity. The only limit to an American's achievement should be his ability, his industry, and his character. These rewards for his effort should be determined only by those truly relevant qualities.

Extract from a speech made by Harry S. Truman to the NAACP, 29 June 1947. From millercenter.org/scripps/archive/speeches/detail/3345

Activity

Read Source A and then answer the following questions.

1 What was Truman's concept of civil rights?
2 What actions did Truman take that show he was a 'vigilant defender of the rights and equalities' of African-Americans?
3 Is it fair to say that Truman offered more than he delivered on civil rights?

What obstacles were there to a more energetic civil rights policy in Truman's time in office?

Discussion point

Historian James T. Patterson takes a less than enthusiastic view of Truman's record on civil rights: 'Speaking for civil rights ... was not the same as taking decisive action. When it came to that, Truman moved slowly.' Patterson argues that Truman did not believe in integration and used racist terms in private. He also points out that Truman failed to issue Executive Orders against discrimination in the armed forces and civil service in 1948. It was only in 1954 that desegregation in the armed services was complete. Even then, there were few African-American officers.

Consider the view that by raising awareness of civil rights issues, and by proposing measures such as an anti-lynching law, Truman made a major contribution to civil rights. Then consider the view that all Truman offered was talk, an over-cautious attitude and a series of failed measures. Which case do you find more convincing?

The 1948 election

By 1948, Truman had implemented a number of successful reforms. For example, he had made several aspects of government more efficient. Congress approved the creation of a new Department of Defense, merging the old Departments of War and Navy. The National Security Council (NSC) was established, as was the Central Intelligence Agency (CIA). In the Cold War context, such measures were regarded as valuable streamlining. However, a proposal to create a Department of Health and Welfare was rejected by Congress, which was anxious not to further extend the state's control over its citizens.

Despite his successes, Truman also faced several difficulties. He took a hard line against communism abroad by launching the Truman Doctrine in 1947, in which he pledged US support for any country threatened by communism. The following year, the Marshall Plan was implemented, giving financial aid to war-torn Europe. In theory this was available to any European country, but in practice only the 'free' (capitalist) countries of Western Europe benefited.

The Truman Doctrine and the Marshall Plan clearly established the USA as a protector of the capitalist world against the spread of communism. Conservative elements in the US accepted this position, but those with more liberal political leanings regarded Truman's anti-communist policies as an open-ended and dangerous commitment to affairs beyond the USA's borders.

Conservative support for Truman did not extend to his domestic policies. Many objected to his liberal attitude on issues such as health reform and civil rights. Organised labour – one of the Democratic Party's main sources of support – was offended by Truman's actions over the labour strikes (see page 23), and southern Democrats were angry about his civil rights policies.

Increasingly regarded as too conservative by the liberals and too liberal by the conservatives, it seemed unlikely that Truman could win the 1948 presidential election. The Republicans had a strong candidate in **Thomas Dewey**, while the Democrats were divided between the Dixiecrats (see page 24) and the northern-based Progressive Party of America (PPA). The opinion polls were unanimous in predicting Truman's defeat.

Republican candidate Thomas Dewey (right) during the 1948 presidential election campaign

Thomas Dewey (1902–71) Dewey was a brilliant lawyer and the governor of New York from 1943 to 1954. With the strong support of US business interests, he ran in the 1944 presidential election campaign, but lost to the sitting president, Roosevelt. Moderate and articulate, Dewey seemed a sure winner against Truman in 1948, but his election campaign was not well run, and he suffered a surprise defeat. He later retired from political life and returned to his law practice.

The Republicans fully expected to win the election, and Dewey's campaign was conducted cautiously in order to maintain the status quo. In contrast, Truman launched a vigorous campaign late in the run-up to the election. He travelled up and down the country, giving spirited speeches in defence of his policies and attacking his opponents. In particular, he criticised the Republican Congress for blocking social and economic reform. Historian Robert Ferrell remarks that 'in 1948 Truman was for the first time in his life a dynamic campaigner'. Contrary to all expectations, Truman won the election and – crucially – the Democrats regained control of Congress.

Truman believed that his victory was due to support for his social reform programme, but many historians have argued that it was circumstances rather than personal popularity or support for his agenda that led to Truman's success in 1948. Four years later, facing stronger opponents, Truman decided not to seek re-election and the Democrats lost heavily. In addition, Truman's victory in 1948 was not decisive – he only gained 49.5% of the popular vote. However, he won without the support of white southerners, and this opened the way for greater civil rights reform. Truman also felt confident enough to relaunch his programme of social reform.

A triumphant Truman displays a premature headline in the Chicago Daily Tribune *in 1948*

What do you think was the main reason for Truman's election victory in 1948?

The Fair Deal

Formally announced in January 1949, but reflecting earlier policy statements, the Fair Deal had echoes of Roosevelt's New Deal of the 1930s. It proposed:

- more civil rights reforms
- unemployment benefits
- support for house-building
- federal aid for education
- tax relief for low earners
- a repeal of the Taft–Hartley Act
- a higher minimum wage
- help for the agricultural sector.

After 1948, Truman had enough support in Congress for some of these proposals to become law. A total of 800,000 houses were to be built by 1955, and the minimum wage rose from 40 cents to 75 cents an hour. Social Security was extended and a Displaced Persons Act allowed 400,000 refugees from Europe to enter the USA. The Hill–Burton Act approved federal and state support for public hospitals. However, much of the Fair Deal was blocked by an alliance of Republicans and Dixiecrat conservatives. More policies were proposed than achieved, but Truman kept alive the idea that government was responsible for the welfare of its people. In the 1950 midterm elections, however, the Republicans increased their seats in Congress once more, and the Fair Deal effectively came to an end.

There has been some historical debate about Truman's success with the Fair Deal. Conservative historians such as Larry Schweikart and Michael Allen argue that by raising the minimum wage, making an additional 10 million people eligible for Social Security benefits, and through federal slum clearance and housing projects, Truman successfully continued the New Deal of the 1930s. Many liberals agree with this view. In an address to Physicians for a National Health Program in 1999, Dr Karen S. Palmer claimed that Truman was more radical in his healthcare proposals than the New Deal had been: 'It was Truman who proposed a single egalitarian system that included all classes of society.'

An alternative modern view is that there was a lot of support for continuing the New Deal policies, but that Truman was not a driving force in their planning, and only offered limited leadership. The real influence came from the ongoing support for state intervention that had developed during the years of the Depression and the Second World War. In particular, the Republicans had accepted the reforms brought about by the New Deal, and Truman offered little that was distinctive.

SOURCE B

Admirers of Truman contend that he was ... a saviour of liberalism and the New Deal ... But Truman's role ... should not be exaggerated. Much more important in preserving the New Deal were political forces established before Truman took office. By 1945 most Americans had accepted Roosevelt and programmes such as Social Security.

Patterson, J. 1998. Grand Expectations: The United States. Oxford, UK. Oxford University Press. p. 164.

Some historians are sceptical about how much was really achieved by the Fair Deal. For example, Hugh Brogan questions the results of the programme, pointing out the poor quality of the new federal housing and the government's failure to pass a health bill, an anti-lynching law or a bill on fair employment practices.

Activity

Plan a short essay entitled 'How Important was Truman's Fair Deal?' In pairs, consider how you might deal with the issue of importance – was it important for what it actually achieved or important for what it stood for in post-war America? Write an introduction to your essay that sets out the issues about importance, and then consider what points you would use to support your argument.

Why did Eisenhower win the 1952 presidential election?

Truman's second administration

At the same time as Truman was pushing through domestic reform, he was also dealing with events in the wider world. This included Germany – and Berlin – which, after the war, had been temporarily divided into zones of occupation run by the USA, Britain, France and the USSR. In 1948, following the West's unilateral imposition of a new currency for its zones, the USSR blockaded Berlin. The USA and Britain co-ordinated the Berlin Airlift, by which supplies were flown into the besieged city. In addition, in 1950 communist North Korea invaded South Korea, drawing the USA into a three-year war in the region.

Truman's administration was also weakened by increasing concerns in the USA about the influence of communists in government and the so-called 'Red Scare' – a more widespread fear of communist infiltration in US society. In 1945, there were accusations that official US documents had been leaked to a left-wing journal called Amerasia.

In 1949, the USSR successfully exploded its first nuclear bomb – a development that many Americans believed was only possible because US atomic secrets had been passed to the Soviets by spies. This led to the arrest and execution of **Julius and Ethel Rosenberg** in 1953.

> **Julius (1918–53) and Ethel (1915–53) Rosenberg** Husband and wife Julius and Ethel Rosenberg were communist supporters. After Ethel's brother David Greenglass was arrested for spying, Ethel and Julius were named as co-conspirators in the wartime spy network. Despite protesting their innocence, they were both executed in 1953. Documents released in the 1990s confirmed Julius Rosenberg's guilt, but Ethel's involvement remains uncertain.

Communist supporters in the USA made up less than 1% of the population, but many people believed that they had infiltrated key positions in society. Truman responded to these concerns in 1947 by introducing a loyalty programme. The loyalty of all federal employees was assessed by the FBI and a civil service commission. Membership of certain organisations, including the Communist Party, was regarded as incompatible with loyalty towards the USA. In all, around 3 million people were investigated and 212 were dismissed from their jobs. In part, the continued spread of the Red Scare was due to the high-profile case involving a leading government advisor, Alger Hiss.

Hiss was an intellectual from a wealthy background who worked in Roosevelt's State Department and who had been a confidential aide of the president. In 1948, Whittaker Chambers, an editor at *Time* magazine, accused Hiss of being a Soviet spy. Chambers claimed that Hiss had recruited him and led him to take part in copying and hiding official documents that were then passed to the Soviets. Hiss was found guilty of perjury in January 1950 and sent to prison for five years.

Alger Hiss takes the oath before giving evidence to the House Un-American Activities Committee in 1948

In the wake of the Hiss trial, the government arrested leaders of the Communist Party for violating the Smith Act, which made urging the violent overthrow of government illegal. Then, on 9 February 1950, Wisconsin senator **Joseph McCarthy** made a speech in which he claimed to have a list of 250 communists working in the State Department. A committee was established to investigate this claim, and McCarthy made various accusations. However, Truman ordered the release of FBI files on the accused, which demonstrated no evidence of disloyalty or communist activity.

Joseph McCarthy (1908–57) McCarthy became a Republican senator for Wisconsin in 1945. In 1950, he began his campaign against suspected communists in the US administration. In 1952, he used the House Un-American Activities Committee, but had no real evidence to back up his claims. McCarthy began to lose credibility in 1954, after failing to supply any proof during a televised hearing. Despite this, he went on to accuse the army and even Eisenhower of communist activities.

The committee condemned McCarthy as a trouble-maker, but he had a great deal of support amongst Republicans in Congress, and the Red Scare continued. Truman opposed but could not stop the McCarran Act, a law against communist activity that even allowed for the establishment of concentration camps for subversives. In 1952, a congressional immigration act banned communists from entering the USA.

The 1952 election

In the midst of this growing hysteria, Truman was accused of being 'soft' on communism. In addition, he was associated with the lack of progress being made in the Korean War, poor handling of a steel strike in 1952 (in which he brought the steelworks under government control), and revelations of corruption in government. He was also accused of failing to halt the spread of organised crime in the USA.

As his popularity declined, Truman stood down from the presidential race. The Republicans chose the popular war leader Dwight D. Eisenhower as their candidate, with the anti-communist Richard Nixon as his running mate. They campaigned strongly against the Korean War and the two 'Cs' in government – corruption and communists. They also offered lower taxes and less government interference. All these strategies won the support of the people, and Eisenhower took the popular vote by a majority of 6 million. The Republicans also won a majority in the Senate and the House of Representatives, as well as a high number of state governorships. For the first time since 1933, the Republicans were back in power.

SOURCE C

Truman oversaw the conversion of the American economy from its World War II footing to one that emphasized both consumer and military production. Truman protected the New Deal and—with a rise in the minimum wage in 1949 and the enlargement of Social Security in 1950—built upon its achievements. He pushed forward the cause of African-American civil rights by desegregating the military, by banning discrimination in the civil service, and by commissioning a federal report on civil rights. Just as important, Truman spoke out publicly on the matter. Finally, Truman engineered one of the most unexpected comeback victories in American political history.

From millercenter.org/president/truman/essays/biography

SOURCE D

Some historians argue that Truman responded too slowly and weakly to Senator McCarthy and that his support for African-American civil rights was underwhelming. Finally, many historians contend that Truman grievously erred in 1946 and 1949 by advocating liberal initiatives that expanded the welfare state and increased government intervention in the nation's economy, for which a conservative polity had no appetite.

From millercenter.org/president/truman/essays/biography

Activity

Using the information given in this chapter and any other resources available to you, find as much support as you can for the two views expressed in Sources C and D. Which view do you find most convincing? Is it possible to combine the views?

Truman: an assessment

It is probably an exaggeration to suggest that Truman played no part in preserving or extending the liberal policies of the New Deal. In particular, he demonstrated decisiveness in his stand against the Dixiecrat opposition to civil rights reform. However, internal policy was limited by the US Constitution and the power of Congress to block legislation.

Truman raised key issues and tried to adjust domestic policy to encourage social change. More radical actions would have been rejected by Congress and occupied time that Truman could not devote to internal policies while dealing with wider Cold War issues.

Much of Truman's presidency was concerned with foreign rather than domestic affairs, and the Fair Deal was hindered by the need to allocate resources to the Korean War in 1950. Fears of communist infiltration within the USA grew from events in the wider world and revelations about espionage that were beyond Truman's control. He and other opponents of anti-communist hysteria found it difficult to stop the Red Scare gaining momentum.

Some historians have condemned Truman for not doing more, but it is also possible to argue that he battled courageously with opposition in Congress, and fought to protect the ideals of the New Deal in a hostile national and international environment.

To what extent did the Republicans pursue a distinctive domestic policy?

Dwight D. Eisenhower

The new president, Dwight D. Eisenhower, grew up in Abilene, Kansas, where his family ran a creamery. In 1911, he won a place at West Point military academy. As a military trainer, he did not see combat in the First World War, but from 1927 he worked as a military historian and then a planner. He rose to the rank of brigadier general, and was known for his skilful organisation in military exercises.

A leading Allied army general during the Second World War, Eisenhower later became NATO's first supreme commander. He dealt diplomatically with his fellow generals, and he had a good understanding of global affairs. The USA had a tradition of soldier presidents, and many felt reassured by Eisenhower. During the election, his role as a national hero secured him a lot of 'floating votes', but he also benefited from the splits in the Democratic Party and Truman's unpopularity in his last years in office. Eisenhower stood out as a man who had not previously been associated with local politics or played a part in government.

Eisenhower's views on social policy were different from Truman's, and he believed in individual responsibility rather than government backing. He was a supporter of big business (his first Cabinet contained eight millionaires) and distrusted large and powerful government. From the start, Eisenhower declared his aim of reducing federal influence and spending, in line with pre-war Republican policies. His Cabinet reflected that of the Republican governments of the 1930s – Hoover had also chosen people with business associations.

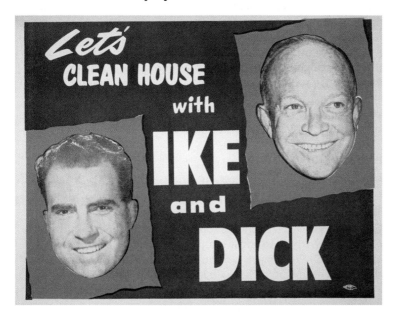

A Republican campaign poster from 1952, showing Eisenhower and Nixon

Eisenhower's style of government was based on his experiences in the army, and he relied on his Cabinet members, his advisors and his chief of staff **Sherman Adams**. He allowed his subordinates the freedom to implement policies in the way they believed best, rather than maintaining strict presidential control.

Sherman Adams (1899–1986) Adams was a Republican politician and former governor of New Hampshire. As a businessman, he believed strongly in controlling government expenditure and he encouraged Eisenhower in making changes to US economic policy. Adams resigned in 1958 after being accused of taking bribes.

Activity

Use the internet to find out more about the lives of Truman and Eisenhower before they each took office. Write a brief comparison of their personalities and backgrounds. Who do you think was better suited to the role of president?

The situation by 1953

Eisenhower inherited significant and costly foreign policy commitments from the outgoing administration. He also faced demands from the American public for greater economic freedom and a reduction in government interference in daily life. In addition, there was increasing pressure for social change, notably in civil rights. Perhaps most significantly, the new president had to deal with the same anxieties about national security and fears of communism that had played a key part in the Democrats' defeat. In practice, Eisenhower found he could do little more than Truman to control the tide of anti-communist agitation in the USA during his presidency.

Anti-communist hysteria

By the time Eisenhower took over, the anti-communist movement had grown even more influential. In private, Eisenhower was critical of communist hysteria in general and McCarthy's actions (see page 32) in particular. However, he did not openly condemn anti-communism. Under pressure from McCarthy's supporters, embassies burned books believed to have been written by communists. One Indiana school board even banned books featuring Robin Hood, claiming that the legendary figure was a communist, stealing from the rich. McCarthy was made chairman of the Senate Permanent Investigation Subcommittee, which allowed him even greater freedom to investigate suspected communists in public life.

In 1954, Congress banned the Communist Party. Increasing numbers of federal employees were dismissed as security risks – a total of 2400 in 1954 alone. McCarthy even began accusing Protestant clergymen of being communists, but still Eisenhower did not confront him. It was only when McCarthy attacked a respected army dentist that he began to fall from public favour. The trial was televised, and McCarthy's disrespectful behaviour and lack of proof angered both the viewing public and many people in positions of authority. His support declined, and by 1955 McCarthy had been publicly reprimanded by the Senate and alienated by Eisenhower's administration.

A cartoon from 1953 commenting on how McCarthy appeared to be controlling Eisenhower

Financial matters

During the 1952 election campaign, Eisenhower and the Republicans promised to reduce federal spending and taxation. After taking office, Eisenhower initially cut back on military spending, but there was no reduction in other areas of federal outlay. He failed to meet his aim of balancing income and expenditure, and there were budget deficits for most years in the period 1953–62.

Where possible, Eisenhower attempted to reduce the power of the federal government. For example, he sold off atomic material and production factories to private firms. He reallocated federal rights over offshore oil deposits to individual states. On the other hand, in 1956 Eisenhower implemented a large-scale federal road-building plan that was to be financed by taxes on fuel, cars and commercial vehicles. He reduced other federal taxes by $7 billion, but did not fulfil his stated aim of reducing Social Security. In fact, in 1954 Social Security was actually extended to self-employed people, and the minimum wage was raised from 75 cents to $1 an hour. Another key development during this period occurred in 1958, when the Defense Reorganization Act was passed. This allowed greater control over defence spending by an enlarged military establishment.

Agriculture

Throughout the 1950s, agricultural overproduction and low prices continued to be a problem. Eisenhower adopted a policy of cutting subsidies, but this only resulted in farmers producing more to try to make up for lost income from the state. In 1954, a law was introduced that allowed the government to purchase surplus crops for export and direct food aid abroad.

The president introduced the Soil Bank law in 1956, by which farmers would be paid not to use land for farming, but to put it into a 'soil bank' for future use. Eisenhower hoped that this would restrict production and maintain prices. Money was also given for land to be used for conservation rather than farming. However, agricultural prices continued to drop, and the farming community grew increasingly resentful.

The 1956 election

The Democrats made some gains in the midterm elections held in 1954, but Eisenhower had worked well with Congress and the Republicans did not feel this would be a significant threat to their success in the next presidential election.

For the 1956 campaign, Richard Nixon was once again Eisenhower's vice-president, although he was not the preferred candidate of the president himself. One significant difference in this election campaign was the amount of support the Republicans won from African-Americans. **Adam Clayton Powell**, an influential mixed-race congressman from New York, gave his support to Eisenhower and swayed many African-American voters. Many big cities – traditionally Democrat – also swung to Eisenhower. The sitting president won re-election with 58% of the vote. However, the congressional elections were a victory for the Democrats, who retained control of the Senate and gained seats in the House of Representatives.

Adam Clayton Powell (1908–72) Powell was a mixed-race clergyman and politician from a wealthy family. Initially a Democrat, Powell became the first non-white congressman to be elected in New York. He opposed segregation, but disliked the power that the white Southern Democrats seemed to have over the party, and switched to support Eisenhower in the 1956 election.

Eisenhower's second term

Throughout his second period in office, Eisenhower faced significantly greater opposition from Congress than he had before. A recession in 1957–58 resulted in a rise in unemployment and a drop in production. The president feared that introducing any kind of spending programme would cause inflation, but despite his objections Congress passed a $1 billion subsidy for housing and more road construction.

The Soviet launch of the world's first satellite, *Sputnik*, in 1957 also forced Eisenhower's hand. The USA could not be left behind in the 'space race', and he approved funding for the establishment of the National Aeronautics and Space Administration (NASA) in 1958. The USA's need to keep pace with the USSR in space technology also led to a new, federally directed educational curriculum and greater spending on education, in order to properly train future scientists and help the USA take the lead.

In addition – and partly in response to rising unemployment – the Republican government accepted increased investment in Social Security, and a new Department of Health, Education, and Welfare was established. Farm subsidies also increased. By 1959, the budget deficit stood at $12.5 billion, a fact that caused enough concern to bring a halt to reforms and federal spending.

Although there were some successes during Eisenhower's second term, such as the addition of Alaska and Hawaii as states in the union, fewer gains were made overall than during his first term. This was partly due to fears about inflation and overspending, but the increased Democrat influence in Congress was also a significant factor. In particular, the Democrats began winning greater public support under the leadership of their young rising star John F. Kennedy.

Civil rights in the Eisenhower presidency

Civil rights was already a key issue in American life when Eisenhower took office, and it was a problem that the new president could not ignore. To begin with, Eisenhower followed the moderate level of reform that Truman had started. He completed the desegregation of the armed forces. In addition, he appointed the first African-American, **J. Ernest Wilkins**, as undersecretary of labor, and more African-Americans won senior government posts. Eisenhower encouraged trade unions to admit African-American members, and he demanded the desegregation of interstate dining facilities on trains.

J. Ernest Wilkins (1894–1959) Wilkins was an eminent African-American mathematician and lawyer. He held several positions in Eisenhower's government before being appointed undersecretary of labor in 1954. Four years later, following a disagreement with the administration, he left this post and was replaced with an anti-civil rights conservative. Wilkins later played a prominent role in the US Civil Rights Commission.

Eisenhower's 1953 appointment of Chief Justice Earl Warren to the Supreme Court led to a major development in civil rights. A case heard by Warren in 1954 – *Brown v. Board of Education* – resulted in a ruling that segregated education in public schools was unconstitutional and should be ended 'with all deliberate speed'. There was a backlash in several southern states, which refused to honour the ruling and desegregate their schools. Eisenhower himself made no move to support the efforts at desegregation, and expressed doubts about the court ruling.

The Montgomery Bus Boycott 1955–56

While this issue remained unresolved, further civil rights events arose. Most significant of these was the Montgomery Bus Boycott, which occurred after an African-American woman, Rosa Parks, refused to give up her seat on a bus to a white passenger in Montgomery, Alabama. Parks was arrested and fined, inciting anger amongst the town's African-Americans.

Local activists were joined by the Baptist minister Martin Luther King in organising a boycott of local buses, which gained national attention. In 1956, NAACP lawyers won a Supreme Court ruling that transport segregation laws were unconstitutional. King formed his Southern Christian Leadership Conference (SCLC) in 1957, and became a leading force in the civil rights movement.

Little Rock, Arkansas 1957

By 1957, the situation over desegregated schooling had reached crisis point. In September that year, the governor of Arkansas refused to force the high school in the town of Little Rock to accept nine

Federal troops escort black students from their classes in Little Rock, Arkansas, in 1957

African-American students who had enrolled there. As the students tried to enter the school they were prevented by angry mobs of white segregationists. The event made headlines at home and abroad, and Eisenhower finally stepped in to enforce federal law. Paratroopers were sent to escort the nine students to their classes in safety, and the president made a televised address about the damage caused by such open displays of hostility and defiance of US law.

The use of federal troops to intervene in southern race relations had not been seen since the American Civil War (1861–65), and was undoubtedly a significant step forward for the civil right movement. However, racial tensions continued and Eisenhower was forced to intervene further to enforce anti-racism laws. In 1958, he ordered the release of two black boys aged seven and nine who had been imprisoned for 'rape' for 14 years for kissing a white girl.

The Civil Rights Act 1957

In 1957, Eisenhower proposed a Civil Rights Act that dealt mainly with voting rights for African-Americans. Despite Democrat opposition led by Senator **James Strom Thurmond**, the act was passed by Congress with the help of Texas senator and future president Lyndon B. Johnson. This act established the Civil Rights Commission to investigate discrimination in voting practices.

James Strom Thurmond (1902–2003) Thurmond was bitterly opposed to desegregation, and during the 1948 presidential election he stood against Truman as an independent southern segregationist candidate. He later became senator for South Carolina, and worked hard to block civil rights reforms in Congress. Originally a Democrat, Thurmond became a Republican in 1964 in opposition to that year's Civil Rights Act.

The commission found that only 1.5 million out of an eligible 6 million African-Americans voted in the South because of restrictions the states placed on voter registration. In response to these findings, the position of civil rights attorney general was created so that injunctions could be placed on anyone preventing African-American voters from exercising their rights.

The legislation proved difficult to enforce, however, and civil rights groups began to adopt more militant tactics to make their voice heard. In February 1960, the first sit-in protest over segregated lunch counters took place in Greensboro, North Carolina, when a group of African-American students refused to leave a white-only counter. Similar protests broke out elsewhere, often provoking a violent white reaction. The issue of civil rights seemed set to continue for many years.

Activity

Read the following views on how Eisenhower dealt with the issue of civil rights.

View A: *Eisenhower's actions over the civil rights issue were of great significance in promoting the growth of civil rights in the USA, and earn him a place among the great US presidents.*

View B: *Like most of Eisenhower's presidency, limited reaction to events characterised his policy towards civil rights. He was forced into action more to uphold federal authority than anything else, when in reality he had little sympathy for the policies he was supporting.*

Which view do you find the most appropriate and justified? In pairs, discuss the evidence for both views and come to a conclusion.

Theory of knowledge

The actions of historical figures

When passing judgement on the stature or greatness of figures from the past, should historians take account of the effects of their actions or the motives and attitudes behind them? If Eisenhower's actions resulted in progress in civil rights and helped end segregation, does it matter that he may have taken those actions reluctantly, and for reasons that had as much to do with exerting federal authority and promoting the USA's image abroad as protecting the interests of African-Americans?

The 1960 election

As Eisenhower's second term drew to an end, Republican hopes for staying in power rested with the vice-president Richard Nixon – now their presidential candidate. The Democratic nominee was John F. Kennedy. Although Kennedy represented a youth and energy that Nixon lacked, the record of the Eisenhower years ensured the Republicans a continued base of support, and a Democratic victory was far from assured.

In fact, the 1960 election was one of the most closely run in US history. The debates that took place as part of the campaign – televised for the first time – resulted in no clear winner. The results of the election itself were quite evenly matched. Only a small number of votes gave Kennedy the victory, and the Democrats lost seats in both the House and the Senate. For all this, though, the 1960 election ushered in a new era in US domestic policies.

The debates that took place between the presidential candidates Kennedy and Nixon were televised, marking a new era in political campaigning

Eisenhower: a summary

Throughout his presidency, Eisenhower was increasingly regarded as a leader who reacted to events rather than controlling them. However, the successes of his time in office should not be underestimated. These included:

- passing the first post-war Civil Rights Act
- continuing to offer financial support to farmers
- developing the transport infrastructure through bringing in a major highways programme
- developing and modernising the education system
- expanding Social Security so that, by 1961, 90% of Americans were covered in some way
- fulfilling some of his promises to return power to the states (although civil rights policies were believed by some to oppose states' rights)
- introducing an era of relative prosperity, with more cars, urban development and higher living standards.

Against these positive developments are the fact that unemployment remained high and there were many poor areas of the country. Civil rights was a serious issue, and when Eisenhower left power there were still unresolved problems in enforcing legislation and undermining deeply held racist attitudes. He had been driven into taking action by Supreme Court decisions and civil rights initiatives, rather than being led by his own policies and ideals.

In addition, Eisenhower had been unable to maintain the initiative and Congress had come under Democrat control. High defence spending had led to budget deficits and undue influence from heavy industry and the armed forces – and this was something Eisenhower warned about in his farewell address.

In this speech, Eisenhower's use of the term 'military-industrial complex' (see Source E below) was significant. By this, he was referring to the growth of the influence of US military leaders and the considerable armaments industry that arose during the Second World War – and which reached significant proportions during the Cold War. The political left feared this alliance between the military and capitalist powers, and for a Republican leader to use the term 'military-industrial complex' was a sign of the concern even in US conservative circles about the cost and potential dangers of the arms build-up.

SOURCE E

We must guard against the acquisition of unwarranted influence, whether sought or unsought by the military-industrial complex. The potential for the disastrous rise of misplaced power exists and still exists.

Extract from Eisenhower's farewell address, 17 January 1961. Quoted in Mooney, P. and Brown, C. 1979. Truman to Carter: Post-war History of the United States of America. *London, UK. Arnold. p. 69.*

End of chapter activities

Paper 3 exam practice

Question

Assess how successful the domestic policies of Truman and Eisenhower were in achieving their aims.
[20 marks]

Skill focus

Understanding the wording of a question

Examiner's tips

The first step in producing a high-scoring essay is to look **closely** at the wording of the question, and every year students lose valuable marks by failing to do so. It is therefore important to start by identifying the **key or 'command' words** in the question. In the question above, these command words are:

- assess
- successful
- domestic
- aims.

Key words are intended to give you clear instructions about what you need to cover in your essay – hence they are sometimes called 'command' words. If you ignore them, you will not score high marks, no matter how precise and detailed your knowledge of the period.

- **assess:** this is not the same as 'describe'; it asks for some analysis and judgements about relative importance
- **successful:** this also requires a judgement rather than just a description of what happened; consider how you will measure success
- **domestic:** the question clearly asks you to focus on internal policies, such as health, education, Social Security and civil rights, rather than on international issues and foreign policy
- **aims:** Truman's aims were related to the post-war situation in the USA and also to his beliefs in continuing the reforms of the New Deal; Eisenhower's aims were based on the changed situation by 1953 and the need to redress the balance between the role of the federal government and that of the individual in US life.

For this question, you will need to cover the following aspects:

- **Truman's aims as the US made the transition from war to peace:** the need to maintain economic control and to avoid a return to the high levels of unemployment of the pre-war years
- **the changes brought about by the end of the war:** hopes for a better and fairer society, such as greater civil rights for African-Americans and an extension of social services and health care
- **the achievements:** the beginnings of civil rights reform; the extension of social reforms; the transition from war to peace without economic decline
- **the limitations:** the opposition of Congress; resistance to change in the South; the need to divert resources to defence; problems that arose with trade unions; the distraction of the Red Scare
- **the situation when Eisenhower came to power:** the need to please his supporters by reducing federal spending and encouraging economic reform, without causing social and economic hardship by reversing the gains made by the New Deal and the Fair Deal
- **the problems Eisenhower faced:** ongoing anti-communist hysteria; the need for heavy defence spending as the arms race developed with the USSR; demands for civil rights and the poor image that southern resistance projected to the world
- **the achievements:** did Eisenhower keep a balance between ending government control and maintaining welfare spending? Did he deal well with the McCarthy campaign? Did he offer key support to civil rights by sending in federal troops?
- **the limitations:** did Eisenhower allow McCarthy's campaign to go on for too long? Was the Civil Rights Act too limited? Did he fail to prevent economic downturn and yet still maintain government spending at a higher level than he and many Republicans had wished? Did he fail to control the growing power of the military-industrial complex?

Common mistakes

Under exam pressure, two types of mistakes are particularly common, both of which can be avoided by focusing carefully on the wording of the question.

The first is to begin by giving some pre-1945 context, but then to continue writing a narrative account of the period, focusing on domestic events and the elections of 1948 and 1952. Such a narrative-based account will not score highly, as it will not explicitly address the question. Also, simply listing policies and their results is not enough to gain high marks. You need to make clear judgements about their success in relation to their aims.

The other – more common – mistake is to focus **entirely** on the dates. This will almost certainly lead you to write a general account of what happened during this period. Such a narrative-based answer will not score highly, as it will not explicitly address the 'assess' part of the question. Select **relevant** events from the period and use them to develop an argument that is **analytical** and uses **supporting evidence**.

Activity

In this chapter, the focus is on understanding the question and producing a brief essay plan. Look again at the question, the tips and the simplified markscheme on page 223. Now, using the information from this chapter, and any other sources of information available to you, draw up an essay plan (perhaps in the form of a spider diagram) that includes all the necessary headings for a well-focused and clearly structured response to the question.

Paper 3 practice questions

1   Compare the domestic achievements of Truman and Eisenhower.

2   Why did the Democrats win the presidential election of 1948 yet lose in 1952?

3   Why was civil rights such an important issue in US domestic politics between 1945 and 1960?

4   'There were more similarities than differences between the domestic policies of Eisenhower and Truman.' To what extent do you agree with this assertion?

5   How well did US governments between 1945 and 1960 deal with the social changes resulting from the Second World War?

3 The domestic policies of Kennedy, Johnson and Nixon

Key questions

- What was distinctive about Kennedy's style, ideas and policies?
- How much impact did Kennedy have on civil rights?
- What was Johnson's 'Great Society'?
- How far did Johnson fulfil his aims for the Great Society?
- What did Nixon achieve during his presidency?
- Which of these presidents had the greatest impact on domestic affairs?

This chapter deals with the ongoing responses of three different presidents to the issues faced by the USA in the post-war years, notably civil rights, the management of the economy to maintain living standards, and the preservation and modernisation of the reforms of the New Deal, the legacy of which continued into the 1960s and 1970s. This chapter also investigates the personality and governing style of each president. Kennedy's image was a major factor in his popularity, regardless of the realities of his domestic achievements. Johnson exercised greater personal control over administration and internal change than his predecessors, and federal legislation reached a post-war peak with his Great Society programme. Nixon was also deeply concerned about maintaining personal power.

Overview

- Kennedy was a dynamic young leader with a sense of idealism. During his presidency, the Peace Corps initiative took young Americans into service abroad, demonstrating a commitment to international freedom.
- This commitment was exemplified by Kennedy's visit to Berlin in 1961, after the communists constructed the Berlin Wall to separate eastern and western parts of the city. The fight for international freedom from communism took a less positive form the same year, with Kennedy's ill-judged support for an invasion of Cuba.
- Kennedy's preoccupation with foreign policy reached a climax when the USSR placed nuclear missiles in Cuba, and the president was forced to negotiate with the Soviets to avoid nuclear war.
- Kennedy spoke out in favour of domestic reform and support for civil rights, but little progress was made in these areas due to congressional restrictions and Kennedy's own preoccupation with foreign affairs.
- After Kennedy's assassination in 1963, Johnson assumed the presidency and attempted to continue the reforms his predecessor had started.
- Johnson introduced a large number of measures, but not all were successfully implemented. This was largely because foreign affairs once again distracted the president – this time in the form of the escalating conflict in Vietnam.
- Domestic reforms were scaled back as defence spending rose, but Johnson's Great Society measures were the most extensive since the 1930s, and their importance is still the subject of debate today.
- Nixon was a highly controversial leader. Innovative in foreign policy and by no means a reactionary at home, he became preoccupied with maintaining personal power – to the extent that he supported segregation in the South and condoned illegal spying activities on his political enemies.

- The Watergate scandal resulted in Nixon's resignation in 1974, and cast a shadow over his success as president. In the last decade, however, historians have begun to take a more sympathetic view of Nixon, in particular his domestic achievements and his attempts at securing peace in other countries.

What was distinctive about Kennedy's style, ideas and policies?

The new president

John F. Kennedy was born into a wealthy Catholic family, the son of a businessman and former US ambassador to Britain. He served in the navy from 1941 to 1945, and gained a medal for heroism. Kennedy was elected as a Democrat congressman in 1946, and became a senator in 1953. Kennedy had natural political charisma: he looked good on television, had an attractive wife (Jacqueline Lee Bouvier) and was an eloquent public speaker. After his election to the Senate, it quickly became clear that he was a likely candidate for president in the 1960 election, and his family's wealth allowed him a stream of publicity and access to a presidential-style staff to support him in a long campaign. In his speech accepting the Democratic nomination for the presidency, Kennedy famously stated, 'We stand on the edge of a New Frontier'. Many people interpreted this to mean that he would lead the US in breaking new boundaries in all areas of federal policy, but in reality the phrase was indicative only of a new energy after years of what Kennedy considered to be 'over-cautious' leadership.

Despite Kennedy's broad appeal, many voters felt that the solid achievements of the Eisenhower era should not be ignored. In a close-run election against the Republican candidate Richard Nixon, Kennedy won by only 120,000 votes out of 70 million cast. He took office in January 1961 as the youngest person and the first Roman Catholic ever elected president of the USA.

Activity

Use the internet to find some key images of and speeches given by Kennedy that set him apart from other political leaders. Create a short presentation entitled 'The Kennedy Image'. Try to find some sound clips that demonstrate Kennedy's effectiveness as a public speaker.

What were the key differences in style between Kennedy and older politicians such as Truman and Eisenhower? Why had style and personality become so important by 1960?

Kennedy and domestic policy

Although domestic policy featured prominently in Kennedy's election campaign, there was little mention of it in his inaugural speech in January 1961. At the time, the USA was engaged in a stand-off with the USSR over Berlin, as well as becoming increasingly involved in the conflict in Vietnam. In addition, the Soviets were supporting the communist regime in Cuba, and the US was losing its previously overwhelming lead in the arms race. All these factors made Kennedy believe that he would be judged by his approach to foreign affairs, and that foreign policy must be the key feature of his presidency. In private, Kennedy asked Nixon: 'Who gives a **** whether the minimum wage is $1.15 or $1.25 compared to something like Cuba?'

Events in the wider world made it difficult for Kennedy to prioritise domestic issues, but there were factors closer to home that also hindered progress in this area:

- Since 1946, presidents had a poor record of getting legislation through Congress. The US Constitution protected its citizens against an overly powerful Executive branch, and the House Rules Committee had established a strong group of conservatives that blocked discussion of reforming legislation.
- There was a strong tradition of 'states' rights', which stood against federal interference in matters that supporters felt were the responsibility of state governments.
- The Democratic Party contained a strong white supremacist element from the South, which would block civil rights reforms.
- Kennedy was personally much more interested in foreign policy than in the more mundane issues of tax, welfare, economic subsidies to farmers and Social Security.

John F. Kennedy giving his inaugural address in January 1961

Kennedy's reforms

When Kennedy came to power, the USA was facing several domestic problems. The country was in a recession and suffering a 7% unemployment rate. The civil rights movement was growing increasingly militant. Congressional opposition to reforms could not be easily overcome, and out of 355 administrative measures introduced, only 172 passed; 16 out of 23 major bills were defeated.

Given these facts, it is not surprising that the success of Kennedy's New Frontier policy has been questioned. However, consideration should be given to the reforms that *were* implemented during his presidency. In an attempt to help those worst affect by the recession:

- the minimum wage was raised from $1 to $1.15 and then to $1.25
- states were empowered to extend unemployment benefit for a longer period
- a $4.9 billion Housing Act was passed and an Area Development Act giving federal aid to 'distressed areas' was introduced.

These measures helped counter the effects of the recession, but increased defence spending – necessary for Kennedy's foreign policy – also stimulated the economy. As the economic recovery gathered pace, the government introduced additional measures to stimulate growth, encourage social reform and improve the international standing of the United States:

- The Trade Expansion Act gave the president power to cut customs duties in an effort to increase trade with Western Europe.
- The Manpower Retraining Bill allocated over $400 million dollars to retrain workers.
- The Public Works Act set aside $900 million for schemes to help designated areas of high unemployment (this was, however, considerably less than the $2 billion Kennedy wanted).
- Major federal projects included setting up a large atomic power station at Hanford, Washington, and the Communications Satellite Act to launch space satellites to relay communications worldwide.
- There were successful bills to increase funding for research on mental illness and to regulate the production of drugs.

Failed plans

However, several of Kennedy's domestic initiatives were rejected by Congress. These included education reforms, a reform of farm subsidies and a proposal for a new Department of Urban and Housing Affairs. In addition, a scheme for medical insurance for retired workers over 65, to be paid for while they were in work, met with resistance from medical and insurance interests and was blocked by conservative opposition in Congress.

Furthermore, a number of intended measures were never carried out before Kennedy was assassinated. These included a Civil Rights Bill and a programme for waging 'War on Poverty'. Kennedy also had a Tax Cuts strategy, but this was never fully implemented.

How significant was opposition from Congress when assessing Kennedy's domestic achievements?

The debate

The new style that Kennedy brought to the White House led to high expectations of domestic reform, and there has been much debate about how far he was successful in this area during his 'thousand days' in office. Kennedy's assassination in 1963 generated a wave of emotion that made it hard to be critical of his administration in its immediate aftermath. It also led many to speculate about what he might have gone on to achieve, rather than assessing his actual achievements. His widow, Jackie, encouraged talk of 'Camelot' – a semi-mythical heroic kingdom that equated to Kennedy's presidency.

The early histories of Kennedy's period in office were written by people close to him – notably his advisors Arthur Schlesinger Jr. and Theodore Sorensen. Both these men published books about Kennedy in 1965, and between them they quote the following reforming measures that Kennedy undertook:

- a minimum wage that was 'the first major increase since 1938'
- the 'most comprehensive farm legislation since 1938'
- the 'first accelerated public works program since the New Deal'
- the 'most far-reaching tax reforms since the New Deal'
- the 'most comprehensive housing and urban renewal policy in history'
- 'the longest American expansion of the economy'
- 'a national assault on the causes of poverty'.

In 1991, a generally sympathetic study of Kennedy by James M. Giglio (*The Presidency of John F. Kennedy*) said that 'Kennedy fell short of accomplishing his domestic objectives. Programmes for Civil Rights, medical assistance to the aged, education and poverty, failed to materialise.' However, Giglio goes on to point out that Kennedy promoted economic growth, unemployment fell, New Deal commitments such as Social Security, the minimum wage and reduction of discrimination against women were updated, and a major housing programme launched a period of urban renewal.

By 1996, however, views on Kennedy's domestic achievements had changed. Historian James T. Patterson states: 'Kennedy's record in the realm of domestic policies was hardly stellar.' Patterson believes that Kennedy was an uninspiring leader who made little effort to win congressional support for domestic reform. Kennedy apparently told Sorensen to 'drop the domestic stuff altogether' when drafting his inaugural speech. Many of Kennedy's policies, Patterson claims, helped interest groups and not the people. For example, a Housing Act of 1961 did more to assist developers and construction unions than the poor. In addition to this, Patterson points out that acts aimed at helping depressed areas were not sufficiently funded. Congress scrapped the Area Development Act in 1965.

SOURCE A

Historian Robert Dallek refers to a gap between the claims Kennedy had made by the 1962 midterm elections and the reality of the situation.

Journalists ... pointed out that he [Kennedy] had lost his aid to education and Medicare fights and that many of the Kennedy laws were not new frontier measures, but extensions of earlier programmes ... For all Kennedy's efforts to talk up his legislative accomplishments, a defensive tone revealed his own doubts and his limited interest in domestic affairs.

Dallek, R. 2003. John F. Kennedy: An Unfinished Life. London, UK. Penguin. p. 491.

Activity

Look again at the summary of measures adopted and those that Kennedy intended to implement on page 52. Split into two groups. One group should produce a poster highlighting Kennedy's achievements, and the other group should create a poster outlining his failures and limitations. Use the information in your posters to reach a judgement about how successful Kennedy was in dealing with domestic affairs.

Kennedy: an assessment

Kennedy's legislative achievement seems more limited than the earlier histories suggest. Conservative opposition in Congress was clearly important, but when Kennedy threw the full weight of his authority behind a measure, he was often successful. However, the president did not exert this authority frequently in domestic affairs, nor did he make concerted efforts to persuade Congress to back his proposals, as Lyndon Johnson later did.

Another factor to consider is whether the reforms Kennedy introduced were the right ones. For example, his tax reforms were heavily criticised and many proposals lacked enough funding to be fully implemented. Kennedy launched his mental health reforms as a result of concerns about poor conditions in mental institutions. However, the real consequence of this was that higher numbers of mentally ill people re-entered society – a situation that brought its own problems which were never addressed. Kennedy's War on Poverty was not a priority in his first two years in office, and was still in its planning stages when he died.

How much impact did Kennedy have on civil rights?

Civil rights were already a key social issue when Kennedy came to power. The new president wanted to proceed cautiously, 'in a way that will maintain a consensus of national opinion'.

African-American appointments

To begin with, Kennedy continued Eisenhower's policy of appointing more African-Americans to senior positions, notably making **Thurgood Marshall** a judge in the Court of Appeals and Carl Rowan US ambassador to Finland. In his role as US attorney general, Kennedy's brother **Robert Kennedy** also employed African-American lawyers in the Justice Department and appointed them to the federal district court.

Thurgood Marshall (1908–93) The great-grandson of a slave, Marshall grew up in Baltimore, Maryland. He became a civil rights lawyer and represented the NAACP in the famous *Brown v. Board of Education* case in 1954. He was appointed to the Court of Appeals by Kennedy, and was later promoted to Supreme Court justice by Johnson – the first African-American to hold this position.

Robert Kennedy (1925–68) Kennedy was the younger brother of John F. Kennedy, and was one of his senior advisors. He was the US attorney general throughout Kennedy's presidency and became an influential civil rights activist. After his brother's death, Robert was elected as senator for New York. In 1968, he began his own campaign to become president, but was assassinated in June that year.

Civil rights reform

Kennedy also enacted several reforms designed to tackle discrimination. He established the Commission on Equal Opportunity Employment to ensure fair treatment for all federal employees. Segregation was banned in federal housing, and only integrated schools were awarded federal grants in 'impacted areas'.

In 1962, poll tax payment was abolished as a qualification for voting in federal elections. Only those who earned more than a certain amount of money had to pay poll tax. As many African-Americans did not achieve this level of income, they did not pay the poll tax and were therefore ineligible to vote. After payment of poll tax was dropped as a voting qualification, however, five southern states still insisted on a minimum amount of income-tax payment in order to qualify for voting rights. This was still more than many African-Americans paid.

Continued problems in the South

These modest changes were little more than a continuation of policies initiated by the previous administration, but the demand for reform grew rapidly in the USA in the early 1960s. Civil rights groups organised Freedom Rides, in which black and white activists rode buses into southern states to test the transport desegregation laws. In the deeply segregationist South, the Freedom Riders met with abuse and often violent assault, which local authorities did little to prevent. US marshals were called in to stop the violence, but only limited action was taken against the state authorities.

Discrimination in education made headlines again in 1962, when **James Meredith** was denied entry to Mississippi University despite a Supreme Court ruling. The governor of Mississippi defied the court and refused to allow Meredith his place at the university. Against a backdrop of violence, 400 federal troops were sent to escort Meredith to the university in safety in September 1962.

James Meredith (b. 1933) African-American James Meredith grew up in Mississippi, where he was educated at segregated schools. Determined to challenge segregation and to push Kennedy towards civil rights legislation, he applied to Mississippi University. Meredith's application was denied, but with the help of the NAACP he appealed to the courts. The case was carried right through to the Supreme Court, which ruled that he had been discriminated against on grounds of his race, and ordered that he be admitted to the university. Meredith later had a distinguished career promoting civil rights.

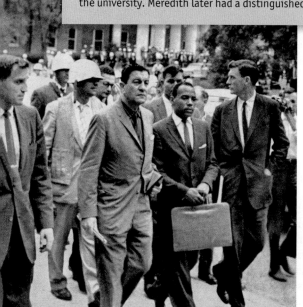

James Meredith enters Mississippi University under the protection of federal marshals in September 1962

The problems continued the following year in Birmingham, Alabama, when the police chief, 'Bull' Connor, launched violent attacks against African-American protesters. Once again, the federal government was forced to intervene. In June 1963, the governor of Alabama, **George Wallace**, tried to prevent two African-American students entering Alabama University. Kennedy federalised the Alabama National Guard.

George Wallace (1919–98) Wallace was a former bomber pilot who served four times as governor of Alabama between 1963 and 1987. He was an ardent white supremacist, who despised Kennedy and what he regarded as the 'Eastern Establishment'. Wallace's failed attempt to stop two students enrolling in the state university in 1963 (known as the 'Stand at the Schoolhouse Door') did not deter him, and later the same year he tried to prevent integration in four primary schools in Huntsville. Wallace was crippled by a gun attack in 1972.

By the middle of 1963, the South was in a turmoil of protests and violent attacks. Membership of the extreme white supremacist group the Ku Klux Klan was reported to have reached 50,000, and local governments in the South were ignoring federal authority. Kennedy realised that racial attacks were severely damaging to the USA's reputation abroad, offering opportunities for Soviet propaganda to brand US talk of 'liberty' mere hypocrisy. The assassination of Medgar Evers, the Mississippi secretary of the NAACP, in June 1963 proved a turning point. The government could no longer simply react to individual occurrences of violence and discrimination in the South – it had to take broader measures to prevent them.

The Civil Rights Act

On 11 June 1963, Kennedy delivered a televised speech in which he called for a Civil Rights Act that would address the problem of discrimination against African-Americans and guarantee their equal treatment in all areas of life. Despite his impassioned address, Kennedy was doubtful that such a bill would pass through Congress, and he feared that just proposing it would end his chances of re-election. However, Martin Luther King (see page 40), one of the leaders of the famous March on Washington in August 1963 in support of African-American rights, expressed his approval of Kennedy's proposal.

More than 200,000 civil rights supporters gather at the March on Washington in August 1963 to demand 'jobs and freedom' for African-Americans

Kennedy's attitude towards civil rights is one of the most debated points of his presidency. Sorensen called the Civil Rights Act 'the most comprehensive and far-reaching Civil Rights Bill ever proposed'. Schlesinger believed that civil rights were an integral part of Kennedy's domestic policy, citing the president's claim that 'an increased minimum wage, federal aid to education and other social and economic reforms were all civil rights bills'.

Modern views are less enthusiastic. In his 2006 book *The Bystander*, historian Nick Bryant argues that civil rights took second place to the Cold War throughout Kennedy's administration. He claims that 'Kennedy was often tone deaf about civil rights' and never provided 'the kind of principled leadership that black activists needed'. Bryant believes that Kennedy simply began a policy in which 'grand gestures … obviated the need for truly substantive reforms'. Dallek also believes Kennedy took a cautious approach to civil rights, and suggests that there were 'more than moral considerations' in the president's decision to embrace a Civil Rights Act in 1963 – namely fear of increasing black violence.

Civil rights under Kennedy: an assessment

Kennedy was undoubtedly driven by events when it came to civil rights. It is unlikely that he would have proposed the Civil Rights Act if violence in the South had not reached the levels it did in 1963. Kennedy knew that he lacked the power over Congress to push such a bill through, and he needed the conservative southern Democrats on his side to ensure the success of other legislation.

In his June 1963 speech, Kennedy seemed heartfelt in his portrayal of civil rights as a moral issue – one that transcended states' rights and legalism. However, it should be remembered that this came more than two years into his presidency. By this point, African-American incomes were half those of white Americans, and black unemployment was more than double the figure for whites. In the South, membership of racist groups was high; their activities went largely unchecked and there was almost constant infringement of black constitutional rights. In light of these facts, civil rights was a pressing issue, and it is easy to argue that Kennedy should have done more to tackle the root cause of the problem right from the start. On the other hand, Kennedy made several important speeches on the issue of civil rights, which highlighted the problems and brought them more firmly into the national consciousness. He also risked his political future by setting the Civil Rights Act in motion.

Kennedy had his detractors at the time, but his reputation was transformed by his assassination in November 1963. He became a heroic figure, cut down in his prime before he could carry through his dreams of social reform. One consequence of this strong public reaction to Kennedy's death was that Congress found it difficult to oppose any initiative that he had launched. Most significantly, perhaps, the Civil Rights Act was passed in 1964, paving the way for further reform under Kennedy's successors.

Activity

The following is an extract from an online article about Kennedy:

John F. Kennedy's assassination on 22 November, 1963, was a defining moment in both the history of the United States and the lives of millions of people around the world. He was the figurehead for a sea change of attitudes at the beginning of the vibrant 1960s in a country fast becoming disillusioned with its foreign policy and desperate for civil rights reform.

Take it in turns to continue this article round the class, giving your views of Kennedy's domestic achievements.

What was Johnson's 'Great Society'?

A plain-speaking Texan, Johnson had already enjoyed a long career in politics by the time he became president. He played his part in Roosevelt's New Deal (see page 10) as director of the National Youth Administration in Texas, and was elected to Congress in 1937. Kennedy chose Johnson as his vice-president during the 1960 election campaign largely because of his political experience. However, after the election Johnson never found a place in Kennedy's closest circle of advisors, and he resented the strong influence the Kennedy family had in government. Despite the fact that the two men had not enjoyed a close political relationship, Johnson pledged to continue Kennedy's work.

Johnson is sworn in as president two hours after Kennedy's assassination

A new style of government

Johnson's presidential style was very different from that of his predecessors. He demanded total loyalty from his staff and insisted on maintaining personal control of most matters of policy. He became one of the most-photographed presidents in history, taking every opportunity to project his image to the American public. Johnson also earned a reputation for humiliating his subordinates (some say he even issued orders to them while he was seated on the lavatory).

Johnson's accession marked a major shift in policy as, to begin with at least, the new president focused on domestic rather than foreign affairs. This was partly in deference to the public's expectation that he would complete the work Kennedy had begun on domestic reform. However, Johnson believed that Kennedy had been too conservative when it came to internal policy, and he was much more committed to domestic change than his predecessor had been. As a congressional insider, Johnson was also more skilled at persuading Congress to support his measures.

The Great Society reforms

The new president had a vision for transforming the USA into a 'Great Society', which he outlined in a speech delivered at the University of Michigan in May 1964. He asked the students gathered there: 'Will you join the battle to build the Great Society, to prove that our material progress is only the foundation to build the richer life of mind and spirit?' Johnson established 17 different task forces to draft a range of reforms, and instituted a flurry of legislation, in what has been called 'the most intense period of reform in US history'.

The sheer scale and complexity of Johnson's domestic policy can be daunting. The table opposite gives a summary of some of the key legislation passed during his administration.

Activity

Using the table on page 61, list the measures that fall under the following categories:

- civil rights
- culture
- housing and welfare
- education
- environment.

Split into groups. Each group should select a category and do some further research into the legislation and its short- and long-term effects. Prepare a PowerPoint presentation explaining the impact of your chosen category.

Measure	Date	Description
Higher Education Facilities Act	1963	Federal aid for colleges, libraries, new technical institutes and 30 new community colleges.
Civil Rights Act	1964	Enforced the constitutional right to vote, provided protection against racial discrimination in 'public accommodations', authorised the attorney general to protect equal rights in public facilities and education.
Food Stamp Act	1964	Gave direct help with food for the poor.
Economic Opportunity Act	1964	Created the Office of Economic Opportunity (OEC); $1 million funding in 1964 and another $2 million in 1965 and 1966.
Urban Mass Transportation Act	1964	$375 million in aid for urban rail systems to ease traffic.
Wilderness Act	1964	Preserved areas of natural beauty and set up national parks.
Clear Air, Water Quality and Clean Water Restoration Acts	1964	Established controls on pollution.
Elementary and Secondary Education Act	1965	$1 billion in federal aid to public education in areas with high numbers of poor families.
Higher Education Act	1965	140,000 scholarships and low-interest loans granted for poorer college students; Teacher Corps established.
Housing and Urban Development Act	1965	Federal funds provided for urban renewal, including recreation centres and a rent supplement scheme.
Social Security Act	1965	Provided for two health-insurance programmes: Medicaid (for people on low incomes) and Medicare (for those over 65 or with disabilities).
National Endowment for the Arts	1965	Federal funding for arts projects; there was also a National Endowment for the Humanities.
Voting Rights Act	1965	Outlawed literacy tests as a means of assessing someone's right to vote, and provided safeguards against state governments restricting voting rights.
Immigration and Nationality Services Act	1965	Abolished national origin quotas in immigration law.
Jobs Corps	1966	To help develop skills among disadvantaged young people.
Demonstration Cities and Metropolitan Development Act	1966	Model Cities Program for urban redevelopment; co-ordinated existing plans and extended them to depressed cities.
National Traffic and Motor Vehicle Safety Act	1966	Created the National Highway Traffic Safety Bureau to give federal government more control over road safety.
Freedom of Information Act	1966	Allowed information and data from federal agencies to be publicly available except in matters affecting security.
Federal Jury Reform Act	1968	Protection from racial discrimination by juries.
Civil Rights Act	1968	Banned housing discrimination on racial grounds, and extended rights in registration and voting to Native Americans.
Bilingual Education Act	1968	Provided aid in local districts for children with limited English.

How far did Johnson fulfil his aims for the Great Society?

The table on page 61 gives an idea of the huge expansion of the activity and regulation of the federal government in a short period of time. Even at the time, there were some who believed that the legislation was rushed through in an effort to please everyone. The debate about the effectiveness of Johnson's Great Society reforms continues to this day.

Negative perspectives

Modern conservative historians tend to regard Johnson's measures as socially destructive. They argue that such legislation broke up traditional family structures by creating welfare dependency, and ultimately brought little benefit to those they were supposed to help. Historians Larry Schweikart and Michael Allen claim that 'the Great Society programs had not had any measurable impact on the percentage of poor in America as compared to the trends before the programs were enacted'.

The view from the political left was not much more encouraging. Howard Zinn also expressed doubts about the effectiveness of the Great Society: 'Those blacks who could afford to go to restaurants and hotels in the South were no longer barred. More blacks could go to universities and colleges … None of this was halting the unemployment, the deterioration of the ghetto, the rising crime, drug addiction and violence.'

James Patterson believed that Medicare and Medicaid 'fell short of national health insurance'. Many Americans were not eligible for this cover, and in fact the US had fewer people covered by health insurance than any other industrialised nation in the world. Even those who were covered by Medicare and Medicaid found that there were many exemptions to what they could claim.

By the time Johnson left office, many people felt that social reform had moved too far away from the community and was too tightly controlled by the state. Johnson was also criticised for not doing enough to address the cause of poverty – unemployment. Ronald Reagan later claimed that Johnson and the Democrats had waged war on poverty and poverty had won.

The historian Allen J. Matusow produced some devastating criticism in his book *The Unraveling of America: Liberalism in the 1960s* (1984). The Jobs Corps, which aimed to train disadvantaged young people and solve the 1 million youth unemployment problem, did not have a high success rate; 28% of its trainees were still unemployed after six months. In addition, most training was for entry-level proficiency in low-income work. By 1976, 20% of Americans were still living below the poverty line. Income distribution had not shifted significantly, and 40% of the poor did not receive welfare benefits or Medicaid. Michael Katz points out Johnson's refusal to adopt a policy of job *creation*. The main strategy of the Great Society seemed to be preparing people for employment through education and training, but there were no plans to provide the employment itself.

In any case, by 1966 the most intense period of social reform was coming to an end, and Johnson himself was starting to lose confidence in his vision of a Great Society. Significantly, he blocked a major literacy project and failed to introduce any radical new measures in the face of increasing racial tensions in 1967.

Positive perspectives

A Cabinet paper of 1967 reported that unemployment for that year stood at 25.9 million – down from 28 million in 1958. Other statistics also suggest that Johnson's early reforms did contribute to social improvements that continued to develop beyond his years in office:

- The proportion of elderly poor dropped from 35% to 16% between 1959 and 1980.
- The proportion of families on welfare benefits went from 33% in 1960 to 90% in 1971.
- In 1964, the hospital admission rate for families earning under $1000 a year was 107 per 1000; by 1968 it was 123 per 1000; those on low incomes saw doctors more frequently than those on middle incomes by 1970.

In 1999, **Joseph Califano** defended the Great Society in an article in *Washington Monthly*, entitled 'What Was Really Great About the Great Society?'

Joseph Califano (b. 1931) Califano was a distinguished lawyer and Johnson's top domestic aide. He took a leading role in the legislation of the Great Society, working on labour relations, health care, education and civil rights issues during Johnson's administration.

In this article, Califano outlined several significant benefits that he believed Johnson's reforms were ultimately responsible for. Some of these are listed on page 64.

- Over a 30-year period, a quarter of a trillion dollars was made available to college students.
- In 1964, only 41% of Americans finished high school and only 8% held college degrees; by 1999, more than 81% finished high school and 24% finished college.
- 79 million people signed up for Medicare in the period 1965–99 and Medicaid helped more than 200 million people in the same period.
- Because of the 1965 Health Professions Educational Assistance Act, the number of doctors graduating more than doubled by 1999.
- In 1999, the Great Society's food stamp programme helped to feed more than 20 million people in more than 8 million households.
- Between 1967 and 1999, the school breakfast programme provided breakfast for nearly 100 million school children.
- Life expectancy in 1964 was 69.7 years; in 1997 it was 76.5 years.
- Infant mortality dropped by nearly 75% between 1963 and 1999.
- The Corporation for Public Broadcasting supported 350 public television stations and 699 public radio stations.
- The 1968 National Trail System Act established more than 800 recreational, scenic and historic trails.
- In Johnson's first year in office, only 300 African-Americans served as elected officials in the USA; by 1998 there were 9000.
- In 1960, life expectancy for African-Americans was 63.6 years; by 1997, this had risen to 71.2 years.
- In 1960, the infant mortality rate for African-Americans was 44.3 for every 1000 live births; in 1997, it was 14.7.
- In 1960, only 20% of African-Americans completed high school and 3% finished college; in 1997, those numbers had risen to 75% and 13% respectively.
- In 1996, Social Security raised 12 million senior citizens above the poverty line.
- The 1968 Housing Act later provided homes for 7 million families.

SOURCE B

This reduction in poverty did not just happen. It was the result of a focused, tenacious effort to revolutionize the role of the federal government with a series of interventions that enriched the lives of millions of Americans. In those tumultuous Great Society years, the President submitted, and Congress enacted, more than 100 major proposals in each of the 89th and 90th Congresses. In that era of do-it-now optimism, government was neither a bad man to be tarred and feathered nor a bag man to collect campaign contributions, but an instrument to help the most vulnerable in our society.

Califano, J. 'What Was Really Great About the Great Society?' Washington Monthly, October 1999.

Theory of knowledge

History and statistics

What are the problems for a historian such as Califano in using statistical evidence to support a programme in which he was deeply involved? For example, is there a definition of 'poverty line'? What controls are in place to allow an objective assessment of what might have happened over 30 years *without* these programmes? Are historians over-influenced by statistics?

The civil rights issue

Johnson's civil rights legislation initially focused on segregation (mainly a southern issue) and constitutional rights – both issues addressed by the 1964 Civil Rights Act. However, by 1965 the civil rights movement had become more focused on social and economic inequality and lack of opportunity for African-Americans. Civil rights had also become a national issue, not merely a southern one.

Amid the prosperity of white urban areas, African-Americans lived in areas with high crime rates, and suffered unemployment and poor housing. Inner-city areas became ghettos, and tensions often erupted in confrontations between young blacks and the police. In August 1965, riots broke out in the Watts district of Los Angeles, leading to 34 deaths, 899 injuries and 4000 arrests.

Armed police patrol the streets during the Watts riot in Los Angeles in 1965

By 1966, the civil rights movement was divided between the integrationists, who believed that civil rights should be about equality and integration, and the separatists, who rejected the white system altogether and aimed for 'Black Power'.

Throughout 1966, there were race riots in 42 cities. Violence continued into 1967, and in April 1968 the assassination of Martin Luther King sparked riots in 168 cities and towns across the USA. Johnson failed to respond with further civil rights legislation. Despite all his welfare reforms, the gap between white and black seemed to have widened during Johnson's tenure.

Discussion point

Who played a more significant role in civil rights issues – Johnson or Kennedy? Debate the issue in groups of three, with one person arguing for Kennedy, another for Johnson and a third taking notes and reporting back to the class on the discussion.

What did Nixon achieve during his presidency?

The 1968 election

In March 1968, Johnson decided not to run for re-election. He had grown increasingly disappointed by the results of his extensive reforms, and investment in further social projects became impossible as money was diverted to the escalating conflict in Vietnam. For a short time it seemed that Robert Kennedy would be the next Democratic candidate for president, but his assassination in June threw the Democratic Party into turmoil.

Eventually, at the Democratic Convention in Chicago, **Hubert Humphrey** was chosen to run in the presidential race. However, the Democrats' reputation suffered a blow the same day, after the police carried out attacks on anti-war protesters who were demonstrating outside the convention.

Hubert Humphrey (1911–78) Humphrey was a Democrat from Minnesota and a former mayor of Minneapolis. He was elected to the Senate in 1949, and served as Johnson's vice-president from 1965 until Johnson left office in January 1969. During this period, Humphrey supported liberal and civil rights reforms. He was later re-elected as Minnesota senator, and held the position until his death.

Once again, Richard Nixon was the Republican candidate. Nixon was the son of a shopkeeper. He had studied law and later served in the navy, but in 1946 he was elected as a California congressman and began his political career. While serving in the House, Nixon played a leading role in the Alger Hiss case (see page 31), proving Hiss was a spy.

In the Red Scare climate of the time, Nixon's overt anti-communism proved popular. He became a senator in 1950, and two years later Eisenhower chose him as his vice-president. In fact, Eisenhower had little respect for Nixon. In 1960, when asked to name a contribution Nixon had made to his administration, Eisenhower replied, 'Give me a minute and I'll think of one'.

Nixon lost the presidential race against Kennedy in 1960, but he returned in 1968 and gained financial support from business contributors who were anxious not to see further extension of federal legislation. Throughout his campaign, Nixon gained popularity through his stand against such issues as urban rioting and the rise in city crime, and due to his open dislike of too much social legislation and welfare – programmes that were greatly resented by taxpayers. Nixon also supported the war in Vietnam, and appealed to what he later called 'the silent majority' – those who, like him, disapproved of the widespread anti-war campaigns. Nixon defeated Humphrey in the election by a 0.7% margin.

Nixon's focus

Nixon's friend Bryce Harlow said, 'When Dick was finally elected president, he attained eighty per cent of all his goals in life. He has no idea of what he will do after he is sworn in.' In fact, Nixon was full of anger at the many political opponents who had slighted him over the years, and it soon became clear that he relied on a close-knit staff more than his Cabinet. Many believed that he regarded the presidency not as the fulfilment of a life's ambitions, but as a period in which constant political campaigning for the next election had to be done.

Although he had campaigned strongly on domestic issues, Nixon found domestic policy increasingly sidelined by foreign affairs, just as Kennedy and Johnson had. The Vietnam War split opinion across the USA, and by the time Nixon came to power it was clear that a US victory was unlikely. He expressed concern about a divided America, but he had no sympathy for social unrest and was angered by the ongoing anti-war demonstrations. When four students were killed by National Guardsmen during a protest at Kent State University in Ohio, the president demonstrated no regret. When shown photographs of the dead and injured, he seemed more concerned that the images portrayed the police in a bad light.

Nixon's greatest political achievement was in foreign affairs. In 1972, he made a visit to China to re-establish diplomatic links with the communist regime there. Some were outraged that a Western leader should extend the hand of diplomacy to Mao Zedong, but it seems that Nixon's strong anti-communist ideals were not as important as political advantage at this time.

At home, Nixon faced a rapidly changing USA. Generally, there was less respect for authority. The Supreme Court – which had championed the liberal cause in civil rights – also championed other causes, such as opposition to capital punishment. Some white radicals began taking direct action. Among these groups were the so-called Weathermen, a white terrorist group. In addition, Nixon faced continuing opposition from activists such as the Black Panthers to white economic and social domination.

Welfare reforms

The public mood of the time was for change, and Nixon's political sense drove him towards a liberal domestic policy. In private, however, he was outspoken against liberals and reformers. However, the Republicans were not the majority in Congress, and this was a limiting factor for Nixon when shaping his domestic programme.

The Family Assistance Plan

Nixon's most forward-looking proposal was a Family Assistance Plan (FAP). This was introduced to replace a programme called Aid to Families with Dependent Children (AFDC), which had been established as part of the New Deal in 1935 and extended in 1960. The FAP intended to equalise welfare benefits across the country, rather than vary these from state to state. The plan also directed federal aid to the poor without the intermediary services that had been established by the Great Society. It provided for a minimum income of $1600 a year for a family, plus $800 of food stamps. One condition of receiving this assistance was that the applicant would actively seek work.

By introducing the FAP, Nixon not only hoped to help poorer families in states where benefits were low, but also to address criticisms that there was too much welfare bureaucracy and that welfare discouraged work. However, the plan met with controversy in Congress.

Conservatives felt that it encouraged dependency on the state and rewarded single parents for their 'irresponsibility'. It was also seen as far too bureaucratic and dependent on too many social workers.

Ultimately, Nixon lacked the support in Congress to push the plan through. Unlike Johnson, Nixon made little attempt to bring Congress round to his way of thinking; nor did he use the press to spread his ideas to the US public in the way that Johnson had.

Other welfare plans

For all his talk of reducing dependency on the state, Nixon maintained high levels of welfare spending, and support for poorer families rose by $50 per person in the period 1968–72. Democrats in Congress voted in favour of bills that would allow more money for those on Medicaid, food stamps and AFDC. In 1972, Congress also passed a Supplemental Security Income programme, which increased payments and linked them to inflation. Social insurance spending increased from $27 billion in 1969 to more than $64 billion in 1973. Nixon disapproved of these measures, but took no official stand against them in case it damaged his popularity with the people.

New Federalism

Not to be outdone by his predecessors in terms of a domestic slogan, Nixon followed the Fair Deal, the New Frontier and the Great Society with what he called 'New Federalism' – indicating a change in the way that the federal government spent taxpayers' money. As part of this, Nixon proposed a 'revenue-sharing' scheme, in which grants were allocated to states and local areas to spend as they wished. This would have given a more equal balance of power between the federal and local governments, but the Watergate scandal and Nixon's resignation (see page 72) meant it was never properly implemented.

The environment

Nixon also was aware of a growing interest in environmental issues in the USA, and although he felt indifferent towards such concerns himself, he supported environmental legislation to win popularity.

The National Environmental Policy Act of 1970 required all contractors engaged in federal projects to provide an estimate of their environmental impact. Reforms begun during the Great Society were continued, including those to improve health and safety at work and to prevent pollution, including the Clean Air Act (1970) and the Water Pollution Control Act (1972). Legislation was also passed to protect the natural world, in the form of the Endangered Species Act (1973). Some of these measures seemed to put economic growth at risk, and several regulations made by the Environmental Protection Agency were contested by big business.

Native rights and affirmative action

In the area of Native American rights, Nixon made several concessions. For example, the Blue Lake in New Mexico was returned to the local Native Americans who regarded the lake as sacred. An Indian Education Act gave federal support for Native American education programmes. Many of these measures lacked any fundamental significance, but Native Americans were encouraged by the symbolism of these gestures.

Civil rights legislation already banned discrimination in employment, but there was no mechanism to help disadvantaged groups gain jobs. Nixon's labor secretary, George Schulz, therefore showed a progressive impulse in his Philadelphia Plan of 1969, which made federal contracts dependent on firms taking on a quota of African-American apprentices. This initiative led to a policy known as 'affirmative action', and goals and timetables for the hiring and training of more African-American workers were established using the economic leverage of lucrative federal contracts.

Nixon signs a bill returning the Blue Lake to the Taos Pueblo people in December 1970

Congress was not keen on the Philadelphia Plan, and unions and employers disliked affirmative action. However, Nixon and his government were supported by the Supreme Court, which made illegal any tests for new employees that discriminated against African-Americans. Such an emphasis on jobs for black Americans marked a change in federal government thinking.

Desegregation and integration

While the reforms outlined above all seemed to look to the future, internal politics was still entangled with issues from the past and, as Nixon's presidency progressed, civil rights once more emerged as a problem.

Education in the South was still not desegregated, and the Supreme Court ruled that southern school boards should not delay integration any longer. However, Nixon did not openly support this ruling. He used his power as president to block measures to stop continued federal funding to schools that were still segregated, but this measure was not regarded as determined enough. The president's apparent lack of support for speedy integration caused an outcry from the NAACP, and resulted in several legal cases.

In *Alexander v. Holmes Board of Education*, the Supreme Court demanded 'unitary schools, now and hereafter'. To continue its offensive, the Supreme Court next ordered that school children should be bussed to different schools to forcibly end segregation. This radical policy ran counter to the whole idea of neighbourhood schools and upset many white families. It was also unpopular among African-Americans, who objected to what they saw as 'social engineering'.

Behind the scenes, Nixon discouraged officials from enforcing the bussing law. He also expressed his disapproval publicly, stating that he would 'hold bussing to the minimum required by law'. In 1973, proposals to merge certain school districts to ensure a balance between races were rejected, reinforcing local control over education.

> To what extent was there continuity between Johnson's and Nixon's domestic achievements?

The New Economic Policy

Despite his populist measures, the midterm elections held in 1970 were not a success for Nixon. Unemployment had risen by 33% and prices by 11%, combining the worst features of stagnation and inflation – called 'stagflation' in the press. Nixon again responded to the public mood by introducing his New Economic Policy in August 1971. Abandoning orthodox economic principles, he imposed a freeze on wages and prices, introduced a 10% tariff on imported goods, and accepted a devaluation of the dollar to boost exports. These sudden and dramatic changes were intended to demonstrate Nixon's willingness to be both daring and forceful in his domestic policy.

Nixon's ability to respond flexibly to such problems earned him respect from the public. As his first four years in office came to an end, many looked back on his genuine achievements and felt that this was a president who still had more to offer the country. His foreign policy had also proved successful. These factors combined to win Nixon re-election later that year.

The Watergate scandal

In 1972, workers on the Campaign to Re-elect the President (CREEP) bugged telephones in the Democrat headquarters in the Watergate hotel in Washington. Shortly after, two agents were caught breaking in to fix bugs that were not working. An investigation was launched, and by 1973 the connection to Nixon's campaign had been discovered.

Nixon ordered the CIA to block the police investigation into the affair, but two reporters from the *Washington Post* found an FBI agent who was willing to tell them what happened. As the investigation continued, the authorities discovered that Nixon had been tape-recording meetings in the White House, and he was ordered to hand over these recordings. The vice-president, Spiro Agnew, resigned in October 1973 after he was accused of corruption. Nixon found himself facing charges of financial irregularity. As further evidence of the president's involvement in the cover-up emerged, Republican leaders and close advisors encouraged Nixon to resign. To avoid impeachment (being formally charged with illegal activity by Congress), Nixon stepped down on 8 August 1974.

 ## Theory of knowledge

History and judgement

How far is it a historian's job to condemn corruption and illegality by those in power?
Is it possible to disregard Nixon's improper use of power and offer a balanced judgement on his policies?

Nixon announcing his resignation to the nation on 8 August 1974

Nixon: an assessment

It transpired that Nixon had authorised surveillance of people he considered his enemies long before Watergate, and it was also discovered that he had used the CIA and FBI for political purposes. These facts, and his taped private conversations, diminished his reputation. Nixon has also been criticised for his domestic policies, which many believed reacted to the public mood rather than offering a coherent programme of reform. His ideas were sometimes liberal and progressive and sometimes conservative, and some of his most original plans were never implemented. During his first term, Nixon gained a great deal of support. After this, however, as corruption and impropriety were revealed, it became impossible for anyone to stand by him.

In recent years, several historians have revisited Nixon's presidency and started to review it in a different light. In *The Nixon Presidency*, Michael Genovese argues that he 'presided over an expansion of the welfare state, but his interest in domestic policy was sporadic and his achievement limited'. Iwan Morgan suggests that 'Nixon's achievements in the domestic sphere were greater than he was wont to brag. Only Roosevelt and Johnson could claim a superior record of reform.'

Which of these presidents had the greatest impact on domestic affairs?

Of the five post-war presidents considered in this book, only Johnson was able to push through most of his legislative programme. The others were weakened by the restrictions that the Constitution placed on the president's powers. They also found that their domestic policy had to be shaped by the preferences and political leanings of Congress and the rulings of the Supreme Court.

All five men had to deal with major changes in society and with key civil rights issues. For the most part, heroic campaigns by black organisations and leaders, Supreme Court decisions and politically brave stands by presidents gave constitutional rights to African-Americans. However, there was less progress in social and economic areas of civil rights than there was in the attainment of legal and political equality. Ironically, the leader most sympathetic to the South, Nixon, did most in this respect by introducing affirmative action over jobs.

Throughout the period 1945–79, the welfare state and the power of the federal government expanded. This was most dramatic under Johnson, whose Great Society stands as one of the most rapid and extensive periods of lawmaking in history. However, none of the five presidents instituted a national health service, and none offered a radical redistribution of income and equality of opportunity. All five administrations found foreign policy a major preoccupation. In nearly every case, the need to spend time and money on foreign problems disadvantaged domestic reform.

End of chapter activities

Paper 3 exam practice

Question

Were changes to civil rights the most important achievement of Kennedy's and Johnson's domestic reforms in the USA?
[20 marks]

Skill focus

Planning an essay

Examiner's tips

As discussed in Chapter 2, the first stage of planning an answer to a question is to think carefully about the wording of the question so that you know what is required and what you need to focus on. Once you have done this, you can move on to the other important considerations:

- Decide your **main argument/theme/approach before** you start to write. This will help you identify the key points you want to make. For example, this question clearly invites you to make a judgement about whether the named factor – civil rights – was the most important out of a range of other possible factors. Deciding on an approach will help you produce an argument that is clear, coherent and logical.
- Plan **the structure of your argument** – i.e. the introduction, the main body of the essay (in which you present precise evidence to support your arguments), and your concluding paragraph.

For this question, whatever overall view you have about the relative importance of civil rights, you should try to make a **balanced** argument by considering the opposing view. Was social and economic reform more important, given the limitations of civil rights legislation to prevent discontent? Was it important for Johnson, but less so for Kennedy? A good starting point is to consider why civil rights might be the most important factor and develop the argument from there.

Whatever the question, try to **link** the points you make in your paragraphs, so that there is a clear thread that follows through to your conclusion. This will ensure that your essay is not just a series of unconnected paragraphs. Include **linking phrases** to ensure that each 'factor' paragraph is linked to the question. For example:

Civil Rights were the most important element for both Kennedy and Johnson **because** ...

However, many other aspects of domestic change also had an impact on African-Americans, **for example** ...

Although the passing of Civil Rights Acts and the securing of constitutional rights was important, these were driven by key decisions by the Supreme Court, such as …

However, although Supreme Court decisions were significant, and both presidents passed important social and economic legislation, their actions and policies on civil rights were the most important because …

There are clearly many factors to consider, which will be difficult under the time constraints of the exam. Producing a plan with brief details (such as dates, main events/features) under each heading will help you cover the main issues in the time available. It will also give you something to use if you run out of time and can only jot down the main points of your last paragraph(s). The examiner will give you some credit for this.

Common mistake

Once the exam has started, one common mistake is for candidates to begin writing **straight away**, without being sure whether they know enough about the questions they have selected. Once they have written several paragraphs, they run out of things to say – and then panic because of the time they have wasted. Producing plans for **each of the three questions** you have to write in Paper 3 at the **start** of the exam will help you assess whether you know enough about the questions to tackle them successfully.

Activity

In this chapter, the focus is on planning answers. Using the information from this chapter, and any other sources of information available to you, produce essay plans – using spider diagrams or mind maps – with all the necessary headings (and brief details) for well-focused and clearly structured responses to **at least two** of the following Paper 3 practice questions.

Remember to refer to the simplified Paper 3 markscheme on page 223.

Paper 3 practice questions

1 How effectively did US presidents deal with civil rights issues between 1963 and 1973?

2 To what extent does Kennedy's domestic policy confirm his reputation as a great US president?

3 How successful was Johnson's attempt to create a 'Great Society'?

4 Assess Nixon's domestic achievements.

4 Canadian domestic policy 1957–80

1957 Jun: Progressive Conservatives win election, ending 22 years of Liberal rule

1958 Mar: Progressive Conservatives win landslide election victory

Agricultural Stabilization Act introduced

1959 Feb: Avro Arrow contract cancelled

1960 Jun: Liberals replace Union Nationale as governing party in Quebec

Aug: Canadian Bill of Human Rights passed

1962 Jun: Diefenbaker wins election but as minority government

1963 Jan: NATO commander insists Canada honour its commitment to NATO

Apr: Liberals win election but fail to gain overall majority

1965 Feb: Canadian flag adopted

Nov: second Liberal electoral victory without overall majority

1967 Canadian centenary

1968 Apr: Pearson retires as prime minister; replaced by Pierre Trudeau

1969 Sep: Official Languages Act passed

1970 Oct: October Crisis

1971 Multiculturalism Act passed

1974 Jul: Bill 22 makes French only official language in Quebec

1976 Nov: Parti Québécois defeats Liberals and takes power in Quebec

1977 Aug: Bill 101 – 'A Charter of the French Language'

1979 May: Trudeau defeated; Clark takes office with minority Conservative government

1980 Feb: Trudeau returns to power

Key questions

- Why was the period of Progressive Conservative rule in Canada so short-lived?
- How successful was the Pearson administration?
- What were the causes and consequences of the Quiet Revolution?
- Why was Trudeau able to remain in power for so long?

This chapter considers the domestic policies of the four prime ministers who governed Canada between 1957 and 1980. It explains why Liberal dominance ended in 1957 and how, despite a landslide victory in 1958, the Progressive Conservatives were removed from power five years later. The chapter also investigates why the Liberals were able to dominate the period from 1963, assessing the success of their economic and social policies. In addition, this section examines Quebec's transformation into a modern state through the 'Quiet Revolution' and explains how the issues of terrorism and separatism were defeated. The chapter concludes by explaining why the Conservative ministry of 1979 was so short-lived, and discusses the subsequent Liberal return to power.

Overview

- John Diefenbaker's election victory in 1957 ended a Liberal dominance that dated back to 1935. The prime minister secured the largest government majority in the 1958 election, but a series of errors in handling policy, particularly over defence, and Diefenbaker's abrasive personality brought down the government in 1963.
- The Liberal leader Lester Pearson remained in power until 1968, despite never having a majority government.
- Pearson's administration passed significant welfare reforms, oversaw economic growth and helped to bring greater unity to the country, symbolised by the new flag.
- Unrest in Quebec troubled the federal government in Canada, and although the 1960s witnessed the modernisation of the province, terrorism developed throughout the decade at the hands of the separatist Front de libération du Québec (FLQ).
- The problems in Quebec reached a peak with the October Crisis of 1970, which was subsequently defeated by the success of both provincial and federal reforms.
- The 1970s were dominated by Pierre Trudeau, who continued Pearson's social developments and oversaw the introduction of multiculturalism and economic nationalism.
- Although Trudeau fell from power in 1979, the Conservative government under Joe Clark lasted only nine months and Trudeau was re-elected in 1980.

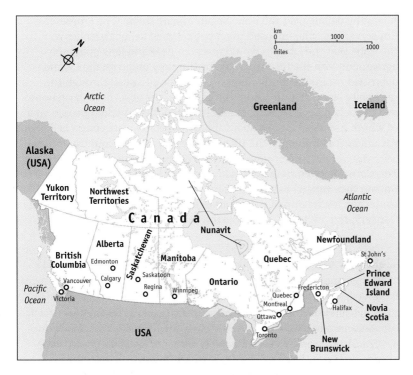

A map of Canada showing its provinces and main cities

Why was the period of Progressive Conservative rule in Canada so short-lived?

Background

The Liberal Party was the dominant force in Canadian politics for most of the early 20th century, broken only by the short-lived Conservative government of Richard Bennett from 1931 to 1935. In an attempt to change their image and win support, the Conservatives joined forces with the Progressive Party in 1942, but this had little impact on their popularity with the Canadian people. By 1957, the Liberals had enjoyed an uninterrupted 22 years in power and the Conservatives had lost five elections in a row.

However, the Liberal government's reputation was declining. It was increasingly regarded as autocratic, and lost a great deal of support in 1956 after failing to back Britain during the Suez Crisis. More significantly, the 'Pipeline Debate' the same year further damaged the Liberals' prestige. This controversial incident began when the minister of trade and commerce, C. D. Howe, organised a deal with US investors to build a gas pipeline from western Canada to Montreal.

A lengthy debate over the issue began in parliament. The Progressive Conservatives, who opposed the pipeline, used delaying tactics in the hope that the Liberals would miss the deadline for signing the agreement with the US. Frustrated by the slow progress, the Liberals overruled traditional parliamentary procedure to push through the necessary legislation to secure the pipeline. The government's actions were widely perceived as an overreaction by the Canadian people, many of whom had reservations about the pipeline and were concerned about the amount of influence the USA already had in their country.

The Conservatives were outraged, and in the wake of the Pipeline Debate they turned nationalist sentiment to their own advantage. Under the leadership of the populist **John Diefenbaker**, the Progressive Conservative Party secured a narrow victory in the 1957 election.

John Diefenbaker (1895–1979) Diefenbaker grew up in Saskatchewan and interrupted his training as a lawyer to fight in the First World War. He later sought election to parliament a number of times before winning a seat in 1940. He also made several attempts to secure the leadership of the Conservative Party, and was finally successful in 1956. Diefenbaker became the only Progressive Conservative prime minister to win three elections, although not all with an overall majority. He built a reputation on his skill for public speaking, and his style prompted the *Toronto Star* to describe him as 'humbug and flapdoodle served up with an evangelistic flourish'.

Diefenbaker's personality

Diefenbaker built his election campaign around smart slogans, and he inspired many Canadians with his talk of 'A new Canada! A Canada of the north!' Historian Donald Creighton states that Diefenbaker seemed to 'combine the inspiring vision of the prophet, the burning sincerity of the evangelist, and the annihilating attack of a prosecuting counsel determined on the conviction of a monstrous criminal'. However, the new prime minister soon proved 'less an alternative to the Liberals than an epilogue', according to historian Robert Bothwell.

What do you think Bothwell meant when he referred to Diefenbaker as an 'epilogue' to the Liberals?

Known as 'the Chief', Diefenbaker tried to run both his party and his government with iron discipline, but according to critics he was 'all heart and no brains'. After his landslide victory in 1958 – the greatest in Canadian history – it became clear that he and his government lacked the experience necessary to deal with the issues Canada faced. Their policies appeared confused and impractical.

In the face of economic decline and other domestic troubles, Diefenbaker's early rhetoric seemed empty, and the public lost faith in his ability to push through reforms of any substance.

Economic problems

Diefenbaker was unfortunate to come to power just as the post-war boom ended and Canada entered an economic downturn that lasted until 1961. Unemployment remained high, at 6–7% throughout the period 1958–61. Diefenbaker attempted to alleviate some of the problems by increasing unemployment benefits from 16 to 52 weeks, and by expanding seasonal unemployment benefits for people who worked in industries that only operated at certain times of year. However, these efforts did not tackle the cause of the problem, and many Canadians continued to suffer in the poor economic climate.

John Diefenbaker reads a petition from Canadian farmers in 1959

Diefenbaker also made a significant blunder as a result of his desire to make Canada less economically dependent upon the USA. He publicly announced that Canada would move 15% of its trade from the USA to Britain; this amounted to $625 million a year, almost double the previous British import figure. More importantly, Diefenbaker's pledge was impossible to fulfil, as it was contrary to the conditions of the 1947 General Agreement on Tariffs and Trade (GATT), which prevented favourable terms being given to a particular country.

The government made some attempts to stimulate the economy. It introduced tax cuts and new spending schemes – notably a programme to build road and rail links in northern Canada. It also expanded funding for education through grants to universities and technical and vocational schools.

Agriculture

Diefenbaker recognised the need to protect Canada's valuable agricultural industry during the economic downturn, and he introduced the Agricultural Stabilization Act in 1958.

This established a minimum price for certain goods regardless of their market value, and offered credit and insurance to farmers. In 1961, the same act was extended to consolidate small farms, modernise farm housing and improve farming techniques. It also provided for trees and pasture to be grown on land that was no longer fertile enough for crops. Ultimately, though, it was external events that saved Canadian agriculture. A drought in China, coupled with the USA's refusal to trade with the communist country, offered Canada a lifeline. As a result of Canadian grain sales to China, prices rose from $1.60 to $2.19 a bushel and net farm income in Canada went up threefold in three years.

The exchange crisis

Diefenbaker faced opposition to his plans for stimulating the economy from several quarters, but few were more outspoken than the Liberal governor of the Bank of Canada, James Coyne. Coyne made several speeches in which he encouraged Canadians to spend less and live within their means. He wanted to raise taxes, cut imports, and establish a fixed exchange rate between the Canadian and US dollars. These ideas all went against Diefenbaker's desire to increase spending to reverse the economic downturn, and Coyne's remarks caused a drop in confidence among businesses and consumers. This decline triggered an outflow of funds that eventually caused an exchange crisis.

Diefenbaker's government attempted to solve the exchange problem in the budget of June 1961. In the budget, the Conservatives proposed that the Canadian dollar be devalued (allowed to drop in value against the US dollar), and the rate was fixed at 92.5 US cents per Canadian dollar in May 1962. However, there was a general feeling that this rate would not be maintained and that the Canadian dollar was still over-valued. Investors withdrew their money and either swapped their dollars for gold – which drained the country's gold reserves – or invested in US dollars, which they believed were more stable.

By June 1962, the exchange crisis was so severe that the government had to embark on a policy of austerity and ask for foreign help to make the Canadian dollar more secure. Diefenbaker's political opponents accused the government of incompetence, and fake 'Diefendollars' with a picture of the prime minister in place of the queen were circulated, further undermining the government's credibility.

Theory of knowledge

History and the individual

John Diefenbaker dominated both his party and the period. It can be difficult for historians to separate key personalities from the events that occurred around them. The 19th-century British prime minister Benjamin Disraeli said: 'There is properly no history, only biography.' How far does your study of history support this view?

The Arrow crisis

Diefenbaker's premiership coincided with the height of the Cold War, and his handling of issues related to the conflict played a critical role in his eventual downfall. In particular, the 'Arrow crisis' highlighted the government's failure to deal appropriately with difficult decisions.

The Arrow was a state-of-the-art fighter plane designed to intercept Soviet aircraft over the Arctic. Although the Arrow was considered essential for Canadian security in the Cold War climate, it was nonetheless a costly project. As expenses mounted, the government formally announced that it was stopping further development of the Arrow in February 1959.

Although privately the Liberals were also preparing to abandon the scheme if they came to power, it did not prevent them criticising the Conservative government's decision. The Liberals argued that the abandonment of the Arrow project marked the end of Canadian sovereignty, as the country's air defence would now have to rely on US equipment. The cancellation of the Arrow also resulted in the loss of 14,000 jobs for skilled workers, many of whom left Canada to seek work abroad.

It was Diefenbaker's management of the situation, however, that drew the most criticism. Firstly, he incorrectly pronounced that the plane was outdated anyway due to the more developed technology of long-range missiles that was now available. He also declared that Canada was a nuclear-free zone, but promptly allowed the US to place two squadrons of Bomarc anti-aircraft missiles – which were to be armed with nuclear warheads – on Canadian soil.

The defence minister resigned in disgust at Diefenbaker's ignorance and contradictory policies, and the government was left open to further accusations of incompetence. Historian Desmond Morton summed up the situation: 'The Arrow cancellation was the right choice made the wrong way ... Diefenbaker had taken one hard look at the costs of technological independence and fled.'

Failed policies and the recovery of the opposition

Even some of Diefenbaker's apparently successful policies seem hollow on closer scrutiny. The clearest example of this was the 1960 Bill of Rights, which guaranteed equality in terms of race, religion and beliefs. Such a bill was widely popular, especially amongst minority groups, but in reality the Bill of Rights was little more than an attempt to win popularity. Without being enshrined in the Canadian Constitution it was difficult to enforce its terms. As Canada was a federal state, the bill also lacked authority in provincial courts. Ultimately, very few people would benefit practically from it.

As Diefenbaker's lofty ideals came crashing down, the opposition parties gained ground. The political allegiances of different sections of society began to change. The Conservatives' economic errors lost them the backing of the business community, and they came to rely instead on support from rural areas and the agricultural communities for whom their policies had been more successful. At the same time, Diefenbaker's 'One Canada' policy – seeking equality for and unity among all Canadians, whether French- or English-speaking – offered no concessions to the province of Quebec. There, the French Canadian majority began to support the Liberals.

The Social Credit Party also enjoyed a revival at this time. This conservative-populist group supported a theory of monetary reform called social credit, in which economic power was returned to citizens through an even distribution of wealth. This would be provided in the form of cash vouchers to boost spending, and thus stimulate the economy. The Social Credit Party increased its presence in parliament from 19 seats in 1957 to 30 seats in the 1960 election.

By the time of the 1962 election, Conservative support had dropped dramatically. Although they won the largest number of seats, they had to continue ruling without an overall majority, as the table below shows.

1962 election results	
Party	Seats
Progressive Conservative Party	116
Liberal Party	100
Social Credit Party	38
New Democratic Party	19

Nuclear policy

After the Arrow crisis, it was clear to many that Diefenbaker had no coherent policy on nuclear weapons. The fact that he had allowed US surface-to-air missiles on to Canadian soil was a matter of grave concern, not only to those who objected to nuclear weapons, but also to those who felt that US influence in Canada was already too strong. Such concerns had arisen earlier in Diefenbaker's premiership, when he signed the North American Air Defense Agreement (NORAD) with the USA. This established an integrated air-defence system under the joint control of both nations. However, at that time Diefenbaker refused to allow nuclear weapons into Canada; he also denied tactical nuclear weapons to Canadian troops serving under NATO in Europe.

In January 1963, the NATO commander told Diefenbaker that Canada was failing to honour its agreement with NATO by refusing to accept nuclear weapons. Sensing an opportunity, the opposition changed tack, and the Liberal leader Lester Pearson announced that the Conservative government should honour its pledge to NATO.

As support ebbed away, the Conservatives tried to win the backing of the Social Credit Party. However, before committing their support, members of Social Credit wanted the Conservatives to give a clear and decisive explanation of their defence policy. Dissatisfied with the answer it received, the Social Credit Party joined forces with the Liberals and the New Democratic Party to bring a vote of no-confidence against the government. At a critical moment in the Cold War, Diefenbaker's inability to reassure his political opponents and the Canadian public about defence of their country ensured his downfall. In the 1963 election, the Liberals took power once more.

Discussion point

How far does your study of Diefenbaker's ministry support the view that it is impossible to fully understand the history of a country without considering foreign policy?

Activity

Copy and complete the chart below to show evidence of Diefenbaker's successes and failures. In the last column, make a judgement about how successful Diefenbaker was in that area by awarding a mark out of six – the greater the success, the higher the mark. Explain the marks you have awarded. When you have completed the chart, write a paragraph that reaches an overall judgement about Diefenbaker's administration.

Issue	Evidence of success	Evidence of failure	Judgement/6
Electoral performance			
Economic performance			
Social policy			
The Arrow crisis			
Nuclear policy			

How successful was the Pearson administration?

Liberal electoral successes

Despite the failings of Diefenbaker's government and the Liberals' promise of '60 Days of Decision' – during which they would make plans to revive the Canadian economy and the country's credibility in foreign affairs – the party was unable to win an overall majority in either the 1963 or the 1965 elections (see tables on page 86). It gained support from the business community, the professional classes, the army and the civil service. However, in 1963 Diefenbaker led a surprisingly energetic campaign against his challengers, and to many people he still seemed preferable to the comparably unexciting Lester Pearson.

1963 election results		1965 election results	
Party	Seats	Party	Seats
Liberal Party	128	Liberal Party	131
Progressive Conservatives	95	Progressive Conservatives	97
Social Credit Party	24	New Democratic Party	21
New Democratic Party	17	Social Credit Party	5

Discussion point

Why do you think that Pearson was unable to win an overall majority in either the 1963 or the 1965 elections?

Economic policy

Pearson's administration got off to a bad start with the budget. The finance minister, Walter Gordon, was an ardent economic nationalist, and he immediately introduced plans to block the foreign takeover of Canadian industry. His programme was unpopular with the business community – which relied on foreign interests – and Gordon was soon forced to revise his plans.

Despite this, Pearson presided over the start of a 20-year period of almost unbroken prosperity in Canada, and the economic upturn naturally reflected well on the prime minister. By 1966, unemployment was relatively low, at 3.4%, and the purchasing power of incomes began to rise significantly. However, this prosperity was regional and several areas continued to suffer economic problems, including Newfoundland, central Ontario and rural Quebec.

Development areas

In order to tackle the issues in poorer regions, Pearson introduced a fund for rural economic development, which provided grants for schools, adult education and land purchase. Elderly farmers who left the land were also offered guaranteed minimum incomes. Development areas were established in places where unemployment was high. The Liberals also allocated more money to the Atlantic Development Board (which had been established by the Conservatives) and set up the Area Development Agency, which offered grants to companies that settled in the development areas. Gradually, the number of regions covered by the scheme was extended so that even more Canadians benefited.

The Auto Pact 1965

Perhaps the most important scheme Pearson introduced was the 1965 Auto Pact. This agreement removed the duties (import taxes) on trucks, cars and vehicle parts moving between Canada and the USA, creating a 'one-industry' free-trade area. The pact helped to guarantee levels of production and investment in the Canadian automobile industry, which was also nationalised. With the rise in exports came a resulting rise in the numbers employed in the car industry. As a result, by 1970 Canadian automobile production was showing a small profit.

The rise of the unions

The economic picture was not all success under Pearson. Throughout the 1960s, strikes increased as union membership grew and the right to strike was extended to civil servants. Typically, strikes were rare as they could take place only after a period of negotiation between unions and employers, often with compulsory arbitration by an independent body. However, the rise in union membership gave the workers greater influence during these negotiations, which led to more frequent cases of stalemate. During Pearson's premiership, strikes occurred over wages, working conditions and benefits – an indication that the unions were trying to use the improved economic climate to regain living standards eroded previously.

Despite the rise in the number of strikes and a series of trade crises, Pearson's time in office is remembered as one of economic growth, rising exports and domestic investments. Visual evidence of the boom could be seen across the country in the form of the steel mills constructed in Quebec, the expansion of the Montreal and Toronto subways and the Nova Scotia heavy water plant for atomic energy, among many examples.

Prime minister Lester Pearson, with the premiers of Ontario and Quebec – John Roberts (left) and Jean Lesage (right)

Theory of knowledge

History and economics

'The study of economic history requires different skills to that of any other field of historical study.' How far do you agree with this view?

Social policy

Very little social legislation was introduced in Canada in the 1950s, but this changed in the following decade. In the five years of Pearson's premiership – and remarkably without the Liberals having a majority in parliament – widespread reforms were passed. In part, this was a direct result of the improved economic situation, which allowed investment in other areas. There was also pressure from the media to increase social provision, and Pearson knew it would secure his continued popularity with the people.

Throughout Pearson's time in office, the state took on more and more social responsibilities, and became increasingly interventionist and paternalistic. Some critics accused the government of pursuing socialist policies, but it continued to rely heavily on the private sector and there were far fewer objections in Canada to federal intervention than there were in the USA in the 1960s. The scope of Pearson's social policies was wide, and included a War on Poverty like that in the USA (see page 52), heavier investment in welfare programmes and a widening of the social safety net in the form of insurance schemes.

Tom Kent, Pearson's main policy advisor, regarded the changes to health care as 'the most important of all the social reforms introduced by the Pearson administration'. Moves towards a national health-insurance scheme began in 1957, but the Liberals extended the programme from acute hospital stays and diagnostic treatments to include doctor services. There were four principles behind the act:

- universality of coverage
- a comprehensive definition of services to be provided by doctors
- the transfer of benefits between provinces
- public administration of the scheme.

The healthcare proposals caused some debate in Conservative provinces, but ultimately the scheme was approved and the costs were divided between the federal and provincial governments.

The Canadian Pension Plan was also a major step in improving the lives of many Canadians. This established a mandatory investment fund, which pooled the money deducted from wages to provide a minimum standard of living. Not only was the scheme contributory, it was also universal and portable, meaning it could be carried from one province to another if an individual moved out of his or her native province. The federal government also agreed to increase the share of personal income tax that the provinces received, which allowed provincial governments to further expand their social service provision.

Pearson was acutely aware that one of the greatest limits on economic advancement – for individuals and the nation as a whole – was the lack of educational facilities in some of the less affluent provinces. His government therefore placed a great deal of emphasis on providing funds to improve a range of education services in these areas, in the hope of benefiting the population in the longer term (see the section on economic policy on page 86).

There were other attempts to introduce social modernisation to Canada. Capital punishment was temporarily suspended (it was formally abolished in 1976), and amendments were made to the criminal code dealing with both divorce and sexual morality. The position of women also improved, largely as a result of the establishment in 1966 of the Committee for the Equality of Women in Canada, which forced the government to launch a Royal Commission to investigate their status.

National unity

The greatest challenge Pearson's government faced was the problem of Quebec. This is covered in detail on pages 91–99, but the situation there highlighted a larger problem in Canada as a whole: the country's cultural and linguistic diversity meant that there was no strong sense of national unity. The federal structure of government gave the provinces a great deal of power, and this led to concerns that certain regions would soon want greater independence – and perhaps even to break from Canada altogether. To bridge the divide between French-speaking and English-speaking parts of Canada, the Liberals launched campaigns promoting bilingualism and encouraging a greater understanding of the different cultures within the country.

Perhaps the most enduring legacy of the moves towards increased unity came with the retirement of the British Union flag and the introduction of the distinctive Canadian Maple Leaf flag in February 1965. The Canadian MP John Matheson remarked that 'the search for a flag was really a search for a country'. Even this decision faced opposition, however – notably from former prime minister Diefenbaker, who called the new flag the 'Pearson Pennant'. In the end, the issue was only decided after the government ruled an end to the debate and forced a vote.

The new Canadian flag is raised for the first time at Canada House in London on 15 February 1965

The new flag provided a symbol around which the nation could unite – an issue that became increasingly important as Canada approached its centenary in 1967. However, when Pearson retired in 1968 there were still many questions to answer about Canada's future and, most significantly, that of Quebec.

Activity

On page 85, you copied and completed a chart on the success and failures of the Diefenbaker administration. Now copy and complete the chart below to carry out the same exercise for Pearson's administration. Using the information in the chart, write a paragraph that reaches an overall judgement about the success of the Pearson government.

Issue	Evidence of success	Evidence of failure	Judgement/6
Electoral success			
Economic policy			
Social reform			
National unity			
Quebec			
Other			

What were the causes and consequences of the Quiet Revolution?

Background

In June 1960, the Union Nationale in Quebec was defeated by the Quebec Liberal Party. The death of former Union Nationale leader **Maurice Duplessis** and his successor paved the way for a Liberal victory, but this was more than just a symbolic change in the provincial government of Quebec. It marked the start of a major transformation of the social, cultural, industrial and political landscape of the province. This period has been called the Quiet (or Silent) Revolution, because Quebec's transformation from an 'anachronism in North America', as one commentator described it, to a modern and energetic society was expected to take place rapidly but largely passively.

Maurice Duplessis (1890–1959) Duplessis was the founder of the Union Nationale party. He rose to power through exposing the misconduct and patronage of the Liberals. However, his period in office was little better and became known as the 'Great Darkness' because of the corruption and scandal that characterised it. Duplessis favoured the rural areas of Quebec over the urban, upheld the provincial rights of Quebec against the federal government, and made little investment in social services in the province. As a result, Quebec fell behind other parts of Canada in development and modernisation.

Long-term causes

Unlike most other areas of Canada, the population of Quebec was predominantly French and Catholic, and many of its inhabitants resented British and American cultural dominance there. During the 1940s and 1950s, Quebec nationalism was confined to defending provincial rights against federal interference, but cultural and political changes in the wider world altered the situation in Quebec. After the Second World War, old empires collapsed and there was a growing campaign for decolonisation in many parts of the world. In 1962, the French colony of Algeria was granted its independence – an event that encouraged French Canadians in their desire for greater freedom from central government control.

At the same time, the position and influence of the Catholic Church was changing. The new freedoms available to society in the post-war world made religion seem less important to many people than it had before. In 1962, the Council of the Catholic Church (known as Vatican II) convened to discuss how to respond to this new world. The decisions made by this council led to greater liberalisation of the Church after decades of conservatism.

Nonetheless, the Catholic Church remained influential in Quebec. It had significant control over education in the province but failed to administer this properly. Higher education was only available to a minority of French Canadians. In the early 1960s, only 63% of French Canadians reached Grade 7 and 13% finished Grade 11, compared with 36% of English-speaking Canadians. French Canadians were growing increasingly dissatisfied with this situation, believing it was preventing their social advancement.

Meanwhile, industrial changes and their social consequences, which had been evolving since the Industrial Revolution, were also challenging traditional values. These developments have prompted historians such as Jacques Rouillard to argue that the Quiet Revolution may in fact have accelerated the natural evolution of an anti-French society, rather than turn it on its head. Rouillard believed that, although the Quiet Revolution was a period of great innovation, it grew out of the revolutionary social and political civil rights and women's movements that developed in North America after the Second World War.

The idea that the Quiet Revolution was a continuation of earlier developments has some validity. Significant progress was made in Quebec while Sir Wilfrid Laurier was prime minster (1896–1911) and under the premiership of Adélard Godbout (1939–44), who nationalised the electricity industry in Montreal and introduced both universal suffrage and compulsory schooling until the age of 14. This interpretation was also supported by Donald Creighton, who argued that 'in reality, it differed from its predecessors only where its scope and intensity had been increased by the special circumstances of the past quarter century'. Provincial developments were not unique to Quebec. Under the premiership of Louis Robichaud (1960–70), New Brunswick also enjoyed a period of rapid modernisation, adding further weight to the view that the changes in Quebec were part of a wider movement.

Discussion point

Was the Quiet Revolution the result of events in Quebec or wider changes affecting North American society as a whole?

Short-term causes

The government in Quebec had been controlled by Duplessis and his Union Nationale party since 1944, and despite accusations of corruption, Duplessis enjoyed widespread support. He spoke scathingly of the Liberals, accusing them of being left-wing and even pro-communist. He argued that foreign companies and investments were denying Canadians the benefits from natural resources such as iron ore, which was being exploited by US-based firms at the expense of local businesses. This, Duplessis said, was the reason so many French workers lived below the poverty line.

The Catholic Church was powerful in Quebec, but it worked quite harmoniously with Duplessis, who claimed that 'the bishops eat out of my hand'. This began to change in the 1960s. A book called *Les Insolences du Frère Untel* ('The Impertinences of Brother Anonymous'), written by the Catholic Jean-Paul Desbiens, was an open attack on the existing system of public education in the province. Desbiens also criticised the poor quality of the French language in Quebec, which he referred to as *joual* (a dialect associated with the working classes of Montreal). He called for wide-reaching reform in all aspects of education. The book quickly sold 100,000 copies and caused many to question the influence of the Catholic Church in Quebec.

However, it was Duplessis' death in 1959, followed by that of his successor, Paul Sauvé, that really opened the way for a new political regime. Duplessis had given the people of Quebec pride in themselves. He had begun to break the power of the Catholic Church and, most importantly, he left a budgetary surplus that would be used to fund the developments and reforms of the 1960s.

The loss of strong leadership in the Union Nationale gave the Liberals their opportunity. Campaigning under the slogans *Il faut que ça change* ('Things have to change') and *Maîtres chez nous* ('Masters in our own house'), **Jean Lesage** (see page 94) swept to power in Quebec in 1960. Described by Duplessis as 'the only person I know who can strut sitting down', Lesage introduced widespread reforms that transformed Quebec from a 'sleepy, priest-ridden society to a modern entity'.

Jean Lesage (1912–80) Born in Montreal and educated in Quebec, Lesage graduated with a law degree, and later served in the Canadian army reserve. He became leader of the Liberal Party in Quebec in 1958 and is generally regarded as the 'father of the Quiet Revolution', holding the office of premier of Quebec from 1960 to 1966. During his period in office, he oversaw the ending of the dominance of English-speaking Canadians and the Catholic Church in Quebec. These were replaced by an increased role for the government, which modernised much of Quebec society and economy.

Activities

- Construct a spider diagram to show the causes of the Quiet Revolution. Mark the long-term causes in one colour and the short-term causes in another.

- Draw a chart with two columns. In the first column list the causes and in the second explain the significance of the cause.

- Which factor do you think was the most important in bringing about the Quiet Revolution? Why?

The consequences of the Quiet Revolution

It was an English Canadian journalist who coined the term 'Quiet Revolution', suggesting that the changes would be both limited and conservative. As it happened, this was not entirely the case, and many new initiatives were less manageable than the Liberals envisaged. The changes encompassed economic, social, cultural and political aspects of life. The moderniser Lesage was fortunate that his Cabinet supported many of his ideas. Among these Cabinet members were the minister of education, Paul Gérin-Lajoie, who campaigned to increase Quebec's provincial jurisdiction, and the minister of natural resources, René Lévesque, who pushed for nationalisation of resources and an end to English dominance in industry. The federal government recognised this desire for change and supported the new reforming premier of Quebec.

SOURCE A

It is now clear to all of us, I think, that French-speaking Canadians are determined to become directors of their economic and cultural destiny in their own changed and changing society ... they also ask for equal and full opportunities to participate in all federal government services.

Prime minister Lester Pearson, speaking in December 1962.

Economic developments

Lesage wanted Quebec to have its own economic policy, and Lévesque agreed – proclaiming that the 'nation' of Quebec should have its own industries like other countries. Such ideas were widely popular with the people of Quebec, and in the 1962 provincial elections the Liberals were returned to power with an increased majority. Their promise to nationalise the electric company was fulfilled within six months and led to the establishment of Hydro Quebec. Not only did this show the strength of the government, it also marked the start of a series of major projects. These included the further development of hydro-electric power and the establishment of a range of public companies, such as SIDBEC for iron and steel, SOQUEM for mining, REXFOR for forests and SOQUIP for petroleum.

The profits generated by these companies gave the province a certain amount of financial autonomy, and they were used to fund many of Lesage's social policies. At the same time as establishing large companies, the Quebec government also created the Société Générale de Financement to encourage Quebec's inhabitants to invest in and increase the profits of small companies.

Such economic development caused a profound change in the employment structure of the province. The service sector grew dramatically in both size and importance, increasing from 37.2% of those employed in 1946 to 59.7% by 1966. Economic growth also had an impact on population distribution, as more French-speaking Canadians moved to the cities. At first, very few were able to access higher-level jobs and there were hardly any French speakers among the economic élite in the boardrooms. However, nationalisation changed this, opening up jobs to French speakers and allowing a new middle class to gain greater wealth and power.

Social and cultural changes

The need for change in education had been a main cause of the Quiet Revolution, and it was one of the first areas addressed by Lesage's new policies. In 1961, a Parent Committee was established to investigate the present system and make recommendations for change. It was this committee that pushed for control of education to be taken out of the Church's hands. In 1964, the Ministry of Education was established; Catholic and Protestant schools were allowed to continue operating, but they were brought under secular control. The ministry also raised the compulsory school-leaving age from 14 to 16, which gave greater educational opportunities to all. At the same time, school was made free of charge for all children up to Grade 11 (age 16 or 17), school boards were reorganised and the curriculum was standardised.

Education was not the only area to see major changes. In 1963, Quebec introduced its own pension plan and in 1964 a new Labour Code was agreed. This made it easier for workers to form unions and gave public employees the right to strike. The government also took on responsibility for health care and, as with education, created a ministry. Public services were expanded as a genuine welfare state was created.

The greatest cultural consequence of Quiet Revolution in Quebec was the rise in status of the French language. In 1969, the Canadian prime minister Pierre Trudeau introduced the Official Languages Act (see page 101), and in 1974 Canada became bilingual on a federal level. At the same time, however, the Liberal premier of Quebec, Robert Bourassa, passed a bill adopting French as the only official language of the province. Businesses that operated in English, or even in both languages, faced restrictions. Children who wanted to attend English-speaking schools had to pass language tests to prove their English-language skills.

This was a bold and deliberate statement about Quebec's desire to have an increased say in its own affairs, but in fact the bill was resented by both sides of the divide. English speakers felt that it went too far, whilst Quebec nationalists argued that it did not go far enough. As a result, the Liberals lost support and were defeated in the 1976 election by the Parti Québécois (PQ), led by the former Liberal minister **René Lévesque**.

René Lévesque (1922–87) Lévesque was a former television news reporter and a Liberal politician. He founded the Parti Québécois in 1968, and was premier of Quebec from 1976 to 1985. During his period in office, Lévesque attempted to win separation from Canada for Quebec. A referendum was held in 1980, in which 80% voted against the move.

René Lévesque is greeted with cheers by supporters of his leftist Parti Québécois in 1973

Despite his earlier role in the Liberal ministry, Lévesque believed that the Liberal government had provided too little too late, and vowed to take reforms in Quebec further. Once in power, the PQ continued with pro-French policies, and in 1977 it passed Bill 101 – the Charter of the French Language. This banned English on commercial signs and further restricted access to English education. French was the only recognised language of the National Assembly and courts. In passing this bill, the Quebec government aimed to preserve French cultural identity, which it believed was threatened by the free-market economy and demographic changes.

Bill 101 represented the culmination of the struggle between individual rights and collective survival as French Canadians attempted to reconquer Quebec, and the policy caused much debate. The author Daniel Poliquin, an ardent anti-separatist, argued: 'For many Anglophone citizens, language belongs to the private domain, and state intervention was seen as an unspeakable violation of privacy on the part of the government. A mistaken assessment that I can understand, but that in no way lessens my high regard for this just and victorious struggle.'

However, this view should be contrasted with Montreal's Mordecai Richler, who wrote: 'The most vibrant original culture in Canada is French Canadian. But at the same time, it's so fragile that the mere sight of a bilingual street sign is sufficient to propel it into the nearest intensive care unit.'

Discussion point

Which do you think had the greater impact on Quebec, economic or social and cultural changes?

Political change and the October Crisis of 1970

The political changes that occurred in Quebec during the Quiet Revolution were far less 'quiet' than the social and economic developments, and had an impact beyond the borders of the province. During Lesage's period of leadership (1960–66), Quebec opted out of 29 federal-provincial cost-sharing schemes in an effort to exert its independence from federal control. However, Lesage was not a separatist, and during his ministry Lévesque grew increasingly impatient with what he regarded as insufficient reform under the Liberals. As a result, he formed his own party to challenge the Liberal government. He eventually succeeded in 1976, but the separatist movement in Quebec had been gathering pace for more than a decade before this.

On a visit to Montreal for Expo '67 – a World's Fair celebrating Canada's centenary – the French president Charles de Gaulle remarked that Quebec reminded him of an occupied country, and he closed a speech at the exposition with the words 'Vive le Québec libre!' ('Long live free Quebec!'), a statement that legitimised the radical wing of Quebec nationalism and became the rallying cry for the separatist movement. The Canadian prime minister Lester Pearson denounced de Gaulle's comments and declared: 'Canadians do not need to be liberated. Indeed many thousands of Canadians gave their lives in two world wars in the liberation of France.'

De Gaulle's speech encouraged an already-radical anti-American separatist group called the Front de libération du Québec (FLQ). This loose coalition of Marxists and revolutionaries had been conducting a terror campaign since 1963, which included bombings and armed robberies. In March 1969, the FLQ issued a sinister announcement that stated: 'In a little while the English, the federalists, the exploiters, the toadies of the occupiers, the lackeys of imperialism – all those who betray the workers and the Quebec nation – will fear for their lives.'

On 5 October 1970, it seemed that this threat had been carried out. A group of armed FLQ terrorists burst into the home of the British trade commissioner, James Cross, and took him prisoner. They demanded a ransom of $500,000 in gold bullion and the release of 23 FLQ prisoners. On 10 October, the FLQ also kidnapped Quebec's labour minister, Pierre Laporte. In response, the prime minister Pierre Trudeau ordered the army into Ottawa to protect the government. Confronted by a journalist who asked how far he was willing to take this armed response, Trudeau responded 'Just watch me'. He went on to state: 'Democracy first must preserve itself. Within Canada there is ample room for opposition and dissent, but none for intimidation and terror.'

On 15 October, the Quebec premier asked for federal intervention in the crisis. Trudeau responded by invoking the War Measures Act, which gave the government virtually dictatorial powers in the province. Canada was placed under martial law, civil liberties were suspended, the FLQ was banned and the police were given the power to arrest and detain anyone without explanation or trial. This was the first time that the War Measures Act had been used during peacetime, and it caused dissent in parliament. Tommy Douglas, the leader of the New Democratic Party (NDP), argued that Trudeau was using a 'sledgehammer to crack a peanut'.

The response from the FLQ was almost immediate – the next day Laporte was murdered. By December, the police had surrounded the hideout where Cross was being held. He was released by the terrorists in return for their free passage to Cuba, but within a few weeks the police had captured those responsible for Laporte's death.

The October Crisis was a turning point in attempts to bring about separatism, but the measures introduced by the Parti Québécois did not end with Bill 101. In 1980, Lévesque organised a referendum over whether the government could start to negotiate for 'sovereignty association', by which Quebec would be a separate country but allowed to enjoy the economic benefits of confederation.

With public feeling generally in favour of separatism, it seemed the PQ could not fail. However, the campaign for the referendum was badly managed. Women who expressed uncertainty about separatism were labelled 'Yvettes' – a term of derision implying a stereotypical Canadian housewife. Such bullying encouraged many women to vote against the proposal on principle. The language laws also undermined the appeal of separatism, as Quebec already appeared to be master of its own destiny and there was therefore little advantage in separation. As a result of this, Lévesque's proposal was defeated in the referendum, and Quebec remained united with Canada.

Why do you think that separatism ultimately had such little appeal to the people of Quebec?

Why was Trudeau able to remain in power for so long?

Trudeau's image

Pierre Trudeau (see page 100) succeeded Lester Pearson as Liberal prime minister of Canada in 1968. His personality soon won him many admirers. His young and suave image appeared to capture the spirit of a new era, and he was greeted with a wave of hysteria as 'Trudeaumania' swept across Canada. The historian Desmond Morton reflected that 'for a few warm spring months in 1968 Pierre Elliott Trudeau synthesised the dreams, achievements and illusions of the liberation era'.

Pierre Trudeau (1919–2000) Born of French Canadian parents, Trudeau dominated Canadian politics from 1968 to 1984. An intellectual who had been a professor of law before entering politics in the 1960s, he became secretary to Pearson and then minister of justice. Despite acquiring a playboy image, his personal motto of 'reason before passion' reflected his workaholic temperament. Trudeau was adored by supporters for his intelligence and efforts towards the preservation of Canadian unity, but criticised by opponents for his mismanagement of the economy. He remains a controversial figure in Canadian politics to this day.

During the 1968 campaign, Trudeau seemed less a political leader than a film star. His enthusiasm and energy inspired the same in a whole new generation of supporters, and contrasted significantly with the withdrawn personality of the Conservative candidate Robert Stanfield. Even before he came to power, therefore, Trudeau's populist appeal and playboy image overshadowed his real inclinations as a strong reformer and a determined politician, undeterred by extreme circumstances.

This more serious side to his personality was notably revealed during the October Crisis, but glimpses of it could be seen during the campaign. The day before the election, Trudeau attended the annual St Jean Baptiste Day celebrations in Montreal. Whilst sitting in the bandstand with other dignitaries, Quebec separatist agitators forced their way forward and began throwing missiles and stones. Everyone except Trudeau fled. The future prime minister waved away his bodyguard and despite being nearly hit, he refused to move or flinch. The mayor of Montreal, Jean Drapeau, returned to Trudeau's side and together they faced down the demonstrators. If any single act won Trudeau the respect of the Canadian people it was this, and it undoubtedly played a part in securing his electoral victory.

Pierre Trudeau receives film-star treatment from his supporters in 1968

Social change

Trudeau fought the 1968 election campaign under the slogan 'the Just Society', and during his time in power he set out to establish a participatory democracy, expanding the welfare state through his defence of the healthcare programme, and implementing many reforms designed to help parliament run more smoothly. For example, the Criminal Code was amended to safeguard individual rights, and family allowance was raised. In 1971, unemployment insurance was expanded and the ceiling was removed so that its provision became universal.

A multicultural Canada

The greatest social changes came in the field of multiculturalism. Trudeau followed up the findings of a Royal Commission established by Lester Pearson, and introduced a range of measures that adopted a 'multicultural policy within a bilingual framework'.

Trudeau's first notable reform in this regard was the Official Languages Act of 1969. This ensured that Canadians – whether French- or English-speaking – had access to federal services in their own language. It was followed by regulations that required bilingual labelling on all commercial products. In 1971, Trudeau introduced the Multiculturalism Act, which guaranteed equality for all cultural and ethnic groups within a bilingual nation. Funding was provided for ethnic organisations and second-language instruction. This represented a considerable shift in attitude, as multiculturalism was now federally supported. Despite concerns at the time that multiculturalism would be a dividing force in society, it did not lead to the collapse of national unity or chaos. Trudeau's policies were largely successful, and they played a significant role in defeating the separatist claims of Quebec.

In the same way that Trudeau tried to reduce cultural tensions, he also aimed to limit regional inequalities. In 1969, he established the Department of Regional Economic Expansion. He protected the farming community through tariffs, and established import quotas and provincial marketing boards. These policies effectively nationalised the economy.

Native Canadian affairs

One notable failure in Trudeau's social policies were those regarding Native Canadians. In 1969, the government published a White Paper on Indian Affairs. This recommended the abolition of the Department of Indian Affairs and the Indian Act (which gave the federal government control over Indian issues), the transfer of responsibility for Native rights to the provinces, the elimination of reservations, and the ending of the special status for Native Canadians.

Putting these recommendations into practice would bring Native Canadians into mainstream society and encourage equality through assimilation. The proposals divided Canadian society. The Native Canadian senator James Gladstone supported the measures and argued that the goal of absolute equality outweighed the short-term losses. However, most Indian groups opposed the changes. Some argued that Native Canadians had a prior legal and historic claim to the land that could not be changed by an Act of Parliament. Native rights became a major political issue, and Trudeau was forced to back down. The government withdrew its proposals in 1971 and established an Office of Native Claims to deal with outstanding land issues.

Economic policy

Much like Diefenbaker, Trudeau grew increasingly concerned about the growing US domination of the Canadian economy. To combat this, he initiated a policy of economic nationalisation. In 1973, Trudeau introduced the Foreign Investment Review Agency (FIRA). The agency was to screen foreign business takeovers and decide if they benefited Canada, but in practice it did little more than discourage investment and growth.

The establishment of the national oil company Petro Canada in 1975 helped to 'Canadianise' the petroleum industry, which had been dominated by foreign interests up to this time. Trudeau also launched a National Energy Policy in the 1980s, which increased Canadian ownership of the oil industry, forced the western provinces to give the central government a larger share of the revenue, and helped to make Canada more self-sufficient in energy. However, these policies angered both the USA and western Canada, which saw them as an assault on provincial resources.

The success of Trudeau's economic policies remains a matter of debate today. The rise in oil prices that characterised the latter part of the 1970s were largely the result of the Organization of Petroleum Exporting Countries (OPEC) controlling supply, but Trudeau's erratic economic policies did not help.

Policy changes from 1972

Trudeau failed to win a majority in the 1972 election, and remained in power at the head of a minority government that relied on the support of the New Democratic Party, which held the balance of power. This forced Trudeau into a move to the left. The 1973 budget revealed a drop in personal income tax, increased pensions and amendments to social–economic legislation, as the government adopted a more economic nationalist policy. When the 1974 budget was unveiled, however, political opposition to its plans ended in a no-confidence motion in parliament.

In the ensuing election campaign, the Conservative leader Stanfield proposed government-sanctioned wage and price controls to tackle the problem of inflation. Trudeau criticised the scheme and ran his own campaign on the slogan 'Zap! You're frozen' to deride Stanfield's policies. Trudeau won the election, but almost immediately introduced a similar policy. This allowed wages to rise at the rate of inflation plus 2%, and prices to rise only when a cost rise could be demonstrated. The policy failed and was aborted in 1978. Such events highlighted the confusion that surrounded many of Trudeau's economic strategies, and by 1979 the prime minister faced a country in the grip of a declining population and rising national debt.

The fall and rise of Trudeau

Much of Trudeau's time in office was spent dealing with issues in Quebec, and this allowed the Conservative Party to gain ground in more national issues. In addition, Trudeau alienated the western provinces with his oil policy, and many people felt that federal government control had extended too far. The economy was struggling, inflation was rising, and many were weary of Trudeau's arrogance. He delayed the next election for as long as possible, but it was eventually held in 1979. The Liberals took only one seat west of Winnipeg and lost much of urban Ontario. Trudeau resigned as leader of the Liberal Party, but his time in Canadian politics was not over yet.

The result of the election brought Progressive Conservative leader **Joe Clark** into power at the head of a minority government. Clark's political rise had been rapid – so much so that after his election victory one newspaper ran the headline 'Joe Who?' His inexperience soon became clear. He pledged to move the location of the Canadian embassy in Israel from Tel Aviv to Jerusalem; he privatised Petro Canada, causing a rise in the price of petrol; he delayed calling parliament; and he lacked support in Quebec. When parliament did meet, it passed one bill – a minor amendment to old-age pensions – but when the government tried to introduce a tough budget to tackle the economic crisis, it was defeated. After just nine months in power, Clark faced another election. The Liberals pleaded with Trudeau to return, to which he readily agreed. In February 1980, he was reinstalled as prime minister, quoting the poet Robert Frost: 'I have promises to keep, and miles to go before I sleep.'

Joe Clark (b. 1939) A statesman, businessman, university professor and journalist, Joe Clark's rise to political prominence was dramatic. He entered parliament in 1972, but became leader of the Progressive Conservatives in 1976 and was sworn in as prime minister on the day before his 40th birthday in 1979. Although his premiership did not last long, he returned to government in 1984, serving in Brian Mulroney's cabinet.

Activity

Make a copy of the set of scales opposite. On one side list all the achievements of the Trudeau administration and on the other side the failings. Which side do you think is the heaviest and should be Trudeau's lasting legacy? Why? Write a paragraph explaining your answer.

Activity

You have now considered the three Canadian prime ministers from 1957 to 1980. Copy and complete the chart below to summarise their achievements and reach a judgement about their relative successes.

Issue	Diefenbaker	Pearson	Trudeau
Electoral success			
Economic policy			
Social policy			
Handling crises			
Other			

End of chapter activities

Paper 3 exam practice

Question

Assess the causes of the Quiet Revolution in Quebec.
[20 marks]

Skill focus

Writing an introductory paragraph

Examiner's tips

Once you have planned your answer to a question (as described in Chapter 3), you should be able to begin writing a clear introductory paragraph. This needs to set out your main line of argument and to outline **briefly** the key points you intend to make (and support with relevant and precise own knowledge) in the main body of your essay. Remember – 'To what extent … ?' and 'How far … ?' questions clearly require analysis of opposing arguments – and a judgement. If, after writing your plan, you think you will be able to make a clear final judgement, it is a good idea to state in your introductory paragraph what overall line of argument/judgement you intend to make.

Depending on the wording of the question, you may also find it useful to define in your introductory paragraph what you understand by key terms, such as 'Quiet Revolution'. You should briefly explain that the term refers to the reforms that took place in Quebec in the 1960s, ending with the October Crisis of 1970. This latter date is important, as you should not cover events that occured in the 1970s. However, you should also remember that the focus must be on the **causes** and not the reforms themselves.

For this question you should:

- define the terms of the question
- identify the issues or themes that you will consider – either in the form of long-term and short-term causes or religious, social, economic and political factors
- offer your view about the most important reason for the Quiet Revolution, an argument that you should follow throughout the rest of the essay.

Setting out this approach in your introductory paragraph will help you keep the demands of the question in mind. Remember to refer back to your introduction after every couple of paragraphs in your main answer.

Common mistake

A common mistake (one that might suggest to an examiner a candidate who has not thought deeply about what is required) is to fail to write an introductory paragraph at all. This is often done by candidates who rush into writing **before** analysing the question and doing a plan. The result may well be that they focus entirely on the word 'causes' and give a long introductory account of the policies and their consequences – an approach that is likely to result in a narrative of events of the 1960s. Even if the answer is full of detailed and accurate own knowledge, this will **not** answer the question, and so will not score highly.

Sample student introductory paragraph

The Quiet Revolution that began with the election of Lesage's Liberal government in Quebec in June 1960 was completed by the October Crisis of 1970. The revolution witnessed changes particularly to the social, cultural and economic life of Quebec and dramatically altered the position of French Canadians. Although the immediate trigger for the revolution was the death of the Union Nationale leader Maurice Duplessis, and the resultant ending of the party's political dominance, there were both short-term and long-term developments that made the revolution possible. The Quiet Revolution was, at least in part, a response to changes that were taking place within a wider society, with increased industrialisation and secularisation also prompting changes in New Brunswick, and throughout North American society as a whole. Quebec nationalism had been growing for some time, but with events such as Algerian independence, the process that started the revolution can be traced back even further.

This is a good introduction, as it shows a clear understanding of the topic and sets out a logical plan clearly focused on the demands of the question. It demonstrates a sound appreciation that to assess the causes, it is necessary to explain what is meant by the term 'Quiet Revolution', and it explicitly demonstrates to the examiner what aspects the candidate intends to address. This indicates that the answer – if it remains analytical and well supported – is likely to be a high-scoring one.

Activity

In this chapter, the focus is on writing a useful introductory paragraph. Using the information from this chapter, and any other sources of information available to you, write introductory paragraphs for **at least two** of the following Paper 3 practice questions.

Remember to refer to the simplified Paper 3 markscheme on page 223.

Paper 3 practice questions

1 Assess the reasons why, after a landslide victory in 1958, the Conservatives lost power in 1963.

2 How successful was Diefenbaker as leader of the Progressive Conservative Party?

3 'Despite their failure to achieve an overall majority, Pearson's Liberal governments were the most successful in bringing about social and welfare change in Canada in the period 1957–80.' To what extent do you agree with this statement?

4 How revolutionary was the Quiet Revolution?

5 How effectively did the federal and provincial governments in Canada deal with the problem of Quebec?

6 Assess the reasons why Pierre Trudeau was able to remain in power for so long.

5 Argentina under Perón 1945–55

Key questions

- Why was Perón elected president in 1946 and how did he consolidate his power?
- What were the characteristics of Perón's regime and how far does it deserve to be called populist?
- How successful were the social, economic and political policies of Perón's administration?
- Why did Perón fall from power in 1955?

This chapter examines the rule of Juan Perón in Argentina, and explains how a virtually unknown army officer rose from obscurity and a minor role in an army coup in 1943 to become elected president of Argentina in 1946. It reviews the nature and characteristics of his regime, assessing its populist roots and placing it in the context of other political movements of the period. The social and economic policies of the government are analysed, and a judgement reached as to their success. This chapter also considers how Perón attempted to strengthen his position politically and how he dealt with opponents. Finally, it discusses his fall from power in 1955.

Overview

- The army seized power in Argentina in 1943, but it was widely expected that there would be a swift return to civilian government.
- These expectations were exploited by an army officer named Juan Perón, who developed a bond with the working classes through his position as minister of labour. He also strengthened his position by maintaining the support of his former fellow officers.
- Perón was ultimately brought to power by open election in 1946, but it was popular support and protests during the previous year that created the conditions for his candidacy as president.
- Perón's economic policies aimed to bring about social justice and increase support for the regime by their appeal to the working classes. Although he achieved some economic success, this was not sustained.
- Economic decline limited Perón's ability to implement his social reforms. Initially, these improved working and living conditions for many, but as progress slowed, the regime lost much of its traditional working-class support.
- Perón attempted to consolidate his position by creating the Peronist Party, holding mass rallies and granting women the right to vote. Trade unions were forced to elect Peronist supporters, whilst independent unions lost their rights.
- Legislation was passed that allowed Perón to stand for a second term as president. Meanwhile, opposition was stifled and denied access to the media during election campaigns.
- Initial attempts in June 1955 to bring about Perón's downfall were linked to the growing clash between Church and state. However, it was the loss of army support that eventually resulted in Perón's defeat in September 1955.

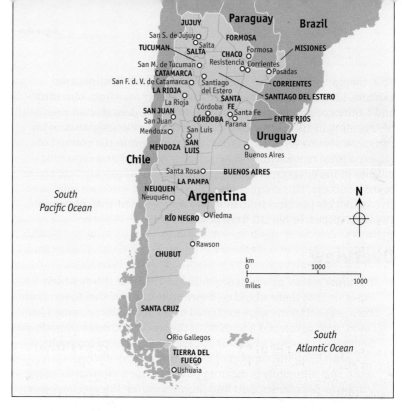

A map showing the major cities and provinces of Argentina

Why was Perón elected president in 1946 and how did he consolidate his power?

Background

In 1930, as the effects of the Great Depression spread through Argentina, the military overthrew the civilian government, claiming that it had failed to maintain order. A new government was installed under army control. The period that followed became known as the 'Infamous Decade', as it was characterised by electoral fraud, government corruption and the persecution of political opponents. The Depression resulted in an economic policy of import substitution industrialisation (see page 16), which gave Argentina greater economic independence. However, politically the period witnessed increasing conflict between right-wing fascists and left-wing radicals.

The outbreak of the Second World War in 1939 changed the political situation in Argentina. Initially it seemed that the government would commit Argentina on the side of the Allies (Britain, France and the Soviet Union) against Germany. However, the army feared the spread of Soviet communism, and there was much public pressure to remain neutral in the conflict. Neutrality was maintained for most of the war, and it was only in March 1945 that Argentina broke off diplomatic relations with the Axis Powers and joined the Allies.

While war raged elsewhere in the world, Argentina experienced domestic crises. After growing popular concern over government fraud and corruption, on 4 June 1943 another military coup overthrew the government of President Ramón Castillo to prevent the fraudulent election of his chosen successor, Robustiano Patrón Costas.

Perón's rise to power

The military coup that brought the army to power in 1943 had popular support, but most Argentineans expected it to result in a moderate administration that would quickly return power to a civilian government. **Juan Perón**'s role in the events of 1943 has been the subject of debate, but recent writing by the historian Jill Hedges argues that he played a significant role in engineering Castillo's fall, while maintaining a low profile to avoid the repercussions if things went wrong.

Juan Perón (1895–1974) Perón was the illegitimate son of working-class parents and his humble origins gave him a common bond with his second wife, Eva. He joined the army and in 1926, he attended the Superior War School to train for higher command. Perón did not support the coup of 1930, and as a result found himself punished by postings in outlying regions of the country. After the death of his first wife in 1938, he was sent to Italy, where he trained with an Italian regiment and visited Nazi Germany, witnessing mass rallies and Nazi organisation. He returned to Argentina in late 1940 and acted as an army instructor. After he was overthrown as president in 1955, Perón went into exile, but later returned and was elected president for a third time in 1973.

Juan Perón and his wife Eva inspecting troops in 1950

Perón's contribution to the coup resulted in his appointment as secretary to the minister of war in the new government and then as minister of labour. He used his power in these positions to build up a solid base of support amongst the armed forces – by arguing for better pay and career opportunities for junior officers, and for increased technology and industrialisation under military control. Perón also won the support of the working classes, claiming that he wanted to 'improve the standard of living of workers, but without social conflict'. His role as labour minister allowed him to build a relationship with the trade unions. Socialists from the main trade union, the General Confederation of Labour (CGT), formed an alliance with Perón in order to get labour laws passed.

Such developments gave Perón significant influence in an administration that was becoming increasingly isolated. Claiming that the government had become dictatorial, leaders of the Radical Party demanded a return to democratic rule, so the military regime was desperate to widen its base of support. Perón's popular appeal went some way to achieving this aim. In January 1944, after an earthquake struck San Juan, Perón took an active role in the relief work. This won him further approval and brought him to national attention. No one was surprised, therefore, when Perón was made vice-president and secretary of war later that year.

Perón now held two important posts in the Cabinet – secretary of war and secretary of labour. As labour secretary, he continued his policy of introducing welfare benefits for unionised workers, in exchange for union support of the government. As a result, the unions lost much of their earlier independence. At the same time, Perón began to spread the idea of an organic national community that offered social justice, stating that 'we must ensure labour's fair share of rewards and put every household under a decent roof'.

He combined this appeal with more blatant nationalism, calling for 'Honesty, Justice, Duty'. This appealed to the Catholic Church, which already enjoyed a strong relationship with the armed forces. The Church disliked liberal, radical forces, and opposed legislation such as state-controlled education and civil marriage, both of which were traditional areas of Church responsibility.

Under Perón's influence, it seemed to the Church that the government would restore traditional values and initiate policies similar to those that Mussolini had introduced in Fascist Italy. There, Catholicism had been recognised as the state religion and religious education had been made compulsory.

Arrest and recovery

On 18 September 1945, Perón gave a speech that became known as the 'From work to home and from home to work' address. In this, he pointed out the success of the social reforms that had been introduced by the government, and how they had made Argentineans 'proud to live where they live once again'. As part of this speech, Perón delivered a scathing attack on government opposition that delighted his audience and angered his enemies.

By this time, Perón's influence and policies had already provoked significant political rivalry, and this speech finally incited his opponents to action. On 9 October, his rivals in the army forced him to resign. A few days later, rumours spread that Perón had been arrested. In fact, he had been taken to the island of Martín García. Perón insisted he be seen by a doctor, who declared that the climate there was affecting his health. As a result, Perón was sent back to Buenos Aires, to a military hospital. However, the rumours that Perón had been imprisoned sparked a public outcry, and mass demonstrations were organised demanding his release.

There has been some debate over who arranged this show of support for Perón. His opponents claimed that **Eva Duarte Perón** played a significant role in mobilising the masses. However, she was not particularly well-known at the time, and it is more likely that Perón's detractors wanted to emphasise her role to make him seem weak – heavily influenced by and dependent on a woman.

Eva Duarte Perón (1919–52) Later nicknamed Evita, Eva Duarte was the youngest of five illegitimate children and spent her childhood in poverty. At the age of 15, she went to Buenos Aires to pursue an acting career. There are many stories surrounding her first meeting with Juan Perón, but it probably occurred during the relief operations following the San Juan earthquake. She became his mistress, but they married in 1945. Eva became active in politics, founding the Eva Perón Foundation to help the poor, and campaigning for female suffrage. In 1951, she was encouraged to stand for vice-president, but opposition from the army and her declining health led her to withdraw from the race. Soon after her death, the Argentinean Congress gave her the title 'Spiritual Leader of the Nation'.

Initially it seemed that Perón's followers in the CGT were responsible, but Eva herself challenged this, stating that 'no one gave the call to come out. The people came out on their own. It was not Perón's wife [sic]. It was not the CGT. It was the workers and the unions who themselves came into the street.'

Whatever the driving force behind this public show of support, Perón's fans mobilised on 17 October, with estimates of the numbers who marched to the Plaza de Mayo in Buenos Aires varying from between 100,000 to 1 million.

In fact, Perón's supporters in government had secured his release before this mass demonstration took place, but such a vast show of solidarity destroyed the political opposition. The event also allowed Perón to strengthen his relationship with the masses through the speech he delivered to the crowds in the Plaza.

Historian Rodolfo Puiggrós has suggested that the workers responded to the situation in such a way because 'the proletariat sought in Perón the political leadership it could not itself provide.' Jill Hedges has described the demonstrations and the speech Perón gave to his supporters in the Plaza as 'the apogee [climax] of the mystical relationship between Perón and the workers, a unique relationship which produced a unique movement by those workers to rescue their leader when he needed them.' The day became known as Loyalty Day, celebrated annually in Argentina as the day on which the Peronist movement was founded.

SOURCE A

I therefore put aside the sacred and honourable uniform given to me by the fatherland in order to put on civilian clothes and mix with that suffering, sweating mass which with its labour makes the greatness of the country. I give my final embrace to this institution which is the prop of the fatherland: the army. And I give my first embrace to this immense mass which represents the synthesis of a sentiment which had died in the Republic: the real civility of the Argentine people. I want now, as a simple citizen, mixing with this sweating mass, to press everyone against my heart as I could with my mother.

Extract from Perón's speech in the Plaza de Mayo, October 1945. Quoted in Monzalvo, L. Testigo de la primera hora del Peronismo. p. 192.

How did Perón appeal to the working classes in the speech in Source A? How did he try to maintain the support of the army? Why do you think that he considered it important to try to keep their support?

Crowds gather in the Plaza de Mayo, Buenos Aires, demanding Perón's release from prison on 17 October 1945

The 1946 election

Perón's restoration was swiftly followed by the announcement of a presidential election to be held in February 1946. Although Perón was an obvious candidate, he was not associated with a particular political party, which meant that he had no solid political backing. This changed in late October 1945 with the formation of the Partido Laborista (Labour Party), which offered Perón its nomination for the presidency. After this, Perón also secured the support of some members of the Radical Civic Union, who backed his measures to assist workers, as well as a few Conservatives who feared the rise of communism in Argentina.

In the run-up to the election, Perón consolidated his support with several populist measures:

- Decree 33.302 in December 1945 provided benefits for workers, including indexed wages (a way of calculating pensions and other benefits that takes into account overall changes in wage levels over time) and an end-of-year bonus that amounted to an extra month's wages.

- He increased employment opportunities through economic expansion, which brought him support from workers and some factory owners.
- There had been a 10% increase in real wages (a person's income after inflation has been taken into account) in the period 1940–44, and Perón benefited from this, as many workers associated the improvement in their economic position with him.
- Perón promised that he would bring about social justice, as 'the new social policy is based on the need to avoid a situation where some men are unduly rich and others unduly poor'.
- He won over the armed forces by increased spending on military equipment, training and expansion. This increased his prestige with – and his power over – the military.

During the campaign, Perón faced a divided and unfocused opposition, causing Daniel Lewis to comment that as early as mid 1944 Perón was challenged by only two real opponents. At home, opposition came from the Radicals and groups who benefited from a liberal economic policy. However, as these groups were from opposite ends of the political spectrum they were unable to form a united front against him.

The other opposition was from the USA, which regarded Perón as a fascist. This opinion had been formed in October 1943, after an event known as the Hellmuth Affair, in which it was discovered that Argentina had plans to buy arms from Nazi Germany. This relationship with their enemy naturally caused deep concern in the USA. After Perón was made minister for war, the US ambassador to Argentina informed the US that its security could only be guaranteed by Perón's downfall. Perón fought back in a spirited election campaign, offering the Argentinean people a choice between himself or control by the USA. In the 1946 election, he became president with 52% of the vote.

Activity

Exam questions often require you to explain the reasons for the rise to power of a ruler, but this frequently results in candidates *describing* rather than *analysing* the events. In order to avoid a descriptive approach, it is often helpful to think in terms of themes. Make a copy of the following chart and then complete it to help explain Perón's rise to power.

Factor	Explanation of role	Importance of factor
Political reasons		
Economic reasons		
Social reasons		
Religious reasons		
Role of individuals		
Other		

SOURCE B

On 24 February 1946, General Juan Domingo Perón was elected president of Argentina in an open poll. This victory was the culmination of his dizzying political rise, which had begun a few years earlier when the military revolution of June 1943 put an end to a decade of conservative governments and brought to power a clique of army colonels with fascist sympathies. The emerging military regime had been groping its way between the hostility that its authoritarian and clerical tendencies had awakened in the middle and upper classes and the diplomatic quarantine organised by the United States in reprisal for Argentina's neutral position in the Second World War. Through clever manoeuvring Perón became the regime's dominant figure and ended the political isolation of the military elite by launching a set of labour reforms that had a powerful impact on the working class.

Bethell, L. 1993. Argentina Since Independence. Cambridge, UK. Cambridge University Press. p. 243.

Activity

Look at Source B, then describe in your own words Bethell's explanation for Perón's rise to power. How far is his explanation supported by events explained in this section of the book?

 ## Theory of knowledge

History and language

Is our perception of events affected by the words an author uses? Should a historian always use words that are neutral, or is the use of emotive language acceptable if it helps to make the topic come alive?

Methods of consolidating power

After his election in 1946, Perón spent several years consolidating his authority. He created his own political party, changed the Constitution so that he was able to stand for re-election, and limited access to the media for those groups who opposed him. Thus, a regime that began as an expression of popular feeling was arguably transformed into an increasingly authoritarian – and even semi-fascist – one that expected full obedience from its citizens and tolerated no opposition.

Winning allies

As soon as he came to power, Perón began rewarding those who had supported his campaign for the presidency. His military allies stood as candidates in Senate elections, and his Cabinet contained a significant number of CGT members. These two groups received further benefits through wage rises and favourable social legislation.

However, Perón knew he needed to broaden his base of support, so he awarded government posts to wealthy industrialists and socialists. He also offered loyal industrialists lucrative government contracts and a near-monopoly over key markets. Such actions were intended to deprive the opposition of support and leadership, strengthening Perón's own position. One group that found its influence diminished under the new leadership was the unions, despite the significant role they had played in Perón's election in 1946. Union leaders considered disloyal were removed, and those who followed the regime's direction were rewarded.

In addition, Perón sought greater political control. He did not want to be dictated to by a political party, so within a year of coming to power, he abolished the Labour Party that had supported his candidacy for president. In its place, Perón formed the Partido Único de la Revolución (later the Partido Peronista, or Peronist Party), under the domination of Perón himself.

Eva's role

Perón was aided in his attempts at consolidating his regime by his wife Eva, whose successful campaign for female suffrage won the support of many women for her husband. Several new organisations were created to further strengthen loyalty to Peronism, including the General Economic Foundation, the General Federation of Professionals and the Union of Secondary Students. These were all controlled by the government and offered alternatives to independent organisations such as the Catholic Youth.

Perón adopted other traditional authoritarian practices. Propaganda was used to glorify the regime. One example of such propaganda was Eva's 'Rainbow Tour', in which she travelled Europe meeting dignitaries such as the pope and the Spanish semi-fascist dictator Francisco Franco. Her poor background was also exploited to reinforce the government's sympathy with the working classes. Mass rallies celebrating key Peronist events, such as Loyalty Day and May Day, were also used to win popular support.

Legislation

Three legislative developments were clearly aimed at consolidating Perón's power. The first was the extension of the franchise to women. The second was the replacement of the 1853 Constitution, which prevented a president from serving more than one term. In 1949, Perón amended this to allow presidents to stand for re-election. At first, Perón stated that despite this move he had no intention of remaining in the post beyond the end of his first term. However, as his first period in office came to an end he was 'persuaded' to run again, and was returned as president with 60% of the vote. In addition, Peronists won control of every provincial government in the country, all the seats in the Senate that were up for election at the time, and a large majority in the Chamber of Deputies in Congress.

The third legislative move to consolidate Perón's power came in the form of changes to the Supreme Court. Three judges who opposed the government were removed from the court and replaced by committed Peronists. In justifying these actions, Perón issued two suprisingly contradictory statements. At first, he claimed that he had removed these judges because they had acted illegally in recognising the governments of 1930 and 1943. Later, he claimed they had been removed from the Supreme Court for impeding certain measures that these governments had attempted to introduce.

The opposition

Although Perón would not tolerate opposition to his regime from any group, left- or right-wing, the violence and terror used against his opponents was not as widespread as that of some other authoritarian regimes in the Americas. Perón preferred more subtle tactics, in particular denying his enemies access to the media in order to stifle their message. Socialist and conservative newspapers were often closed down or brought under Peronist control.

Such limitations were seen most clearly in the 1951 election campaign, when the Radicals found they were unable to purchase radio time to spread their campaign message, and were given very little press coverage. The police were used to break up opposition rallies and the Socialist candidate was jailed after an attempted military coup. Perón thus faced only minor opposition in the election. However, there were still occasions when Perón used violence to silence his opponents. In April 1953, for example, after Socialists attacked Peronists attending a rally in the Plaza de Mayo, Perón urged his supporters to carry out reprisals.

Individuals who challenged Perón were also targeted. Infamously, Perón had two formerly loyal supporters – Cipriano Reyes and Luis Gay – charged with treason after they opposed the abolition of the Labour Party, believing he was trying to bring all his supporters, particularly the CGT (see page 112), under the control of his own Peronist Party. The establishment of the Peronist Party did indeed allow Perón unprecedented control of the CGT, as it was the only trade union that the government recognised, eliminating yet another source of potential opposition. This left only the Church as a possible threat to Perón's power and, to begin with at least, his promise of building a stronger society kept this institution on side.

Discussion point

- Perón remained in power for so long because his policies won mass support for his regime.
- Perón was only able to remain in power because he systematically destroyed any opposition.

Which of these two statements do you think best explains Perón's hold on power from 1946 to 1955?

What were the characteristics of Perón's regime and how far does it deserve to be called populist?

What is populism?

In simple terms, populism is the representation of the ordinary people against the élites. Historian Andrew Heywood states that populism 'reflects the belief that the instincts and wishes of the people provide the principal legitimate guide to political action'. Leaders of populist movements therefore often make direct appeals to the people, claiming that they share common hopes and fears, and inciting distrust of other institutions.

In practice, apparently populist leaders have often used this image to support an authoritarian regime, or 'top-down' process, in which the leader addresses the masses and manipulates them through rallies. Such regimes usually have a charismatic leader who is able to inspire popular support. This type of government was a significant force in Latin American politics throughout the period 1930–60, and can be seen in Brazil under Getúlio Vargas, in Mexico with Lázaro Cárdenas and in Ecuador with José María Ibarra. In many instances these regimes had to adapt to fit the national mood, but they often had fascist overtones.

Activity

In order to begin an assessment of whether the Peronist regime deserves to be described as populist, re-read the previous section and look for evidence that either supports or challenges the key features of a populist regime as explained in the paragraph above. Copy the chart below and fill it out as you read through this section.

Feature	Evidence to support the view it was populist	Evidence to challenge the view it was populist
Represents the ordinary person		
Opposes the élites		
Direct appeal to the people		
Attacks other institutions		

What were the characteristics of Perón's regime?

Peronism, or *Justicialismo*, was never clearly defined for fear of alienating potential or actual supporters. However, by 1951 three books had been published that attempted to outline Peronist beliefs. One of these books described it as 'a doctrine whose object is the happiness of man within the society of mankind through the harmonising of material, spiritual, individual and collective forces, appraised from the Christian standpoint.'

In fact, the very vagueness of Peronism was one of its strengths, as it allowed the party to adopt a flexible range of policies and appeal to a much broader section of society than parties with a more defined philosophy. Although elements of fascism and nationalism can be clearly identified in Perón's regime, historian Felipe Pigna has argued that very few people – at the time or since – considered Perón a fascist. On the other hand, several of his social and economic reforms can be identified with Roosevelt's New Deal in the USA (see page 10), suggesting that the Argentinean president drew on a wide range of ideas and influences.

Such observations suggest that, rather than being ideologically led, Perón was driven by his own convictions or, as Arturo Jauretche has proposed, that he was a realist who responded to events and demands as they arose. However, an examination of Perón's policies reveals some common themes based on nationalism, neutrality, political and economic independence, industrialisation, anti-communism and the grievances of the poor.

Perón: populist or authoritarian?

It would be wrong to dismiss the populist base of Perón's power, at least in 1946. He clearly had the support of the workers and those groups in society who had previously been either ignored or repressed. He appeared to be the champion of the urban poor, promising them opportunities for regular work, housing, food and education. Union membership provided him with a solid base. Yet Perón's electoral support was much wider than this, as he won the votes not only of the workers but also the peasants. This support base broadened even further after he extended the franchise to women, and Eva Perón's profile also contributed to his popularity.

However, the role of the army in ensuring that Perón remained in power should not be underestimated, and the president sought to base his new society on the regimental and hierarchical model of the armed forces. In practice, this meant that he could use the army to enforce his will and 'discipline' society for its own good. This suggests that although the regime appeared to be populist, it was authoritarian in practice.

Critics have challenged the notion that it was a populist regime and argued that it was totalitarian, as Perón wanted to control and shape the social, economic and political life of the nation. Some in the USA compared his regime with those of Mussolini and Hitler, and others suggested that Perón simply used the working classes to bring him power in much the same way as Vargas achieved influence in Brazil.

How successful were the social, economic and political policies of Perón's administration?

The economy

Perón's economic and social policies were closely linked. He hoped that his plans for industrial development in Argentina would create jobs and help close the gap between rich and poor, thus achieving his ultimate goal of social justice. At the same time, he wanted to use the wealth made available by economic growth to fund his social policies.

Perón believed that several measures were necessary to stabilise Argentina after the Second World War. He intended to develop Argentine industry and create an economy that was not dependent upon foreign imports or investment. In practice this was not always possible, and by the time of his second administration (1952–55) the policy of economic nationalism that he had pursued on coming to power was partially abandoned.

SOURCE C

Intelligent state intervention in labour relations, to achieve the collaboration of all those who contribute with their muscle, their intelligence or their capital to the economic life of the nation. To achieve this it is essential to guarantee welfare and just retribution to those who, as the large majority of the human masses of the Republic, may find themselves defenceless before the blind power of money or feel themselves tempted to assume violent attitudes.

Juan Perón, outlining his plans for Argentina after the Second World War.

The first Five-Year Plan

Perón wanted to diversify the economy so that it was no longer dominated by agriculture and food processing. At the same time, he wanted to remove foreign control of companies in Argentina. He therefore instructed his advisors to develop a Five-Year Plan that would not only achieve this diversification, but also bring about improvements in pay and employment levels. The period between 1946 and 1949 therefore witnessed large-scale nationalisation, including the central bank, merchant marines, public utilities, communications, energy, and the social infrastructure such as health care and education. Perón also established a single exporter for grain and oil seed through the Institute for the Promotion of Trade. Foreign interests were removed from many areas, including the railways, communications, docks, grain elevators, warehouses and power companies.

Government support for industrial development not only resulted in a growth of over 40%, it also helped to create jobs, which added to Perón's support among the workers. Factory owners and the armed forces welcomed the growth in both the iron and steel industry and armaments manufacture. There was also record investment in projects to improve the nation's infrastructure: the rail network was modernised, roads were built and power sources were developed with Rio Turbio, the only active coal mine, and the exploitation of both gas and hydro-electric power. The success of the Five-Year Plan was short-lived, however:

- Inflation increased from 13% in 1948 to 31% in 1949 and reached 50% by 1951, sending the country into recession.
- In the first three years, real wages rose 27% for skilled workers and 37% for unskilled before falling in the period 1949–52 (even though purchasing power declined 20% in the period 1948–52, it was still 50% higher than it had been in 1943).

- The Five-Year Plan had projected a growth of 43%, but this was never achieved and after an initial 25–30% growth in GDP, this dropped to zero from 1948 to 1952.

However, the failures were not simply because of government policy. The introduction of the Marshall Plan by the USA (see page 26) changed world markets, as the European nations benefiting from the plan shifted their trade even more in favour of the USA, denying Argentina an export market. This development was made even worse by increased domestic consumption, which meant that there was less to export. This had a serious impact on the amount of government revenue available to fund social programmes.

The second Five-Year Plan

The second Five-Year Plan marked a reversal of economic nationalism, as the government began to encourage US investment. This was attacked by Perón's opponents, but really it was simply a recognition of US dominance in the region. The plan was also criticised for its austerity agenda, aimed at reducing the high levels of inflation. In order to achieve this, the government introduced wage and price controls.

A portrait of Eva Perón hangs in a car factory in Córdoba in 1955

To begin with there was little improvement in the economy, largely due to a drought in 1952, which seriously affected grain production. However, by 1954 inflation had dropped to single figures, and government policies to attract overseas investment appeared to be working. FIAT, Kaiser Motors and Mercedes Benz all established plants in Argentina, and a contract was signed with the Standard Oil Company of California in 1955.

By this time inflation had dropped, the trade deficit had been reduced and real wages had been boosted. However, production levels had stalled and the government was forced to distract workers by calling on the unions to organise mass demonstrations against those who attacked the government. Failure to generate the revenue required for further industrial development weakened Perón's position, and the people began to lose faith in their leader.

Activity

Identify the aims of Perón's economic policy, then copy and complete the first column of the chart below. In the second column, find examples of where Perón's aims were either achieved or there was failure, and record the successes and failures in two different colours. In the final column, make a judgement about how successful the policy was in achieving its aim.

Aim	Evidence of success/failure	Judgement

Social changes

Perón came to power on the promise of bringing social justice to those who had been ignored by previous governments or who had little influence on policy, and there is no doubt that Perón brought about an improvement in the living and working conditions of many Argentineans. His government pushed for full employment, health care, labour benefits and wage rises. These humanitarian policies endeared Perón to the working classes and gave his regime a certain amount of credibility.

Developments in Argentina mirrored those taking place in the USA and across Europe, and public services increasingly came under government control. There was increased investment in health care, with the development of over 4200 medical facilities and training for some health professionals.

Education was also expanded so that in the longer term there would be more skilled workers available. Under Perón, around 8000 schools and 1000 kindergartens were built. Housing was also improved for the workers, with 650,000 public sector homes built.

It was not just living conditions that improved. Workers benefited from government intervention on matters such as minimum wages, working hours and pension plans. Leisure time was increased as holidays were expanded and limits placed on weekend working. Union membership rose from 500,000 in 1945 to 2 million by 1949.

These developments did much to consolidate support for the regime, but not all of it was due to Perón himself. In the social sphere, his wife Eva played a significant role in earning the affection of the people.

SOURCE D

One person had to take care of the big things: the General. Another had to take care of the small things: Eva. I took care of the Nation. Eva, of the personal problems of its inhabitants. With her, with Eva, there was direct contact with the people. For that reason, maybe, some remember her more.

Extract from Perón's memoirs. Quoted in Hedges, J. 2011. Argentina: A Modern History. London, UK. I.B. Tauris. p. 79.

 Theory of knowledge

History and emotion
The personal reminiscence of Juan Perón about the role of his wife (Source D) contains some emotional expression. Why does a primary source often have a more emotive impact than a secondary source? What value and limitations do primary sources have as historical evidence?

Church and state

Initially, the Catholic Church supported Perón's government, but conflict developed between the two as the state increased its role in family life and education. The government introduced a series of measures that were felt by the Church to be an attack on both its rights and traditions:

- In September 1954, equal rights were granted to illegitimate children.
- In December 1954, divorce and prostitution were legalised.

- Religious education in schools and the General Inspectorate of Religious Education were abolished.
- No more tax exemptions were awarded to religious institutions.
- Religious protests were banned (Perón believed they were being used as a front for demonstrations by his political opponents).
- In May 1955, the government announced a referendum on the separation of Church and state.

Although the reforms appeared to advance individual rights, the more the Church was attacked, the more sympathy and support it attracted. Eventually, it became the rallying point for many of Perón's opponents (see page 129).

Why did Perón fall from power in 1955?

Long-term causes of Perón's fall from power

Declining Church support

The drop in Church support was an important factor in Perón's overthrow. In particular, the Church disliked the work of the Eva Perón Foundation, which it felt undermined its role in society and treated the working classes with too much respect. The Church expected the poor to submit themselves to whatever humiliating conditions it imposed before they were deemed worthy of its charity. These included such procedures as inspecting children's fingernails to ensure they were clean before they were given food, and accusing parents of being unable to ensure even basic levels of hygiene. The Eva Perón Foundation carried out its work among the poor in a way that avoided social stigma.

The Church was further alienated when Perón set up the Peronist Union of Secondary Students, which competed with traditional Catholic youth groups for members. In many ways, the Peronist Union was the government's attempt to order civil society as an organised community along the lines of the armed forces, but in which the will of the state had to be followed. This emphasis on the importance of the state naturally conflicted with the Church's ideas about its own status in society.

Early signs of the rising tension between Church and state were seen after Eva's death (see page 128), when the Church rejected the suggestion that she should be canonised for her work with the poor. The relationship continued to decline as the government took steps that seemed to stifle freedom of religion. These included banning religious processions on traditional holidays on the grounds that they had become political rallies against the regime.

Eva's role

Although Perón won the 1951 presidential election, the fact that he nominated Eva as his vice-president lost him significant army support. Eva's own lowly birth – and the connection with the working classes that she represented – offended many. In addition, the idea that she might take on an increased and more formal role in government caused concern among the élites.

However, Eva's death in 1952 also played a part in the loss of support for the regime. She had been a tireless campaigner for the rights of poor Argentineans, and Perón himself was unable to assume this role after she died. Gradually the government grew more distanced from the ordinary people. Observers at the time believed that Eva's death played a key role in the collapse of the regime. However, historians such as Lewis argue that this is an exaggeration, and that much greater emphasis should be placed on the state's failure to fulfil its economic promises. In 1952, inflation stood at 30% and the decline in government revenue meant that it was unable to maintain the extensive social programme that had won it so much popular support.

Argentineans hold up candles beneath a poster of Eva Perón, mourning her death from cancer in 1952

The loss of the unions

The failure of Perón's economic and social policies lost him a great deal of traditional support. In an attempt to distract workers from these failures, the unions were ordered to organise mass rallies against the government's opponents, who were blamed for the lack of progress. These rallies often ended in attacks on the symbols of the opposition, notably the Jockey Club – a favourite haunt of the privileged élites. There were also attacks on the Socialist headquarters and several newspapers.

Such attempts to draw attention from the government's failings were only short-term solutions. By 1954, many unions had lost patience with the austerity measures imposed by the regime, and strikes broke out. When the strikes ended, the government increased worker's wages to try and win back support, but in doing so it alienated employers.

Short-term causes of Perón's fall from power

Matters between Church and state reached a climax in June 1955, at the feast of Corpus Christi. After a celebratory mass, Catholic ministers led a march on Congress to protest against recent anti-clerical legislation. During the march, the national flag was allegedly burned. The government arrested the ministers, as a result of which the Vatican issued a decree excommunicating Perón.

This event inspired a revolt against the president by the armed forces on 16 June. Planes bombed the Plaza de Mayo, and members of the navy launched an assault on the ministry of war, where Perón had gone into hiding. In response, the CGT summoned union members to the Plaza to defend the president, and eventually the military revolt was suppressed. However, reprisals were swift – 12 churches in Buenos Aires were ransacked and a priest was killed.

Following these events, Perón called for calm and attempted reconciliation with the Church. He announced that the 'Peronist Revolution' was over and encouraged everyone to follow constitutional laws. Rather than winning him back support, however, such pronouncements only caused many people to consider him weak. His opponents were now convinced that they had the upper hand.

On 31 August 1955, a statement was issued claiming that Perón would resign. However, this is likely to have been an attempt by the president to mobilise the masses to come out in his support once more, and show his enemies that he still had the backing of the people. In a speech delivered shortly afterwards, Perón threatened to wage civil war against his opponents – a declaration that removed any remaining support that he might have had among the armed forces.

SOURCE E

The overthrow of Perón in September 1955 was even less attributable to the Church than the June revolt. Eventually, it was the army, supported by various civilian groups, which was to bring down the government … Army unease was increased by reports that the CGT had proposed to create armed worker militias, a proposal flatly rejected by Perón but which nonetheless appeared as a further threat to be averted.

Hedges, J. 2011. Argentina: A Modern History. New York, USA. I.B. Tauris. p. 167.

Military uprisings against Perón began on 16 September in Córdoba. Similar uprisings soon began in other parts of Argentina, including in the provinces of Mendoza and San Juan. The navy supported the rebellion, seizing the southern ports of Puerto Madryn and Puerto Belgrano. The government claimed that it had control of the uprising, but as warships began moving towards Buenos Aires it seemed that the final assault was imminent. On 19 September, Perón resigned and urged a peaceful resolution to the conflict. The following day, his entire government stepped down, and on 22 September the nationalist army commander Eduardo Lonardi assumed the presidency.

Perón stood down without any attempt at negotiation, and some historians argue that he did so in order to prevent further violence. Some others claim that after nine years, he was simply exhausted, bored and disillusioned by failure. As Lonardi took over, Perón sought refuge in the Paraguayan embassy and then began a 16-year exile from Argentina.

Activity

Complete a chart like this to summarise the factors behind Perón's overthrow in 1955. In the second column you should explain the role of the factor in bringing about his downfall. In the final column, explain its importance.

Factor	Explanation	Importance

Peronist troops prepare to fire on navy rebels at Río Santiago on 17 September 1955

End of chapter activities

Paper 3 exam practice

Question

How successful were Perón's economic policies?
[20 marks]

Skill focus

Avoiding irrelevance

Examiner's tips

Do not waste valuable writing time irrelevant material. If it's irrelevant, it won't gain you **any** marks. Writing irrelevant information can happen because:

- the candidate does not look carefully enough at the wording of the question (see page 45)
- the candidate ignores the fact that the questions require selection of information, an analytical approach and a final judgement; instead the candidate just writes down all that they know about a topic (relevant or not), and hopes that the examiner will do the analysis and make the judgement
- the candidate has unwisely restricted their revision; for example, if a question crops up on the success of Perón's economic policies, a candidate may include extensive information about social policies because this is the area that they have revised.

Whatever the reason, such responses rarely address any of the demands of the question.

For this question, you will need to:

- look at the aims of Perón's economic policies, as they will provide you with the criteria against which to judge success
- describe the economic measures introduced by Perón's government
- explain how far the measures addressed the economic problems Argentina faced
- differentiate between different aspects of economic policies to show where there was success and failure
- explain the wider implications of the changes – not only did Perón want to bring about economic change, he also wanted to use economic reform to fund social policies and win political support
- assess how successful Perón's economic policies were in each area and reach an overall judgement as to their success.

Common mistakes

One common error with questions like this is for candidates to write about material they know well, rather than material directly related to the question. Another mistake is to present too much general information, instead of material specific to the person, period and command terms. Finally, candidates often elaborate too much on events outside the dates given in the question.

Sample paragraphs of irrelevant focus/material

Although Perón was unsuccessful in reviving the Argentinean economy and creating a broader industrial base, he was more successful in his social policies, which did much to transform the lives of ordinary workers in the country. Perón's aim in social policy was to bring about 'social justice' and he achieved his aims to a far greater extent than in his economic policy. This was most noticeable in the area of health care, where the building of some 4200 healthcare facilities and the provision of free care did much to improve the lives of the less well-off. The same was true of educational facilities; the regime built around 8000 schools and 1000 kindergartens, which in the long term would raise educational standards and therefore improve job opportunities. The workers also benefited from an increase in housing provision, and a reduction in working hours and the length of the working week. Perhaps most notable for the workers was the rise in real wages that occurred during Perón's rule, and this helped to increase support for the regime and the Peronist Party, playing a significant role in helping Perón to consolidate his power.

This is an example of a **weak answer.** Although a brief comment on the social measures – particularly if it is linked to the aims of the economic policy – might be helpful and relevant in assessing the wider goals of Perón's economic policy, there is no need for detailed coverage of all the social reforms. Thus, virtually all of the underlined material shown is irrelevant, and will not score any marks. In addition, the candidate is using up valuable writing time, which should have been spent on providing relevant points and supporting knowledge.

Activity

In this chapter, the focus is on avoiding writing answers that contain, to a greater or lesser extent, irrelevant material. Using the information from this chapter, and any other sources available to you, write an answer to **one** of the following Paper 3 practice questions, keeping your answer fully focused on the question. Remember – writing a plan **first** can help you maintain this focus.

Remember to refer to the simplified Paper 3 markscheme on page 223.

Paper 3 practice questions

1   Assess the reasons why Juan Perón came to power in Argentina in 1946.

2   'Terror was the most important reason why Perón was able to consolidate his power in the period from 1946 to 1955.' How far do you agree with this view?

3   Explain the reasons why Juan Perón received so much support from the unions and working classes in Argentina.

4   How important was the role of Eva Perón in the survival of the Peronist regime from 1946 to 1955?

5   'The loss of support from the Catholic Church was the most important reason for the fall of Juan Perón in 1955.' How far do you agree with this view?

6 The Cuban Revolution

Timeline

1895 Feb: War of Independence begins

1898 Spanish–American War

1901 Jun: Platt Amendment introduced

1902 Cuban Republic established

1903 Platt Amendment formally approved

1928–33 Machado dictatorship

1934 US repeals Platt Amendment

1940 Cuban Constitution established

1940–44 Batista's presidency

1952 coup by Batista

1953 26 Jul: Castro and his forces attack Moncada barracks

1956 Dec: *Granma* lands in Cuba

1957 Revolutionary Directorate attacks Batista's palace

1958 May: final assault on Castro by Batista's forces

Dec: Batista hands power to army

1959 Jan: Batista flees; Castro takes power

Key questions

- What was Cuba's history of revolution?
- What led to Batista's overthrow?
- What were the ultimate causes of the Cuban Revolution?
- What impact did the revolution have on the Americas?

This chapter offers a brief outline of the history of Cuba, showing how previous revolutions against dominant groups or foreign control had failed or had been limited in their results. The political causes of the Cuban Revolution of 1959 are considered through investigating Castro's leadership and the weaknesses of Batista's regime, and by linking Castro to existing political discontent about US influence. The economic causes of the revolution are considered, focusing on the imbalance in the economy between sugar and other products. The chapter then discusses the social causes of the revolution, in particular the inequalities of Cuban life and discontent among several sections of society. Finally, we consider the impact of the revolution on the USA and on states in South America, as well as attempts by both Castro's regime and Che Guevara to spread revolution.

Overview

- The Caribbean island of Cuba was ruled by Spain until it gained independence at the end of the Spanish–American War in 1898.
- Within a few years, the Cuban Republic was heavily dominated by the USA, both politically and economically. Due to its investments in the island nation, in particular its interests in the Cuban sugar industry, the USA supported government regimes there that it hoped would accept US control and, after 1945, oppose the spread of communism.
- Between 1902 and 1922, the USA intervened militarily in Cuba on three occasions in order to ensure its continued influence on Cuban politics.
- In 1933, the army general Fulgencio Batista overthrew the government in a military coup, and began ruling Cuba through a series of 'puppet' presidents, with backing from the USA.
- In 1940, Batista was officially elected president, but he was defeated four years later. He returned in 1952, seizing power before the election could be held and beginning a dictatorial regime.
- Angered at this illegal seizure of power, Fidel Castro and a band of rebels launched an unsuccessful attack on the Moncada army barracks in 1953. After his release from prison in 1955, Castro went to Mexico and began planning Batista's overthrow.
- In November 1956, Castro and his revolutionaries landed in Cuba and began their rebellion. After early losses, they won widespread support. Despite being outnumbered by Batista's forces, they eventually succeeded in ousting the president in January 1959.

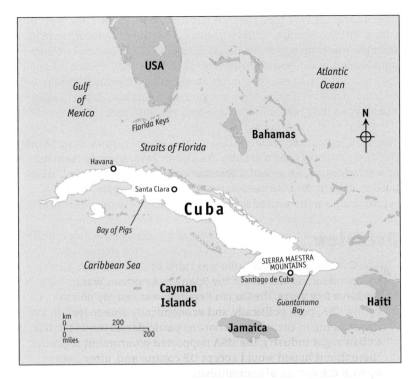

A map of Cuba showing its position in relation to the USA and the Caribbean

What was Cuba's history of revolution?

Spanish rule and resistance 1511–1898

Cuba had a long history of revolution. The Spanish first settled on the island in 1511, and almost immediately met with resistance from the indigenous people. This 'revolution' was quickly crushed, and the Cuban population was soon reduced to a few thousand by repression, disease and suicide. Cuba became a key Spanish possession, providing a base for further conquests in the Americas, and a source of sugar, tobacco and coffee – valuable luxury goods for Europe. To grow these crops, the Spanish brought in African slaves, and by 1800 these made up a quarter of the population. Slave revolts were the next revolutions in Cuba, but all of them failed.

Spain faced further revolution in its Latin American colonies after 1815, but Cuba remained loyal. The élite merchants and landowners were divided into native-born Cubans (*Criollos*) and Spanish immigrants (*Peninsulares*). The immigrant population was higher than that of the native-born Cubans, but both groups feared the emergence of a black revolutionary Cuba and so did not oppose rule from distant Spain, believing that it was essential for keeping the peace in their country.

By the early 19th century, the USA had ambitions to own this wealthy island, but the Spanish would not give up control of Cuba. After 1815, stronger revolutionary movements emerged in the country, but their aims were divided. Some wanted the abolition of slavery; some hoped for unification with the USA; other revolutionary movements were led by freed slaves; and still others sought independence for the *Criollos*. There was a long revolutionary war between 1868 and 1878.

The most significant revolutionary of the 19th century was José Martí (1853–98), who inspired the battle for Cuban independence from its Spanish masters. An ardent Cuban nationalist and intellectual, Martí lived in exile in the USA. He felt that Cuba could lead the way in establishing a more unified Latin America, and he wrote passionately about the need for justice and equality for all races, encouraging measures such as freedom of speech and freedom of the press, which he believed would allow Cuba to develop into a true democracy.

Along with other nationalist rebels, Martí formed the Cuban Revolutionary Party and began planning an invasion of Cuba to overthrow the Spanish. The revolution began in February 1895, in the east of Cuba near Santiago de Cuba, and marked the start of the last phase of the Cuban War of Independence. Martí himself was killed in the fighting in May 1895, but by this point the rebellion had gained enough momentum to continue without his leadership. Slowly the rebels won over eastern Cuba and began to advance on the west. The Spanish commanders responded with brutality, but by 1898 the revolutionaries looked certain to triumph.

Activity

Use the internet to find out more about José Martí. Why do you think he was such an inspiration to future revolutionaries such as Fidel Castro?

The Spanish–American War and US dominance 1898–1925

The USA had its own ambitions to dominate the island that lay just 145 km (90 miles) from Florida, and knew that overthrowing Spanish rule there would allow it to gain a firm foothold. Thus, the USA favoured the rebels in the Cuban War of Independence, and was already considering intervening on their behalf when the US battleship *Maine* blew up in Havana Harbor in February 1898. Although the evidence was inconclusive, the USA blamed the Spanish for the incident and declared war on Spain in April that year. Within three months, the USA had defeated Spain not only in Cuba but also in Puerto Rico and the Philippines.

Cuba won its independence after the Spanish–American War, but the USA ensured that the peace terms allowed it sigificant control of the island. The Cuban military was disbanded – removing a potential source of opposition to US domination. In 1903, the US Congress formally adopted a law known as the Platt Amendment, which had been drawn up in 1901 and imposed on the Cuban Constitution in 1902. This asserted the USA's right to intervene in Cuban affairs at any time. In addition, the US worked to secure a series of Cuban governments that would support its growing interests in the region, including in 1906 after bitter disputes between Cuban political parties, and in 1912 when an association of Afro-Cubans called the Independent Party of Color threatened a revolt. By the mid 1920s, the US had all but won political, economic and military control over Cuba.

Machado's dictatorship 1925–33

In 1925, the Cuban nationalist leader General Gerardo Machado came to prominence. Machado had fought in the War of Independence, he strongly opposed the Platt Amendment, and he offered a strong Cuban government with an emphasis on public works and some social reform. After his election as president, Machado began a campaign for national regeneration that gained wide support. He taxed US capital investments, initiated the construction of a 1127-km (700-mile) central highway, and promoted investments in tourism, industry and mining. For a time, Machado successfully balanced support for US interests in Cuba with defence of Cuban sovereignty, but as time passed his regime became increasingly dictatorial. As the president lost public support, the US also withdrew its backing. In 1933, opposition to Machado culminated in his overthrow, and a Cuban army sergeant named **Fulgencio Batista** helped establish a provisional revolutionary government under the liberal professor **Ramón Grau San Martín** (see page 140).

Fulgencio Batista (1901–73) The son of poor farmers, Batista joined the army in 1921. He developed a large personal following and although he was still only a sergeant at the time, in September 1933 he led the coup that ousted Machado. By 1934, he had established himself as head of the armed forces, and from this time on he was the real power behind several civilian 'puppet' presidents. Batista served as the elected president in 1940–44, and enjoyed genuine popularity. However, after assuming leadership again in a 1952 coup, he became a corrupt right-wing dictator. He was overthrown by Fidel Castro in 1959, and died in exile in Portugal.

Fulgencio Batista giving a radio address on the first anniversary of the coup that brought him to power, September 1934

Ramón Grau San Martín (1887–1969) Grau was a physician who opposed Machado and went into exile in the USA. In 1933, Batista supported Grau's appontment as provisional president, but forced him to resign the following year. Grau led the Auténticos, a major political party. Grau lost the 1940 election to Batista, but won in 1944. Although he promoted reform, Grau's time in power was notable for widespread corruption. He handed over power to his ally Prío in 1948, after which he withdrew from politics.

Cuba under Batista 1933–44

Some immediate changes were introduced under Grau's nominal leadership. The Platt Amendment was abolished and women were given the vote. A minimum wage was introduced and a law passed stating that 50% of employees on farms and in businesses had to be Cuban-born. However, the situation in Cuba was unstable and there were fears that civil war would break out. In addition, political groups including the Popular Socialist Party (PSP) demanded more significant reforms. Realising that Grau was not the man for the job, Batista forced his resignation in January 1934. This marked the start of a period in which Batista himself maintained control of government behind the scenes, with his political allies as the front men.

To ensure stability, Batista adopted reforming policies and worked with the communists in the PSP and the unions. The high point of these reforms was the 1940 Constitution, which was one of the most progressive of its time. The new constitution was not just a democratic framework for the country. It committed Cuba to land reform and social justice, including public education and an eight-hour working day. Under the new constitution, general elections were held in July 1940, and Batista was elected president at the head of the Democratic Socialist Coalition – a group that included both liberals and communists.

During his four-year presidency, Batista carried out widespread reforms, including improving the education system and launching an extensive programme of public works. Batista also reinforced ties with the USA by increasing trade between the two countries, and Cuba benefited from the resulting increase in sugar exports. Cuba joined the Allies in the Second World War the day after the Japanese bombing of Pearl Harbor in December 1941, further strengthening the bond with the USA.

As his presidential term came to an end, Batista hand-picked his successor, but in the elections Grau was returned as president. Batista moved to the USA, but he remained an influential figure in Cuban politics.

Corruption, conflict and a return to dictatorship 1944–52

Grau's return to office in 1944 at the head of the Cuban Revolutionary Party began a period of stagnation and corruption. As a result, the next few years were characterised by social and political unrest. By this time, Cuba was dominated by US capital, which controlled 40% of the sugar industry and 50% of the railways. The capital, Havana, was a major tourist destination, attracting wealthy and decadent members of US society, and US crime interests were firmly established in the city and elsewhere. Political reforms did little to alleviate rural poverty and illiteracy or to diversify Cuba's economy.

The new president elected in 1948, Carlos Prío Socarrás, did little to end political corruption. The reforming Ortodoxos Party, led by **Eduardo Chibás**, demanded wide reforms to address the issues faced by the Cuban people. As public discontent with the government rose, it seemed increasingly likely that the Ortodoxos would win power in the 1952 elections, despite the death of their leader.

Eduardo Chibás (1907–51) Chibás was committed to Cuba's reform and modernisation, and served in Grau's government 1933–34. Opposed to what he saw as corruption, he founded the Ortodoxos Party in 1947, which attracted reforming students such as Fidel Castro. Chibás spoke out publicly against politicians' greed and immorality. He shot and killed himself as a protest against corruption during a live radio broadcast in 1952.

However, at this point, Batista decided to return to active politics. Knowing that Prío would lose the election, Batista joined the presidential race at the head of his own party – the United Action Party. His earlier popularity convinced him that he would win, but he soon discovered that his political opponents were stronger than he thought. Before the elections could take place, Batista staged a coup that removed Prío from power and established himself as provisional president. The police and the army suppressed all opposition, and Batista began a dictatorial regime in Cuba.

Activity

Read back over the chapter so far, then write a paragraph explaining the significance of each of the factors listed below in Cuban history:

- US interference and the Platt Amendment
- Batista's rule 1934–44
- Batista's coup in 1952
- Chibás and the Ortodoxos
- US economic interests in Cuba.

What led to Batista's overthrow?

The causes of the Cuban Revolution are largely rooted in the widespread resentment at Batista's dominance. Not only was he a figure from the past who was deeply associated with US control of Cuba, but there was also considerable resentment at his suspension of parts of the 1940 Constitution, which deeply angered the Cuban people. However, there were additional factors involved, and the politics of the Cuban Revolution cannot be understood without considering the wider influences and ideologies on which the revolutionaries drew.

The political aims of Batista's opponents were not explicitly socialist, and in fact Batista forged links with the communist PSP in order to keep them on side. Instead, the opposition drew inspiration more from the writings of the nationalist José Martí (see page 138) and the heroism of the reforming Ortodoxos leader Chibás (see page 141).

The resisters of the Batista era were also influenced by Cuban revolutionary history, in particular the struggle against foreign domination. Many people felt that in the years since the Cuban War of Independence, Spanish rule had simply been replaced by US control. Some resistance to Batista was influenced by revolutionary ideology common to other 20th-century movements, notably Marxism and Leninism. However, the revolution of 1959 was not Marxist. It was more greatly affected by Cuba's own revolutionary tradition, a nationalist reaction to US influence, and the changes attempted by radical reforming regimes in Latin America, especially in Mexico in the 1930s.

Fidel Castro and the revolutionaries

Castro's background

Fidel Castro was born in 1926, the illegitimate son of a Spanish immigrant, Angel Castro, and his housekeeper. After serving in the revolutionary wars, Angel returned to Cuba, acquired some property, and became a sugar grower. Fidel was educated in church schools and later attended the Jesuit College in Havana, where he discovered and was greatly influenced by Martí's works.

Castro went on to study law at Havana University, where he threw himself into political activity. He was ambitious and became a strong speaker and a student leader, extending his study of Martí and dreaming of power. As part of a student delegation to meet Ramón Grau, he seriously suggested throwing the president off a balcony and declaring a revolution. Castro admired the reformer Chibás and joined the Ortodoxos Party in 1947. He would have been a candidate for Congress in 1952 if Batista had not launched his coup and prevented the election taking place.

Castro was part of a revolutionary armed force that set off to overthrow the pro-US dictator of the Dominican Republic in 1947, but the boat was turned back by the Cuban navy before reaching its destination. Castro also helped to organise a congress of Latin American radical students in Bogotá, Colombia, in 1948. While he was there, the Colombian liberal leader Jorge Gaitán was assassinated. Castro took part in the ensuing riots before police and the army restored control.

The start of the revolution July 1953

Batista's coup of 1952 angered Castro. 'If Batista grabbed power by force,' he said, 'he must be thrown out by force.' Propelled into direct action, Castro began gathering recruits for a revolution against the new regime. These recruits came from a wide section of Cuban society, including professionals, intellectuals and members of the middle classes, as well as the radical Ortodoxos. Some, including Castro's wealthy mistress Naty Revuelta, were members of Cuba's élite.

On 26 July 1953, Castro and his group of revolutionaries – 165 men and women, including his brother Raúl – stormed the garrison at the Moncada army barracks in Santiago in eastern Cuba. The assault failed and the price paid by the revolutionaries was high. Batista's forces killed 61 of the rebels. The rest were captured and either imprisoned or tortured to death. Fidel and Raúl Castro escaped, but gave themselves up soon afterwards to prevent further executions of their fellow revolutionaries. Castro was sentenced to 15 years in prison, but was released just two years later, in 1955, after Batista granted him amnesty in an attempt to improve his own image.

SOURCE A

To those who would call me a dreamer, I quote the words of Martí: 'A true man does not seek the path where advantage lies, but rather the path where duty lies' ...

Our Movement had no link with past politicians: that this Movement is a new Cuban generation with its own ideas, rising up against tyranny; that this Movement is made up of young people who were barely seven years old when Batista perpetrated the first of his crimes in 1934.

I do not fear prison, as I do not fear the fury of the miserable tyrant who took the lives of 70 of my comrades. Condemn me. It does not matter. History will absolve me.

Extract from the speech Castro made at his trial.
From: www.marxists.org/history/cuba/archive/castro/1953/10/16.htm

Activities

Look at the speech in Source A on page 143.

- Why do you think Castro quotes Martí?
- Why do you think he mentions young Cubans?
- Why do you think the last words, 'History will absolve me', became so famous?

Look up the whole speech. How does Castro use other writers, thinkers and arguments to defend himself? How would you describe Castro's style of speaking? Do you think it helps to explain his popularity?

After his release in 1955, Castro went to Mexico to build a new revolutionary movement (this became known as the 26 July Movement, after the date of the Moncada barracks attack). While in Mexico, Castro met the Marxist revolutionary **Ernesto 'Che' Guevara**, who soon joined Castro's cause. Despite Guevara's influence and Castro's own later association with communism, the movement was not Marxist in nature. Indeed, Castro delivered a speech during a fundraising visit to the USA in which he spoke of patriotism and democracy. Socialism was not proclaimed in Cuba until April 1961 – more than two years after Castro took power.

Ernesto 'Che' Guevara (1928–67) Argentinean-born Guevara trained as a doctor, but became a convinced Marxist and was soon participating in revolutionary activities. He took part in a revolution in Guatemala after the overthrow of the socialist government there by a US-backed coup, and then fled to Mexico where he met Castro. From 1959 to 1965, he was part of Castro's revolutionary government and headed Cuba's national bank. Frustrated by Cuba's economic failures, Guevara started promoting worldwide revolution, encouraging change in many countries across Africa and Latin America. He eventually left Cuba to become a guerrilla leader in Bolivia, where he was captured and executed in 1967.

Ernesto 'Che' Guevara (left) and Fidel Castro (right) in Havana in 1960

Castro won backing from several groups, including opponents of Batista in Venezuela and businessmen in Cuba who were anxious to have some insurance if Batista were to fall from power. The Revolutionary Directorate, a student organisation led by José Antonio Echeverría, worked within Cuba to organise sabotage and armed raids to create a revolutionary climate and prepare for Castro's planned invasion in 1956. Their actions included the assassination of the head of Cuban military intelligence in October 1955. Some younger army officers close to the Ortodoxos planned a coup, but this was discovered and their leader, Colonel Barquín, was imprisoned.

The *Granma* expedition and Castro's leadership

By June 1956, the Mexican police were growing unhappy with Castro's presence in their country, and Castro realised that it was time to put his revolutionary plans into action. On 25 November 1956, 82 rebels armed with 90 rifles and some handguns set off for Cuba in the 18-m (60-ft) cabin cruiser *Granma*.

Their arrival was planned to coincide with an uprising in Havana led by **Frank País**. País was a member of the Revolutionary Directorate, and helped co-ordinate urban underground resistance to Batista for the 26 July Movement while Castro was in exile. However, País' rebellion was crushed and government forces were ready when the revolutionaries landed. Pursued by the army, the group dispersed, making their way into the mountains of the Sierra Maestra. In this wild and remote area, Castro hoped they could regroup while avoiding detection. Just 21 of the 82 revolutionaries made it to the rendezvous point.

Frank País (1934–1957) País was the son of a Protestant pastor. He trained as a teacher, but was outraged at Batista's coup in 1952 and was inspired by Castro's attack on the Moncada barracks the following year. He joined the 26 July Movement and became its leader in Santiago. An inspirational young revolutionary, País was killed by the Cuban secret police in 1957.

Batista ordered bombing raids on the mountains, and shortly after the invasion he announced that Castro had been killed. However, in February 1957, a *New York Times* journalist, Herbert Matthews, tracked Castro and his revolutionaries to their hideout in the mountains. The interview with Castro that Matthews published made headlines in the USA, and later attracted attention around the world. This gave Castro a huge propaganda coup and made him the face of the Cuban Revolution.

Castro trains new recruits to the revolutionary cause at his hideout in the Sierra Maestra mountains in 1956

As the revolution gained momentum, Echeverría led 150 supporters and stormed Batista's palace. They failed to kill the president, and Echeverría and 39 others died in the attempt. Castro's rivals were spurred to action; they began rounding up and torturing anyone suspected of sympathising with the revolution. Violence and unrest spread across Cuba, and the rebels gained international attention. They became beloved within Cuba for 'liberating' peasants from their landlords and for their promises to initiate land reform if their revolution was successful. In a manifesto published in July 1957, Castro also promised free elections based on the 1940 Constitution, agrarian reform and a mass literacy campaign to improve the standing of poor Cubans.

On 30 July, País was killed by the Santiago police chief, eliminating one of Castro's potential rivals for the Cuban leadership after Batista's overthrow. A three-day general strike followed. However, the war was not yet won. Castro still had only 300 armed men, but despite this he began to establish a type of revolutionary government in the eastern areas that he controlled.

The final campaigns: Batista's forces fail

In April 1958, Castro's cause received a significant boost when the communists pledged their support for the revolutionaries. The following month, Batista assembled 10,000 men for a final showdown. However, Batista's inexperienced troops, the problems of locating the small guerrilla forces, and declining army morale gave the revolutionaries the upper hand. Realising that Batista's regime was about to fall, the USA withdrew its support – a move that significantly undermined his legitimacy as president and contributed to his failure to defeat the rebels.

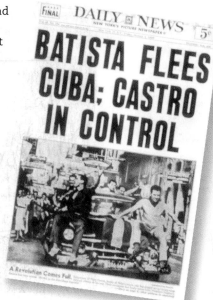

A US newspaper announces Castro's victory in January 1959

As the summer progressed, Guevara led 600 men to the central areas of Cuba to carry the war closer to Batista and cut Havana's communications with the east. In December 1959, at Santa Clara, Guevara's rebels stopped a train taking Batista's reinforcements from Havana to Santiago. This was a turning point in the fighting. The rebels took the city, the key to controlling central Cuba. By this time, it was clear that Batista's support from the Cuban people was practically non-existent. In a last attempt to save his reputation – and under pressure from the USA – Batista held open elections in 1958, but the opposition boycotted them. The army was no longer fighting on the president's behalf, and on 1 January 1959 Batista resigned and handed over power to General Eulogio Cantillo and to the Supreme Court judge Carlos Pedra. He then fled to the Dominican Republic with $424 million of national gold reserves. Two days later, the 26 July Movement took power in Cuba.

What were the ultimate causes of the Cuban Revolution?

The importance of sugar

Sugar lay at the heart of the Cuban economy. The prosperity and development of the island depended on sugar and, since the 1890s, this had meant dependence on the USA. The US had become the biggest market for Cuban sugar and, after the devastation brought by the wars of 1895–98, Cuba became even more reliant on US sales and investment. A trade treaty of 1903 gave Cuban sugar imports a large tariff reduction in the US, and in return Cuba imported US manufactured goods at a cheaper rate. US companies owned 40% of Cuban refineries and sugar-processing plants. US businesses controlled 60% of the sugar harvest.

By the early 20th century, therefore, Cuba had lost control of its most important product. Profits from the industry went to the USA rather than being reinvested in Cuba, and this severely stunted economic growth. There was no incentive for US firms to invest in other Cuban products or in Cuban industries, so the country remained a foreign-dominated monoculture.

Dependence on this single product caused social problems as well as economic ones. The sugar industry did not require year-round workers, so there was a great deal of underemployment. The growth of a world economy meant that Cuba was vulnerable if the world price of sugar fell, as it did from 1925 and especially after 1929 as the Great Depression spread. It was difficult to increase production of sugar to keep pace with a rising population, so although there was more growth in the sugar export market in the 1940s and 1950s, the production per capita and the wealth per capita did not rise significantly. The limited economy could not provide enough work for a growing population.

Cuba depended to an unusual degree on foreign trade. Between 1945 and 1958, overseas trade was on average 54.8% of Gross National Product (GNP). If the total trade was divided by the population of Cuba, the country had some of the highest figures in the world. Cuba's population was therefore dependent on economic factors beyond its control. Between the 1920s and 1940s, the price of Cuba's imports rose more rapidly than the price of its sugar exports, and standards of living began to drop. To maintain them at the levels of the late 1940s, production and sales of sugar would have to rise to 7 million tonnes a year in 1955, but sales only achieved 5 million tonnes. Batista was thus presiding over a country that was unlikely to achieve better living standards.

Sugar cane was grown on over half of Cuba's land, and the industry employed around a quarter of Cuba's workforce. As it became less profitable, US interest began to decline and Cubans were able to retake some control over the sugar industry. By the mid 1950s, Cuban owners controlled 70% of sugar mills, but there was still no reinvestment of the profits in new industries or crops to help the economy become less reliant on sugar.

Sugar cane being loaded on to a railway truck in Cuba in the 1950s

In the first three decades of the 20th century, Cuba experienced some industrial growth. In 1923, manufacturers formed their own National Association to press for more support for industry. By 1930, local industries were supplying around 45% of consumer goods, but there was still a heavy dependence on imports. The Machado dictatorship helped by lowering customs duties on the raw materials that industry needed, and raising them on consumer imports. In this way, the state helped manufacturers such as shoemakers, furniture producers, brewers, distillers, tanners and dairy and food processors. However, the Great Depression of the 1930s restricted the growth of non-sugar production. The USA was the only hope for Cuba to avoid massive recession, and as a result sugar exports to the USA increased and US-manufactured goods dominated the Cuban market. In 1946, Cuban industrialists warned that 'it is imperative that we carry out a major reform of our economic system, which is a colonial one, based on producing raw materials which we sell in only one market at a price and conditions imposed by the buyer'.

Activity

Look at the warning from Cuban industrialists quoted above. Explain why economic reform was so necessary by adding two more paragraphs of your own.

Economic reform

Cuban bankers, industrialists and non-sugar interests all protested to the government about the economic situation. Even the sugar growers and processors saw the need for change, as falling income from the US had left insufficient capital for modernisation. Batista himself realised that reform was necessary, and in 1955 he launched the National Program for Economic Action, which had some success over the following years. This came on top of several other economic improvements that Batista had already instigated:

- There were fewer imports of consumer goods in the mid 1950s than a decade before.
- There was more investment in non-sugar enterprises.
- Cubans owned most of the 2300 business that were not linked directly to sugar.
- The national bank of 1950 was extending credit to new businesses.
- A fall in wages offered cheap labour to new enterprises.

Thus, the Cuban Revolution did not take place against a regime that was unaware of economic problems or in a country experiencing total economic stagnation. However, Cubans invested little in the modernisation of farming methods, for example, or in establishing new manufacturing industries in order to generate jobs.

The considerable trade deficit also meant funds for new investment were lacking. In addition, Cuba was still not in control of its markets. For example, the US pressured the country to accept large amounts of imported rice in return for sugar sales to the US. Cuban rice growers could not obtain investment and their share of the market fell.

Economic problems by 1959

By the late 1950s, there was a strong movement for economic reform amongst urban consumers in Cuba. The country had a predominantly urban population and a rising middle class, which demanded more job opportunities and a scaling back of US control. The unions were concerned about the power of sugar in the economy. In addition to these groups, industrialists and businessmen in non-sugar enterprises were concerned about the lack of economic progress Cuba was making compared to other parts of the world.

However, the largest source of discontent was unemployment and underemployment. By 1956, one-third of Cubans were not in full-time work. Agriculture was the largest employer, at 40%. There was a growing gulf between urban and rural Cuba, and economic inequality was accompanied by social inequalities in education and health.

There was also a gap between the underemployed and unemployed in the Havana province and other urban areas, home to a quarter of the country's population. Standards of living, consumerism and education were higher in the capital and its province. This inequality is significant in that the revolution established itself first in the eastern and central provinces, where living standards were considerably lower. Such economic inequality between regions has often been a major cause of revolution.

The importance of economic problems in causing revolution

The following factors support the idea that economic issues were an important cause of the Cuban Revolution:

- the failure to adjust from a semi-colonial dependent economy dominated by sugar
- the failure of industries and alternative crops to provide enough employment
- the discontent of sections of Cuban society with the limited economic development
- the resentment at US economic power, which fuelled political nationalism
- the growing inequality between urban and rural areas and between Havana and the rest of Cuba

- economic discontent might explain the willingness of many in the middle classes to abandon Batista and support a national regeneration in 1959
- rural poverty and a sense of neglect might explain why Castro was able to sustain his forces in the eastern provinces.

Against this, it might be argued that economic factors were not the key reason for revolution:

- The government was aware of the problem and had made some progress in economic diversification.
- Sugar was still relatively profitable.
- Standards of living in Cuba were not the lowest in Latin America.
- The largest urban centre was experiencing greater prosperity through tourism and the service industries in the 1950s.
- Emigration to the USA, which increased from 3000 a year on average in the early 1950s to 12,000 a year by 1958, brought in money to the country in the form of remittances.
- It would not have been possible for a more effective government to bring about economic change – it was political not economic failure that was more important.

Activity

In pairs, write a short presentation for the class in which you explain how important economic factors were in the Cuban Revolution. Be sure to come to a judgement.

Political factors behind Castro's success

After Batista's coup in 1952, there was effectively a political vacuum in Cuba. His presidency had no real legitimacy, and his support rested on military force and the backing of the USA. Batista resisted change and protected the interests of the Cuban élite and middle classes. However, many of these people were in favour of political reform and there were several reforming Ortodoxos officers in the armed forces in particular.

Castro's strengths

Castro and his revolutionaries were careful not to alienate broad-based support. Castro chose the liberal judge Manuel Urrutia (see page 166) as president, and avoided proclamations of radical Marxism. At the same time, he maintained a relationship with the Cuban communists, and his policies and political promises were popular enough to engage the support of the peasants and workers. Castro offered a wide programme of reform, and middle-class donations to his cause poured in. In his speeches, Castro made frequent references to Martí, a popular Cuban hero among all classes, and Chibás, a crusader against corruption and a supporter of middle-class democracy. Finally, Castro demonstrated considerable political skill in maintaining his position as the key figure in the resistance in several ways:

- He did not join a proposed revolutionary *junta*.
- He did not associate himself with a general strike that failed.
- He retained links with the army.
- He used the publicity of the meeting with the reporter Herbert Matthews to his advantage.
- He maintained good relations with the people in the areas of eastern and central Cuba occupied by his rebel army.
- He hinted that he would be willing to negotiate with the USA on the basis of a moderate reform programme.

Batista's weaknesses

Batista's political weaknesses after he seized power in 1952 also contributed to the rise of the revolution:

- He was unable to reconstruct the mixture of personal rule and progressive social and economic policies that had contributed to his popularity in the 1930s and early 1940s.
- He did not eliminate the corruption that angered many Cubans and would have influenced voting in the 1952 elections if they had taken place.
- Having masterminded the 1940 Constitution, he then betrayed its terms – an act that lost the support of most sections of society, for whom the constitution was an ideal towards which all Cubans should strive.
- He mismanaged the campaign against Castro, which he saw in narrow military terms – underestimating the importance of winning over the hearts and minds of the Cuban people.
- His links with American mafia bosses and his use of US support gave the opposition status as true patriots against a foreign-dominated puppet regime.

It is doubtful if a Marxist–Leninist revolution would have been successful in 1959, and this may be why Castro avoided associating himself with the Marxist ideology that his brother Raúl and key supporter Guevara both embraced. What emerged was a revolution based on the ideals of the past, celebrating Cuban independence, offering an end to corruption and the fulfilment of the moderate social and agrarian reforms promised in 1940. The crucial political factor was probably Castro himself – a charismatic and well-known leader with a heroic reputation. That image kept him in power for nearly 50 years.

Debate: Castro's role in the revolution

Historical accounts tend to link Castro inextricably with the Cuban Revolution. In *The Penguin History of Latin America*, Edwin Williamson presents the narrative in terms of Batista losing the propaganda war. His brutality alienated Church and people, 'but more significant was the romantic image of Fidel Castro projected by the international news media'. It was Castro's brilliant leadership that won the armed struggle and he rode in triumph into Havana.

George Camarcho sees 'the epic story' of Castro's *Granma* landing, the Declaration of the Sierra Maestra issued on 12 July 1957 (which called on Cubans to support the revolution), and Castro's subsequent victory as a sort of seamless narrative: 'Castro was gaining strength. New recruits joined him, he had won the sympathy of the rural population ... His triumph was absolute.' However, the alternative view places more emphasis on the importance of the urban insurrection in the success of the revolution, as Source B shows.

SOURCE B

Most accounts of the Cuban Revolution logically focus on the guerrillas in the mountains. Little is written about even today the struggle that took place in the plains, the broad movement against Batista that unfolded in the major cities and towns of Cuba, a movement that was both open and clandestine. It was in the cities that the outcome of the revolution would, in great part, be determined. There, in every organization, plans were debated, actions carried out; in the labor unions, where the Communists were organizing 'fighting committees', in the universities and high schools, where the Revolutionary Directorate had influence, even in the professional and business organizations of the middle and upper classes.

Cannon, T. 1981. Revolutionary Cuba. New York, USA. Thomas Y. Crowell.

Castro dominated Cuban history after 1959 – so much so, that it is tempting to regard the Cuban Revolution as one part of this leader's life story. However, without the considerable discontent not only of students and younger Cubans, but also of workers and the Cuban middle classes, it is doubtful whether Batista's regime would have fallen to the small armed forces that Castro was able to deploy against it. It cannot be denied, though, that Castro's reputation and mystique gave the Cuban Revolution its distinctive character and appeal.

Social causes of the Cuban Revolution

The Cuban Revolution was not a mass movement. The numbers of people involved in armed resistance – whether in the Sierra Maestra with Castro and Guevara, or in the cities with the other revolutionary groups – were not high. The revolutionary leaders were mostly discontented members of the Cuban middle classes, and Batista had a more humble background than his left-wing enemies. Many middle-class interests accepted the revolution, but there was no mass rising of the Cuban workers.

Basista's social failures

The social causes of the Cuban Revolution are rooted in the failure of Batista's government to address the growing discontent among the Cuban people. By the time Castro launched his rebellion, Batista had lost a great deal of backing. He could no longer rely on support from the army, and many Cubans were drawn towards the ideals of the revolutionaries as an alternative to the social injustices under the old regime. If Batista had offered greater equality between town and countryside, improved living standards among the rural workforce, better health and education, and a greater sense that social justice was a priority, would there have been a revolution at all? On the other hand, if there had been greater economic diversity with more social development in urban Cuba, more migration into a flourishing industry, a greater sense that Cuba's social development lay in the hands of its people, would the revolution have been possible?

Activity

In class, debate the relative importance of social and economic factors in the Cuban Revolution. One group should defend the view that social factors were more important, while the other group defends the view that economic factors were more important. At the end of the debate hold a free class vote, not dependent on which group students are in.

Urbanisation

Urbanisation, which had reached reasonably high levels by Latin American standards in the mid 1950s, might have brought a sense of modernity to Cuba, but it also assisted the revolution. Ideas spread in the cities – the University of Havana where Castro was educated was a source of student unrest, and a high proportion of the revolutionary movement was made up of students. Urbanisation was not accompanied by sufficient employment opportunities, and this created discontent. In addition, urban growth widened the social gap between urban and rural dwellers, and even within the cities there were different rates of prosperity and consumerism. In itself, however, urban growth would not have caused a revolution – for example, Santiago was a smaller and less populous city than Havana, but was much more revolutionary than the capital.

Social inequalities

Inequalities in Cuban society undoubtedly contributed to the revolutionaries' support. Rural illiteracy was considerably higher than urban illiteracy in the 1950s. Overall, illiteracy in Cuba stood at 24% in 1953, but only 11% of city dwellers could not read as opposed to 42% in rural areas. Poor education restricted job opportunities, and education reform was a major demand of rural workers. It was also a key policy outlined in Castro's manifesto, and he gave priority to a massive literacy drive early in the revolution, increasing support for a more radical revolution after 1959.

Health was also a major factor in rural and urban disparity, even though – once again – standards in Cuba were higher than in other parts of Latin America. Cuba's life expectancy of 58.8 years, its death rates per 1000 and infant mortality rates were favourable compared to other countries. The ratio of doctors to patients was also relatively high. Yet average statistics obscured differences between urban and rural areas. Half of all Cubans were undernourished, and rural workers were often underweight. Most rural Cubans could not afford health care of any sort; 60% of doctors and 80% of hospital beds were located in the more developed Havana region. Castro's personal exposure to rural poverty – experienced during his time in the Sierra Maestra – inspired many of the more radical reforms he instigated after coming to power.

The same picture emerges with housing conditions. Although the availability of electricity was greater than in other Latin American countries, only 60% of households had power and 57% running water. However, 87% of urban Cubans had electricity and 83% had water. Thus, a considerable gap existed between town and countryside in access to even basic amenities. The standard of housing also differed greatly and the development of communications such as radio and television was much more apparent in urban areas.

Social diversity was much greater within towns and cities. The Havana area contained half of Cuba's industries and most of the 18 factories on the island that employed a large workforce (more than 500 employees). Because of this diversity, wages rose in Havana but declined elsewhere in the 1950s.

It is clear that by 1959, there were two distinct sides to Cuba. The Havana province enjoyed the benefits of tourism, cars, restaurants, economic opportunities, hospitals, doctors, radio, television and cinema, cultural and social links with the USA, reasonable amenities, and flourishing higher education. It also had a well-educated but discontented young population with an awareness of the moral, political and economic shortcomings of Batista's regime, and a strong sense of the need for greater independence from the USA.

The rest of Cuba, especially rural areas, suffered from unemployment and underemployment, as well as a lack of diversity in social and economic opportunities. The prevalence of disease, widespread illiteracy, restricted schooling and poor communications made this more typical of Latin America. It was here that Castro consolidated his position after 1956 and sustained a resistance with a remarkably small number of followers. Batista's forces were unable to penetrate rural areas, and could not stop the wave of support for the revolution that spread among people who did not benefit from the development of the capital city.

Activity

Copy and complete the table below to assess the importance of political, economic and social factors in bringing about revolution.

Factor	Explanation	Importance
Political		
Economic		
Social		

An inevitable revolution?

In *The Origins of the Cuban Revolution Reconsidered*, Samuel Farber argues that while the structure of Cuba's economy, society and politics had made a revolution possible by the late 1950s, it was far from inevitable. Marifeli Pérez-Stable also makes this claim, stating that it was not inevitable that Castro and his guerrillas would dominate the anti-Batista struggle. If Frank País and José Echeverría had not died, then alternative leaders from Cuba's more advanced rural areas might have dominated the movement and the later government. However, Pérez-Stable is also certain that Batista's regime could not have survived, because a revolution rooted in radical nationalism and support for the ordinary people had simply become inevitable by 1959.

It seems unlikely that Batista could have made the necessary reforms to ensure his long-term stability and popularity. The coup of 1952 offended many Cubans and seemed to betray Batista's own political ideas. For this reason, he would never have survived, despite US support. However, whether it was inevitable that a revolution against him would have taken the form that it did is far from certain. The revolutionary groups of 1959 did not act as a cohesive unit; it was certainly not predictable that the other possible leaders would be killed or that there would be so little resistance from opposition groups to Castro's dominance after the revolution. Nor was it certain that the USA would not succeed in overthrowing Castro as it had other Cuban reformers.

 ## Theory of knowledge

History and inevitability

Can historians talk about inevitability as a concept? Can situations ever develop in which there is really so little alternative to what actually happened, or is there always an alternative? Is the job of the historian therefore simply to explain the events themselves and why the alternatives did not occur?

What impact did the revolution have on the Americas?

In 1959, it was not clear whether Castro's revolution was simply another internal Cuban upheaval or the start of more significant changes in the region. The support Castro earned from the middle classes gave the revolution an air of respectability, and it was not inconceivable that the US could be persuaded to support the new regime, particularly as other countries in the Americas, especially Venezuela, had already pledged their backing. Although the US had backed the forces for change in 1933 (see page 139), its support for Batista dwindled as the revolution turned in Castro's favour. However, despite Castro's visit to the US and speeches associating himself with figures like Martí rather than Marx, the radical social changes he introduced in 1959–60, and changes within the new government, caused the US to regard Castro's regime with suspicion.

The impact on the USA

As Castro's rhetoric grew more radical and US assets were seized after it had taken several economic and military actions against Cuba, hostility grew between the two nations. Eventually, Eisenhower broke off relations and established a trade embargo. The gradual emergence of Cuba as part of the communist world, and Castro's desire to spread 'world revolution', heightened anxieties in the US. Kennedy's decision to support the failed Bay of Pigs invasion in April 1961 drove the Cuban regime towards an open alliance with the USSR, and was a serious humiliation for the USA. When Cuba's new ally put missiles in Cuba, opposition in the USA was so intense that it nearly led to an air strike and an invasion of Cuba in 1962, which in turn could have provoked nuclear conflict. Certainly in 1962 Cuba became the focus of attention not just for the Americas, but for the whole world.

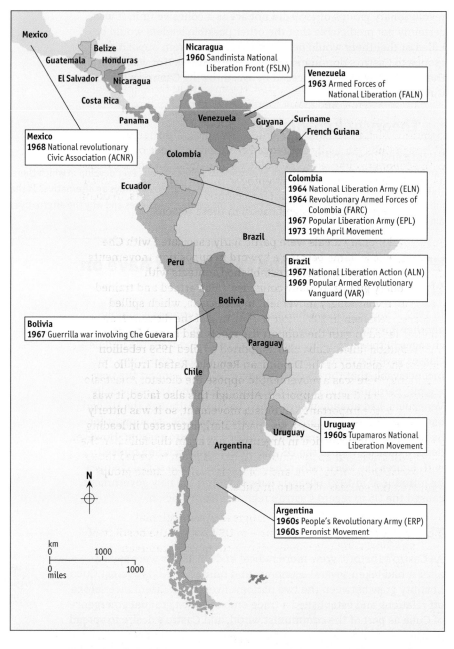

A map showing Central and South America and the revolutionary movements that occurred in the region

Attempts to spread revolution

Having a communist state only a few miles from the mainland encouraged the US to support anti-communist regimes in the Americas. At the same time, Castro wanted to support similar revolutions to his own in the region. His success in the Cuban Revolution had inspired many to believe that small groups of dedicated and heroic guerrillas could bring down established governments and set up new regimes dedicated to social justice. Although Cuba gradually exchanged economic reliance on the USA with economic reliance on the USSR, Castro's government kept alive its revolutionary ideals by intervening in other countries – in Africa as well as the Americas – to support liberation movements. In doing so, Cuba raised its profile significantly in these regions.

Such revolutionary ideals were particularly associated with Che Guevara, whose name became a byword in opposition movements throughout Latin America. He established contacts with revolutionary groups in many countries. Cuba armed and trained a Marxist revolutionary movement in Venezuela, which spilled into open rebellion in 1959 after the ousting of the dictator Marcos Jiménez failed to gain the support the rebels had hoped for. There, the revolution failed. Cuba also supported a failed 1959 rebellion against the dictator of the Dominican Republic, Rafael Trujillo. In Nicaragua, there was a movement to oppose the dictator Anastasio Somoza, which Castro supported. Although this also failed, it was the basis of the important Sandinista movement, so it was bitterly disliked by the USA. Guevara was particularly interested in leading a Cuban-style insurrection in Argentina, but again this failed. In the aftermath of the Cuban Revolution, help was given to armed rebels in Panama, Guatemala, Peru and Colombia. None of these groups emulated the success of Castro in Cuba.

In 1966, Havana played host to a congress of anti-colonial movements from three continents – to US fury and the hostility of the USSR, which did not support active communist intervention in the affairs of other countries. In autumn of that year, Guevara arrived in Bolivia to help lead a revolution there. However, the small group of Cubans was not welcomed by the Bolivian communists, and there was little chance of winning the same level of popular support that Guevara had built in Cuba. US and Bolivian army forces tracked him down and executed him in October 1967. His martyrdom (as many regarded it) had an enormous impact on the region. In Cuba he became more than a national hero, and he remains an emblem of the revolution. The mausoleum built to house his remains, which were sent back from Bolivia, is a monument in Santa Clara of considerable proportions, and a national shrine.

Activity

Divide into two groups. In each group, design a poster about Che Guevara – one from the viewpoint of Cuban communists showing his achievements, and one by right-wing groups in Bolivia showing the dangers he represented. Discuss amongst yourselves how you think Guevara should be remembered – as a revolutionary hero or a trouble-making rebel.

Events in the 1970s and 1980s

Many Latin American states objected to Cuban interference in their affairs. Cuba was expelled from the Organization of American States (OAS), and official trade sanctions were imposed that pushed Cuba further into the Soviet sphere of influence. However, after Guevara's death, Cuban intervention in Latin America lessened.

Throughout the 1970s, Castro recognised that he needed to maintain good relations with the USSR. Gradually, Latin American states restored economic and diplomatic contacts. Castro helped to negotiate a peace between rebels and government forces in Colombia in 1975. Despite this, Cuba continued to support revolution in Nicaragua and was rewarded by the overthrow of Somoza by the Sandinista Marxist guerrillas in 1979. Castro advised the Nicaraguan leader Daniel Ortega throughout the 1980s, but the US-backed insurgency was a drain on the country. Against Castro's advice, Ortega allowed free presidential elections in 1989 and was defeated by the US-backed candidate Violeta Chamorro.

Castro also wanted to support the communists in El Salvador. He helped the different radical groups to unite against the so-called '14 families' that dominated the country in alliance with the USA. Cuba provided weapons and training for the revolutionary Farabundo Martí National Liberation Front (FMLN), and after a long period of warfare in the 1980s, the regime began to negotiate with the revolutionaries.

Despite these successes, the collapse of communism and the difficult economic conditions of the 1990s restricted Cuba's impact in the Americas. The development of a dollar economy in Cuba meant increased links between the Cuban exiles in the USA and more contacts with the US. However, restrictions remain. After 50 years, the Cuban Revolution continues to impact the USA.

End of chapter activities

Paper 3 exam practice

Question

How important were economic factors in bringing about the Cuban Revolution?
[20 marks]

Skill focus

Avoiding a narrative-based answer

Examiner's tips

Even once you have read the question carefully (and so avoided the temptation of including irrelevant material), produced your plan and written your introductory paragraph, it is **still** possible to go wrong.

By 'writing a narrative answer', history examiners mean providing supporting knowledge that is relevant (and may well be very precise and accurate) **but** which is not clearly linked to the question. Instead of answering the question, it merely **describes** what happened.

The main body of your essay/argument needs to be **analytical**. It must not simply be an 'answer' in which you just tell the story. Your essay must **address the demands/key words of the question** – ideally, this should be done consistently throughout your essay, by linking each paragraph to the previous one, in order to produce a clear 'joined-up' answer.

> You are especially likely to lapse into a narrative answer when answering your final question – and even more so if you are getting short of time. The error here is that, despite all your good work at the start of the exam, you will lose sight of the question, and just produce an *account* rather than an analysis. Even if you are short of time, try to write several analytical paragraphs in your answer.

A question that asks you how important a particular factor is, or the extent to which you agree with a statement, expects you to come to a judgement about success/failure or the relative importance of the named factor or individual, or the accuracy of the statement. You need to provide a judgement on the views expressed in the statement. Very often, such questions give you the opportunity to refer to different historians' views.

A good way of avoiding a narrative approach is to refer back continually to the question, and even to mention it now and again in your answer. That should help you produce an answer that is focused on the specific aspects of the question, rather than just giving information about the broad topic or period.

For this question, you will need to cover different aspects of the revolution. Firstly, you should consider the importance of economic discontents and the hopes that different groups had from a change of regime, including:

- the underemployed workers
- the non-sugar workers and farmers
- the commercial and industrial interests who did not benefit from sugar
- the poor and the regions that had not benefited from Batista's regime.

Then you should consider other factors, as the question does not invite simply an explanation of the named factor:

- the social discontents and problems
- the political unrest following Batista's coup
- the hopes for returning to the 1940 Constitution
- the resentment at US influence and the power of US investors and organised crime
- the strong political vision Castro had of a reborn Cuba that linked with the popularity of earlier nationalists and reforms.

You will then need to make a judgement in your concluding paragraph.

Common mistakes

Every year, even candidates who have clearly revised well, and therefore have a good knowledge of the topic and of any historical debate surrounding it, still end up producing a mainly narrative-based or descriptive answer. Very often, this is the result of not having drawn up a proper plan. The extracts of the student's answer below show an approach that essentially just describes the events leading to the Cuban Revolution.

Sample paragraphs of narrative-based approach

> Fidel Castro aimed to reform Cuba and bring about many political, economic and social changes. His attack on the Moncada barracks in 1953 really began the revolution. Like many other Cubans, he was furious about Batista's coup in 1952 and wanted to overthrow the regime to bring about economic changes.

Castro wanted to improve the wages of the poorest Cubans and end the control of the landowners and the USA, who were very powerful in the island. So he gathered a small force and attacked the barracks on 26 July 1953. His forces were defeated and many were killed. Castro himself was captured and put on trial. He was released in 1955 and went to Mexico, where he met the Marxist revolutionary Che Guevara, who was very concerned about economic problems.

This example shows what examiners mean by a narrative answer – it is **not** something you should copy!

[The rest of the essay continues in the same way – there are plenty of accurate/relevant facts about Cuba, Castro and the revolution, but there is no attempt to answer the question by addressing the relative importance of various factors.]

Activity

In this chapter, the focus is on avoiding writing narrative-based answers. Using the information from this chapter, and any other sources of information available to you, try to answer **one** of the following Paper 3 practice questions in a way that avoids simply describing what happened.

Remember to refer to the simplified Paper 3 markscheme on page 223.

Paper 3 practice questions

1   How important were social factors in bringing about the Cuban Revolution?

2   How important was the leadership of Fidel Castro in the success of the Cuban Revolution?

3   Was the weakness of Batista or the strength of the revolutionary movement more important in the success of the Cuban Revolution?

4   Explain the impact of the Cuban Revolution on the Americas.

5   'Batista's fall was inevitable, but Castro's rise to power was not.' How far do you agree with this assertion?

7 The rule of Fidel Castro in Cuba

Key questions

- How and why did Castro's policies change between 1959 and 2006?
- What were the aims and achievements of Castro's economic policies after 1959?
- What was the significance of Castro's social and cultural policies?
- How did the Castro regime deal with different minority groups and social issues?
- What were the successes and failures of Castro's regime?

This chapter deals with the political, economic, social and cultural changes that the Cuban Revolution brought between 1959 and the early 21st century. It describes Cuba's transition from a revolutionary regime to a specifically socialist state, describing how Castro responded to economic problems by shifting emphasis from mass organisations to a more conventional one-party left-wing form of rule with developed political institutions after 1970. The political 'Rectification' campaign of the 1980s is discussed, as well as the attempt to recover the spirit of the initial revolution after the collapse of Cuba's major communist allies during 1989–91, which forced a change in Cuba's plans for developing a modern economy. Throughout this period, however, Cuba's social policies were maintained and offered a distinctive model for a Latin American welfare state. Cultural developments were linked to the political aim of creating a fairer and more equal society. The treatment of different groups within Cuba is discussed in terms of women, black Cubans, gay men and the Church.

Overview

- The revolution of 1959 was not a socialist one, but US hostility and attempted invasion put pressure on Castro, and he declared his socialist aims in 1961. However, he was reluctant to model his regime on the communist countries of China and Eastern Europe.
- Castro regarded himself as a traditional Cuban nationalist, and believed in the power of the Cuban people.
- Economic problems led to a more formal socialist organisation of the country in the 1970s. The broader aim of ending dependence on sugar exports failed, and the USSR merely replaced the USA as Cuba's sugar market.
- Castro's state developed a high level of social care and this, together with effective propaganda, repression of opponents and the engagement of the population in mass politics, kept his regime in power. Potential opposition was eliminated and the hostility of the USA towards its small neighbour inspired Cuba with a sense of national unity.
- The greatest strain on Cuba came after the collapse of the Soviet bloc during 1989–91. The economic consequences were severe, and Cuba found itself short of food, fuel and raw materials.
- This period of emergency meant that concessions were necessary, and a separate dollar economy, greater links with other countries and relaxation of repression and economic controls were all introduced.
- Continuity in Cuban life was maintained through Castro's own rhetoric and the continuation of social services.

How and why did Castro's policies change between 1959 and 2006?

The first government: liberal ministers but revolutionary politics

Initially, Castro and his revolutionaries did not have the backing of a mass movement. Support ebbed away from Batista, but membership of the 26 July Movement was still relatively small by 1959. Batista's self-imposed exile left a power vacuum in Cuba, and Castro and his advisors assembled a new government. It was headed by a liberal judge, **Manuel Urrutia**, and the new ministers were mainly reforming middle-class liberals. However, in practice power lay in the hands of Castro and the former insurgents.

Manuel Urrutia (1901–81) Urrutia was a respected Christian lawyer and politician. He had opposed Batista and campaigned in the USA for help to bring about a return to the 1940 Constitution. He was brought back from exile in Venezuela to take up the post of president in January 1959, but he swiftly fell out with Castro. Urrutia was forced to resign in July after opposing the increasing radicalism of the new state. Exiled from Cuba once more, he worked as a teacher in New York.

From the start of the new regime, politics took on a revolutionary feel, and there was a rapid transfer of wealth to the working classes, the *clases populares*. The middle classes, the landowners, professionals, employers (*clases económicas*) had little choice but to accept this as revolutionary justice. Batista's key supporters were punished, and those accused of crimes against the people faced trials that diverged from traditional rules and procedures. Che Guevara took on responsibility for organising the executions of these criminals, and he and the more radical revolutionaries also drove through agrarian reforms.

Castro and the *barbades* ('bearded ones', but effectively meaning 'rebels') made it clear they would not be bound by legalism or constitutions, as the politics of the past had been shown to be corrupt and ineffective. It is said that before 1959 there were many political parties in Cuba but no democracy, and after 1959 there were no political parties, but democracy.

Unhappy with the radical changes taking place under Castro's influence, the liberals that had been brought in to run the new state soon dropped away, and Urrutia resigned. Castro still did not formally align himself with communism, but he postponed elections, took on the role of president himself, and proclaimed a 'third way' between communism and capitalism, which he called 'humanism'.

However, within the 26 July Movement, Guevara and Castro's brother Raúl were both more openly sympathetic to the left and to socialism. Raúl became defence minister and Guevara was appointed president of the National Bank – both senior positions that meant they had a significant influence on the political path Cuba would take. Still Castro resisted setting up a socialist or even revolutionary political structure. He believed his legitimacy as Cuban leader came from the people, and he would not turn the 26 July Movement into a formal political party.

Despite this, Castro led a revolutionary government dominated by his own supporters, including the revolutionary army and the trade unions. Castro also established several new institutions to carry out his aims for the new Cuba. Among the most important of these were the Committees for the Defense of the Revolution (CDRs) and the Federation of Cuban Women, which were local organisations designed to support the aims and ideals of the revolution, rather like the Russian soviets or local councils.

The radical experiments of the 1960s

In the first 18 months of his rule, Castro initiated several political changes that affected the structure of government and brought ordinary Cubans into the political fold.

- In May 1960, he announced that no elections would be held – there would be no traditional parliamentary democracy or political parties.
- The revolution absorbed the existing radical organisations, including the Revolutionary Directorate (see page 145), which surrendered its weapons to the Rebel Army.
- In October 1960, the PSP and the other political groups united in a new Integrated Revolutionary Organization (ORI). This was not a revolutionary party, more a revolutionary mass organisation.
- Traditional politics had been discredited by corruption to such a degree that direct popular participation replaced them. That is, the Cuban people did not elect representatives, they took part in political meetings themselves. Cubans were encouraged to join the new organisations and make their demands heard.

The USA's hostility towards Cuba also helped radicalise the revolution. In April 1961, John F. Kennedy approved and assisted an invasion by anti-Castro Cuban exiles. On landing at the Bay of Pigs on Cuba's south coast, however, the exiles were quickly halted by Castro's army. The fiasco not only led to a decline in US–Cuban relations, but also the creation of a large Cuban defence force of People's Militias, involving 300,000 people. CDRs were established to identify opponents of the revolution, to stifle counter-revolutionary opinions and to spread government information. These committees quickly became a key element in Cuban life – the way in which Cuba's central government communicated with the people, explained policies and heard grievances.

On 16 April 1961 – partly in response to the Bay of Pigs invasion – Castro formally declared that the revolution was socialist. The threat from the USA had strengthened Castro's already considerable personal power and authority. In addition to this, the need for rapid change required not formal democracy but centralised power and the mobilisation of the masses. Socialist policies would allow this.

The great literacy campaign, which began on 1 January 1961, was an example of this new revolutionary mindset. One of the key aims of the revolution was to bring literacy to the people. Castro felt this was an essential socialist reform, since without it the people could not understand the key political ideas being promoted by the regime. The literacy campaign would also be a great equalising measure for Cuban society, reducing the distinction between town and countryside, rich and poor, middle class and working class. Around 300,000 people were mobilised to assist in rural areas and to develop education there.

Even by 1961, therefore, compromises with liberal forces had been abandoned. A massive shift in income from property owners to wage earners – as well as the greatest series of land and social reforms in Cuban history – had started the country down a new political path. Politics became a huge popular effort headed by a heroic and determined leadership, rather than voting for professional politicians who would discuss laws in an assembly. The defeat of the Bay of Pigs invasion and the development of national defences needed large-scale popular co-operation. The campaign for literacy took urban dwellers into the countryside, and full social equality for women was announced. Health care was extended to rural areas, and programmes were introduced to improve standards of housing and establish greater equality between living standards in urban and rural areas. In this way, revolutionary politics swept away class and racial distinctions.

In the late 1960s, Castro began a push for a much greater level of sugar production. He set a target of annual production that should reach 10 million tonnes by 1970. This also required mobilisation of the masses to support the campaign. Thousands began working towards this record harvest.

The drive for agricultural production was linked with the heroic achievements of the armed revolution; this poster to promote Cuban agriculture says: 'With the faith and courage of the fighters of Moncada'

For some, however, this was not enough. Guevara in particular felt the need for greater socialist planning and institutional development. He believed that the Cuban 'socialist man' should be driven to complete the moral revolution, and that the Cuban Revolution itself was not sufficiently supportive of the socialist ideology of personal sacrifice and the rigid planning that had characterised similar changes in Eastern Europe. The failure of the Castro regime to meet its economic targets prompted a political rethink after 1970.

Activity

Imagine a debate within Castro's government in 1965. What arguments might have been made to continue the new form of popular politics and what arguments might have been put forward that more institutions were needed? Recreate the discussion in groups. Would change improve relations with the USSR and why was that important?

The Cuban Communist Party 1965

In 1962, Cuba became the focus of a major international crisis. To protect the island country from US invasion, the USSR installed missiles in Cuba. The USA imposed a blockade and threatened the Soviets with nuclear war. By the end of the Cuban Missile Crisis, the Soviets had agreed to withdraw the missiles, and Castro felt let down by the weak stance of his new ally – although it had got the USA to promise not to attempt to invade Cuba again. This event confirmed to the Cuban leader that his country needed to depend on itself and mobilise as much internal support as possible for protection. To do this, formal political structures were needed. In 1965, therefore, the Cuban Communist Party was founded to give the mass movements a 'vanguard party' around which to rally. The new party was not made up of former Socialist Party members, but instead was dominated by the rebels. Communism had not shaped Castro's regime – Castro had shaped a new party for himself, and in doing so established a one-party state in Cuba.

Popular Power

Before his death in 1967, Guevara summed up the challenge that Cuba faced: 'To find a way to perpetuate the heroic attitudes of the Revolution in everyday life.' In the 1970s, Castro attempted reforms to fulfil this dream. By this time, Cuba had a great deal of centralised power, but its organisations were weak. Despite high participation in political life and social reform – the Federation of Cuban Women alone had 376,000 members – more was needed to sustain the impetus of the revolution and to boost production to improve the economy.

The solution was a policy that became known as 'Popular Power'. By this, the party still ruled Cuba, and the government and the army administered the state, but stronger popular organisations marked the link with the Cuban people. In 1976, a new constitution was established that set up municipal and provincial assemblies, as well as a national assembly. Elections to local assemblies were the key to Popular Power. From these, delegates were sent to provincial assemblies and from there to the national assembly. The party still maintained control of the organs of government – the Central Committee and the Council of Ministers.

Castro addresses a congress of the Cuban Communist Party in 1976; the party still dominates Cuban political life today

What was achieved?

In practice, the local assemblies had limited control over spending and provision of service, and little influence over the actions of the state. The national assembly could not reject party proposals, and ultimately Castro's decisions overrode all possible debate. The numbers of people willing to serve in time-consuming and – as they soon discovered – ineffective discussions declined, and there was a high turnover of delegates to the assemblies. Therefore, although the new structure defined by the 1976 Constitution was designed to allow public opinion to be expressed, in reality no action was taken to implement public concerns unless they fell in line with Castro's own socialist ideals. The people were nominally in charge of how the state was run, but had no real input into policies and decisions.

Political restructuring was accompanied by economic centralisation, with the creation of the System of Economic Direction and Planning (SPDE) in 1976. Throughout the 1970s, there was also a revival of trade unionism. Local elections to trade union bodies were established from 1970, and congresses were held in 1973, 1978 and 1984. However, the Cuban Trade Union Congress (CTUC) was closely controlled by the party, and had little influence on economic and social policy. Local power as a concept was applied to the workplace, as monthly assemblies were held to discuss how to improve production. The Federation of Cuban Women was also reorganised, and formal congresses held.

In the 1970s, the role of a formally organised party was expanded at the expense of the direct popular movements of the 1960s. In 1974, Castro proclaimed that 'the Party is the soul of the Cuban Revolution'. The Politburo, the Secretariat and the Central Committee – all insignificant in the late 1960s – now became central to running the state:

- The 100-strong Central Committee became the party's ruling body.
- The Politburo was a smaller group within the Central Committee, which dealt with party policy.
- The Secretariat, led by the party's general secretary, was the executive branch of the party.

Between 1975 and 1984, party membership grew from 211,000 to 523,000, and politically the mid 1970s seemed to have launched a period of success for the Cuban government:

- The Cuban people had formal voting rights and could express their concerns in an official forum.
- Mass organisations were formalised, streamlined, and brought under party control.

- The USSR approved of the formalisation of Cuban communism and increased its aid to Cuba, strengthening ties between them.
- Cuba became less isolated – between 1970 and 1975, Cuba won diplomatic recognition from eight Latin American countries.
- Cuba became part of the communist 'family'.
- The country took part in broader international affairs and provided aid to Angola in its fight for independence; this increased Cuba's prestige in Eastern Europe and as an anti-imperialist force.

Activity

A huge wave of emigration from Cuba took place after 1959, including half of Cuba's teachers and doctors, a quarter of professionals and technicians, and 80% of its religious leaders. These people left because they objected to Castro's monopoly of political power and the establishment of a socialist Cuba. What might an exiled Cuban have thought of the 'successes' outlined above? Imagine you are one of these émigrés living in the USA, and write an article that challenges the idea of political success in Cuba.

 ## Theory of knowledge

History and 'success'

It can be difficult for a historian to assess 'success' in historical terms without considering the aims and political viewpoints that drove particular reforms. If 'success' has imposed a political tyranny and restricted the lives of the people of a nation, can a historian still talk about it as a success? Is it the role of a historian to consider success only in terms of the aims of a regime?

Rectification

By the mid 1980s, it had become clear that greater political change was needed. Relaxation of economic controls had led to greater prosperity, but accompanying this was a decline in the moral fervour that had characterised the revolution and the early years of Castro's rule. Aid from the USSR was falling; trade was declining; debt was increasing. Just as the socialist world was adopting more liberal economic policies, Castro took the opposing path, which he called 'Rectification'.

The Rectification programme was launched in April 1986. A government report in July of that year condemned the shift from official production to private enterprise that had taken place in Cuba in the previous few years. Volunteer work had declined, and officials hired family and friends rather than ardent supporters of the communist government. Workers no longer felt there was an incentive to work towards higher production levels, and many of them took to working part of the time in their official jobs and spent the rest of the time in making private profit.

To address these issues, Castro introduced tighter discipline in labour, wage cuts for certain sectors and increases in the cost of services. At the same time, he increased wages for lower-paid workers. These moves were intended to remotivate the Cuban people with socialist ideals – encouraging not profit but concern for social justice and equality. Several other programmes were launched to assist with this:

- 'Micro-brigades' of volunteer workers were enlisted to build houses and community centres.
- A Food Plan was launched that involved thousands of city dwellers working in the countryside.
- Special local groups were created to monitor and report back on excessive wages.
- There was a political campaign against the black market, and any officials buying illegal goods were punished.
- Communist Party members visited factories, schools and local areas to explain the importance of a socialist mentality.
- Workers were encouraged to report corruption and injustice.
- Bureaucracy was reduced.
- The party apparatus was streamlined, and there were secret ballot elections for municipal and provincial assembly leaders.

For all these democratic-seeming changes, Cuba did not become a political democracy. In 1989, the party showed its determination to reinforce socialism and inspire the people with earlier revolutionary ideals by arresting 14 leading army officers accused of corruption and drug trafficking. This affair also exposed Cuba's weakness in managing its top officials.

Rectification: the debate

Rectification can be seen as a response to falling sugar prices and declining Eastern European support. Official production had to be increased, and domestic spending and black markets had to be controlled to meet a trade gap. This is the view taken by historians such as Susan Eckstein. Others, including the sociologist Alfonso Dilla, stress emotional and political motives for Rectification, believing that Castro revived the ideals embraced by Che Guevara, and sought an ethical and patriotic revival in the face of ongoing hostility from the USA in the 1980s.

After 1989: economic change but little political development

The end of the Soviet Union and the decline of the Eastern European market for sugar proved catastrophic for Cuba. Major economic diversification took place, but living standards fell. By 1994, Cuba was in crisis. Castro ceased intercepting Cubans fleeing to the USA, and thousands made it there before US president Bill Clinton stopped accepting Cuban immigrants.

Cuba had to allow a dollar economy to operate alongside the 'official' economy, and Castro was forced to open up the country to tourism in an attempt to revive the economy. Despite these difficulties, the president refused to surrender his communist principles in the way that many regimes across Eastern Europe had done. Right up to Castro's retirement in 2006 he remained true to the policy he established in 1961: 'Within the revolution, everything; against the revolution, nothing.'

Why did Castro's regime survive for so long?

In *The Origins of the Cuban Revolution Reconsidered*, Samuel Farber sees in Cuba 'a left-wing authoritarian populism that evolved into a variety of communist nationalism' that was never a revolution from below. Historian Edward González claimed that Castro was a more typical mainstream communist leader, which he characterised as 'charismatic hardship communism' – where the inspirational leader urges his people to make sacrifices in order to achieve socialist goals, in the manner of Lenin, Stalin and Mao.

Some historians claim that, despite arguments to the contrary, Castro *did* revitalise Cuba's political life. Georgina Suárez Hernández believes that Rectification stimulated the creativity of the masses and strengthened socialism, and there is some evidence to support this view:

- In 1986, around 6.7 million people took part in elections.
- In 1988, 5.2 million participated in local accountability assemblies.
- The Communist Party had 1 million members in the late 1980s.
- Membership of the CDRs remained high.

Marifeli Pérez-Stable is less enthusiastic about Castro's later reforms, arguing that voting and meeting without any means of exercising real control offered little to the masses, and that the key necessity of engaging public loyalty was not addressed at more than a superficial level.

As the international situation changed drastically after 1989, it might seem surprising that there was not more popular unrest in Cuba. Historian Antoni Kapcia offers several explanations for why the ideals of the revolution and Castro's personal popularity continued in Cuba (see Source A).

SOURCE A

- The social benefits that the system has brought. By the 1970s, considerable achievements in social provision, equality, land distribution and employment security (all comparing well with contemporary Latin America) had sufficed to guarantee the continuing loyalty of most Cubans.
- The degree of democracy and popular participation was enough to guarantee loyalty. Testimonies such as those in Richard Gott, 'Fidel Remembered' are evidence of this. Even when the early 90s saw a drastic fall in production and trade, there was residual loyalty to the regime. This was because of the ability of the regime to mobilise people for inspirational campaigns – the 1961 Literacy Campaign and defence against hurricanes and for house building. Also, institutional mass organizations involved women, workers, farmers, children and local neighbourhoods. These were far more successful than the equivalent in other 'socialist states' like East Germany or the USSR and may explain why Cuban communism survived.
- A third reason may be the association of Castro's socialism with nationalism and independence from the USA, a relationship which blighted Cuba from 1898 to 1959. In that respect there is a parallel with Communist China. National pride is a strong element in Castro's appeal and success. The continuing US embargo has always served as living proof of the 'siege' and provided an alibi for economic problems.
- However a major factor is the extensive emigration. This provided a safety valve and weakened any development of internal opposition. Also, dollar inputs in the 1990s from the Cubans in the USA ironically helped to save the regime.

Kapcia, A. 2000. Cuba: Island of Dreams. *New York, USA. Berg.*

However, this explanation can be challenged, as it assumes a loyalty on the part of the Cuban people that may not have been widely felt. Some claim that repression, the continuing support of the armed forces, and the existence of 're-education camps' (UMAPs or Military Units to Aid Production) – which some have seen as similar to concentration camps for opponents – played a more important role in securing support for Castro's later regime. The military draft for men between the ages of 16 and 45, and the association of any 'deviant' social behaviour with political subversion of the revolution, may also have been significant.

Activity

Read Source B, which is an extract from an online blog. Continue the blog, offering several different views about why Castro survived politically for so long.

What were the aims and achievements of Castro's economic policies after 1959?

The economic aims of the 26 July Movement

When Castro came to power, his economic policies reflected concerns about Cuban dependency on the US for its sugar exports, and included plans for import substitution industrialisation – a policy that was common in Latin America in the 1930s (see page 16). This was a strategy to develop a range of industries to make the economy less dependent on the export of a particular crop. Cuba's economy needed capital and modernisation, and the problems of underemployment and rural poverty had to be addressed as matters of urgency.

The basic aims of the new regime, therefore, were to ensure fairer distribution of wealth, which would boost domestic demand; to ensure economic growth in areas beyond sugar production; and to sustain full employment. The government's nationalist tendencies meant that it wanted to use internal capital rather than overseas investment to finance this economic diversification. In fact, these ideas were not especially radical – many of Castro's economic plans had been advocated by reformers, and even Batista's regime had attempted economic diversification.

Early changes and hopes

Castro's earliest reforms were targeted at agriculture and a return to the 1940 Constitution, which had aimed to break up larger estates. The reforms he introduced in 1959 allowed estates of up to 400 hectares (1000 acres) or, if justified, special allotments of 135 hectares (334 acres). Larger holdings – about 10% of Cuban farms – were confiscated and their owners compensated with state bonds. The government set up co-operatives rather than parcelling out land, but anyone cultivating land up to a certain amount was given ownership of that land. A minimum of 27 hectares (67 acres) was granted to those who were already working on the land. The National Institute for Agrarian Reform was established to supervise these changes.

Rents were reduced. Tax concessions were introduced for native businesses and non-sugar producers. Wages were increased and the government encouraged the establishment of small businesses. There were more Cuban industrial enterprises and an expansion of domestic purchasing power to encourage demand. Initially, these reforms brought a certain amount of prosperity to Cuba. Sugar output increased from an average of 5.4 million tonnes in the 1950s to 6.2 million by the early 1960s. A surplus gave the basis for a more ambitious plan of industrialisation after 1961. The reaction to these reforms varied. Employers were alarmed, and members of the professional classes and technical experts began to leave Cuba. There was an outflow of what economists call 'social capital' in skilled managers, and in real capital as overseas trade and investment fell.

As US mistrust grew, another source of trade emerged. Castro signed a trade treaty with the Soviet Union in March 1960 after a visit to Cuba by the Soviet minister **Anastas Mikoyan**. By the terms of this treaty, the USSR would take 1 million tonnes of Cuban sugar and advance $100 million in credit for industrial equipment. In June, Castro confiscated the holdings of the big US oil refineries in Cuba, after they refused to process cheaper Soviet oil. In August, the USA imposed trade embargoes on Cuba and in response Castro nationalised US properties on the island. This escalating animosity between Cuba and the US eventually meant an end to Cuba's most lucrative source of income and a heavy dependence on aid and support from the USSR.

Anastas Mikoyan (1895–1978) Mikoyan was the deputy premier of the USSR under Nikita Khrushchev. He had a long history in Soviet politics, serving as trade minister under Stalin, and he supported reforms in Russia after Stalin's death in 1953. Mikoyan was an influential figure, and his visit to Castro provoked alarm in the USA. It paved the way for close economic ties between Cuba and the USSR.

Economic experiments of the 1960s

Castro's plan after 1961 was to use earnings from sugar exports to gain currency for industrialisation. This, and greater agricultural diversity, would in turn reduce the dependence on sugar. The plan needed fuel reserves for new industries, and in the short term Soviet aid and credit was vital. Castro still hoped for national self-sufficiency and economic independence in the long term, but ultimately his plans failed:

- Sugar production fell to 4.8 million tonnes and then 3.8 million tonnes by 1963 because of diversification into other crops.
- Other crops were not developed enough for Cuba to be self-sufficient, so food imports continued; these used up Soviet credits.
- There were limited markets for Cuban agricultural products abroad (other than sugar); it was unlikely that more varied food production could provide enough income to ensure economic growth.
- The trade deficit rose from a surplus in 1960 to a deficit of 322 million pesos in 1963.
- The loss of technical experts and the inexperience of economic planners made industrialisation difficult.

The drive to industrialise faltered, and from the mid 1960s emphasis was once again placed on sugar production. In 1966, investment in agriculture rose to 40.4%, compared to spending on industry, which fell to 16.7% of total expenditure that year. The demand for labour required by the sugar industry led to a huge labour-mobilisation programme that involved workers from other sectors voluntarily leaving their jobs to work in the sugar-cane fields.

The loss of US markets had to be made up by increased sales to communist countries, but these fluctuated. Castro's plan to achieve a record sugar harvest of 10 million tonnes by 1970 fell short by 1.5 million tonnes and cast doubts on the whole strategy. The fundamental issue was that sugar production alone was simply not enough to sustain the Cuban economy and fund industrial development. In addition, financial resources were going into wages for low-paid workers, free health care and sustaining large armed forces.

The revolution did bring about a reduction in unemployment and seasonal underemployment in the 1960s, but the sharp rise in standards of living that occurred between 1959 and 1961 could not be sustained. In 1962, shortages of basic imported foods led to rationing. In the late 1960s, absenteeism became a major problem for employers, as workers lacked incentives to produce. The state nationalised 58,000 small businesses in 1968 and banned self-employment in an effort to address these problems, but consumption was 5% less in 1969 than it had been in 1962.

Castro sews up a symbolic sugar bag to celebrate reaching the sugar target of 6 million tonnes in 1965; ultimately he failed to reach his ten-year target by 1970

The Cuban economy after 1970

The failure of the 1970 harvest campaign resulted in large-scale changes to Cuba's economic policy:

- There were more incentives for workers, such as bonuses for higher output.
- Economic planning was decentralised, and smaller workshops and agricultural enterprises were established.
- Development focused on alternative products to sugar, including livestock, citrus fruits, rice, coffee and tobacco.
- Producers were given more technical education.
- Greater economic links with Eastern Europe were established, and in 1972 Cuba joined Comecon (the Soviet-led organisation for economic co-operation between communist states).

As a result of these policies, there was greater economic growth in Cuba in the early 1970s, but this was still not enough to allow a significant move away from sugar as the key product. After 1975, economic difficulties surfaced once more. By the mid 1980s, there were growing debts. Income from refining imported Soviet crude oil and re-exporting it fell because of a drop in oil prices. Relaxation of economic controls in the early 1980s increased private production, but this occurred at the expense of productivity in key areas. Cuba had become dependent on its Comecon allies for 63% of its food, 96% of its fuel, 80% of its machinery and 74% of its manufactured goods. It was difficult to find capital for the development of domestic industries or to achieve the diversification and independence that Castro had hoped for.

In an international context, Cuba was significantly restrained. Its natural market, the USA, was closed. New markets collapsed with the fall of the USSR and its Eastern European empire after 1989. Cuban exports dropped dramatically and aid from the communist world ceased. After this, Cuba found itself in a state of emergency that Castro called a 'special period in the Time of Peace'. With little money for imports, rationing and austerity returned after 1990.

The 'special period': the Cuban economy since 1989

Throughout the 1990s, Castro once again introduced reforms designed to tackle the economic crisis:

- State farms were converted into co-operatives, and between 1990 and 1996 state control of farms fell from 82% to 34.2%.
- Farmers markets, banned during the period of Rectification, were once again allowed.
- Foreign investment was encouraged and foreign firms allowed to set up businesses in Cuba; these firms paid the state in US dollars, and the state paid employees in pesos.
- Emigrants were allowed back to attract hard currency; by the late 1990s, around 80,000 exiles were returning for visits compared to 7000 in 1990.
- Special 'dollar shops' accepting US dollars were established by the state to earn hard currency.
- Tourism was encouraged.
- The state paid bonuses to workers in key industries that exported or earned hard currency – for example mining, ports and tobacco.
- Faced with fuel shortages, the state encouraged 'green' policies – natural fertilisers, reduction of motor transport and biotechnology; it also made much of its health facilities to attract tourism.

Despite attempts to attract investment and visitors to stimulate the economy, shortages continued, as did a decline in living standards. By 1994, Cuba had reached an economic low point; 21,000 people left in August and September that year when restrictions on travel abroad were lifted. A survey of 2000 people in Havana found that 77% of Cubans had insufficient income to cover their day-to-day living expenses. The Cuban economy became what some writers called 'post-capitalist', with an emphasis on the provision of services, using an educated workforce to promote biotechnology and pursuing post-industrial environmental policies. During this difficult period, however, there was no severe reduction in health and social services, which still accounted for 32% of GDP in 1998.

Edward González believed that 'economic development was the Achilles heel of the *fidelista* [Castro's] regime'. This was partly due to a lack of sustained strategy and a tendency to react to events, but also to a difficult international situation. Historically, Cuban prosperity depended on close economic links with the enormous US market. When that market collapsed in 1929, nearly all states in the Americas suffered. Profits from sugar gave Cuba one of the highest living standards in Latin America, but Cuba lacked the natural resources, the internal market and the capital for large-scale industrial production. To finance the high level of social and defence spending Castro's new state needed, he had to maintain sugar as the country's key crop. Low productivity remained a problem, and efforts to tackle it were intermittent.

Did socialism continue in Cuba?

Susan Eckstein has argued that the ideology of the revolution persists in Cuba to this day, and that the degree of state control in the 1990s was still strong enough for Cuba to be considered 'socialist'. Progressive social policies were pursued despite economic problems. This is certainly the view of many US commentators, who drew comparisons between Cuba and the failing socialist economies of Eastern Europe. However, Javier Corrales casts doubts on this, claiming that after Rectification, the state in Cuba had to allow such a degree of inequality that it lost its central socialist ethos.

For most of his time in power, Castro resisted the complete Soviet model and was flexible enough to cope with different situations. Economic policy always had a moral and political side. Ultimately, unlike the USSR and China, communist Cuba did not have the natural, technical or human resources to impose a transformative economic plan. In present-day Cuba there is a bewildering disparity between the revolutionary slogans and the celebration of socialism and revolutionary idealism on public occasions and in schools, and the desire of both citizens and the state for hard currency from vistors and the development of commercial tourism.

Activity

To what extent did economic difficulties lie behind political developments in Cuba? Take each development discussed in the section above and explain why it might have been led by economic factors. Then consider other influences – personal, moral and political. Try to take a view.

What was the significance of Castro's social and cultural policies?

Cuban social policies were one of the most distinctive elements of Castro's regime and had a huge significance for the Americas as a whole. They established a model for other nations, and may account for the stability of the government in Cuba. The success of many of Castro's social policies may lie in the fact that he did not begin from a low base – Cuba was certainly not one of the poorest countries in Latin America, nor did it have the most severe social problems. However, there were considerable regional, class and racial differences in living standards in the late 1950s.

Changes to social policy

The changes to social policy brought by the revolution included:

- free and universal health care – a national health service and rural health programme
- free and universal education
- a safety net of benefits for workers through a developed scheme of social insurance to cover old age, sickness and unemployment
- food subsidies
- greater income equality and universal benefits totally run by the state and not by private providers
- racial and sexual equality as official policies.

The effects were important for the Cuban people, and were remarkably far-reaching. Despite the economic problems it faced, the regime maintained unswerving support for its social policies. Although the economic crisis affected the quality of social services in some areas, the overall achievements were impressive:

- In 1958, only 8% of Cubans had access to health care; after 1959 all Cubans did.
- In 1960, the literacy rate was 77%; as a result of the massive literacy campaign this rose to 96% and in 2000 was still at that level.
- In 1959, 45% of children did not attend primary school; by 1980, school non-attendance had dropped to 1.2%.
- Secondary school attendance was 14% of children over 14 in 1960 and 90% by 1990.
- In 1970, only 7% of Cubans attended university; by 1990, this was 21% (although it had dropped to 12% by the late 1990s).
- Infant mortality stood at 35 out of every 1000 live births in 1950, but 7.2 out of every 1000 in 1999 – a figure comparable to the much wealthier USA.
- Deaths of children under five were 54 in every 1000 in 1960, but only eight in every 1000 in 1999.

Nowhere is the distinctiveness of the Cuban Revolution's social policy more apparent than in education. The literacy campaign of 1961 was an extraordinary initiative for a new regime, drawing more than 1 million Cubans into achieving a common aim, and Castro considered education to be an essential part of economic and social reform:

- 10,000 new classrooms were built in rural districts in the late 1960s.
- Travelling libraries were introduced.
- The 1970s saw the construction of huge, modern secondary schools in the countryside.
- In the late 1980s, 939,900 students attended primary schools, 775,350 attended secondary schools, and 262,200 were in other institutions of higher learning.

Young women celebrate the success of the literacy campaign in a parade in Havana in 1961

Social policy: an assessment

Historians have not always found it easy to reach a conclusion about Castro's social policies since 1959, or to reach a judgement about whether he should have persisted with them in the face of severe economic problems. Certainly, the universal nature of the policies meant that there was some waste, as they were not always targeted at the groups that most needed them. The failure to develop any private provision of services might have prevented efficiency and necessary competition. The socialist economy's poor performance did not generate the wealth to provide top-quality social services, especially after 1989. Social policy came under increasing strain throughout the 1990s, and many of the gains made in the early years after the revolution were lost.

In addition, the significant effort put into education and training was undermined by poor employment prospects. The introduction of the dollar economy (see page 174) meant that it was preferable for Cubans to take low-skilled work that could earn dollars rather than professional or skilled work that did not. Aviva Chomsky comments that 'one of Latin America's most educated populations became de-schooled and deskilled'. In addition, economic problems affected the provision of services: neighbourhood centres that provided valuable childcare only had 100,000 places for 1 million working women by the mid 1990s. Fewer economic controls left some groups vulnerable – especially poorer black Cubans – and increased the gap between those with access to hard currency and those without.

However, this pessimistic analysis is countered by those who point out the resilience of local communities in Cuba, many of which developed local support groups in the workforce, among women, among poorer blacks and in neighbourhood councils, to maintain the spirit of the revolution and to take care of the most vulnerable in their society. The state has also shown an ongoing commitment to raising social spending, even in times of acute economic hardship.

> How successful do you think Castro's social policies were in the 1960s and 1970s?

Cultural life after the revolution

After 1959, the Cuban state took an active role in promoting cultural life, within a context of respect for the well-being of the people as a whole. New cultural institutions included the Casa de las Américas (to promote the arts and to establish cultural links with other countries in the Americas and elsewhere), the Cuban Institute of Cinematic Arts and Industry, the Cuban National Theater, the National Ballet of Cuba, the National Symphony Orchestra and the National Folklore Group.

However, interest in the arts largely depended on improving literacy, so the literacy campaign of 1961 was crucial in changing popular participation in culture.

To enforce this, education began to include artistic training and training in an appreciation of the arts. Subsidised concerts, theatre, museums and galleries ensured that cultural experiences were not confined to the wealthy. Free or low-cost art education was provided for children and adults from primary level to specialised art schools and arts courses in higher education. As the Castro regime placed emphasis on national awareness, folklore and ethnic culture were encouraged, and in 1961 the Institute of Ethnology and Folklore was set up; the state established Festivals of Culture from 1962.

Before 1950, the Cuban film industry had been insignificant, producing no more than around 80 films. After 1959, cinema – along with all forms of media communication – came under state control and began to expand. On the whole, Cuban art and cinema has been less widely known than its dance – with ballet and popular dance forms such as salsa gaining world renown. In other areas of the arts, the poster and street art of the revolution made a strong impact both within Cuba and elsewhere in the world. In particular, the heroic image of Che Guevara appeared on posters and wall graffiti, linking art and politics, and reminding revolutionaries everywhere of Cuban ideals.

Guevara's image still appears on posters and billboards across Cuba; this sign says 'Ever onwards to victory'

The significance of Cuban revolutionary culture was considerable. It encouraged national awareness and racial and political unity, and presented a strong image of Cuba to other Latin American states. It also represented a celebration of Cuba's past and encouraged worldwide interest in Cuban culture. However, there were negative aspects to cultural policy under Castro:

- There was no pretence of free expression of alternative political views.
- Culture was used as a tool of a one-party state.
- Some have argued that the promotion of ethnic culture was patronising.
- In the drive for dollars in the 1990s, culture was exploited to create a sort of 'revolutionary theme park'.

How did the Castro regime deal with different minority groups and social issues?

Women

Female equality was proclaimed as soon as Castro came to power in 1959, and women were mobilised in a mass organisation that remains a significant force in Cuban society today. More than 85% of Cuban women belong to the Cuban Women's Federation, and this group now has 73,710 branches throughout the country.

Women found greater employment opportunities and equality of income under Castro than they had before. In the 1950s, 13% of Cuba's working population were women; by 1980 this had risen to 30% and by 1990 it stood at 40%. Women benefited from the social and education reforms, and special attention was given to retraining the many women who lost their jobs in domestic service as a result of the revolution.

It was stated as a revolutionary law in the 1975 Family Code that both men and women had obligations in terms of housework and childcare. Neighbourhood Centers were open from 7 a.m. to 7 p.m. to look after the children of working women. Even during the difficult period after the collapse of European communism, social support for women and families continued. However, some historians have outlined the negative aspects of life for women under Castro's regime (see Source C).

SOURCE C

The FMC's [Cuban Women's Federation] principal task was to defend a revolution whose interests were defined by a male elite. Women participated very little in the making of policies. The changes in social behaviour in a 'machismo' Latin American male culture may have been slower than official policy recommended. The economic problems of the 1990s hit women more. The day to day shortages, the lack of goods in shops and the need to make every possession in the household count to avoid waste and save money fell on women disproportionately. Also, the revival of tourism also saw the rise of *Jinterismo* (prostitution) if not directly then in the exploitation of Cubans in tourist centres for all kinds of tourist needs.

Smith, L. and Padula, A. 1993. *Sex and Revolution: Women in Socialist Cuba.* Oxford, UK. Oxford University Press. p. 133.

Castro pins an award on a member of the Cuban Women's Federation during a ceremony to mark the organisation's tenth anniversary in 1975

The situation for black Cubans

Castro was quick to end segregation for Cuban blacks, and all forms of racism and discrimination were banned. As black Cubans tended to be among the poorest in society, they benefited particularly from wage rises and social services. All reforms affecting black Cubans came 'from above', and thus in Cuba there was no equivalent to the civil rights campaigns that characterised the USA in the 1960s.

However, despite Castro's reforms, black Cubans did not gain economic or social equality, and Castro has been accused of being indifferent to the relatively low economic status of black Cubans. In *Castro, the Blacks and Africa* (1998), Carlos Moore referred to 'Castro's icy silence on anything remotely touching the plight of black Cuba', and in *A Nation for All* (2001), Alejandro de la Fuente wrote of the 'marginalisation of Afro Cubans in social, economic and political life'.

Castro was unsympathetic to the ideals of the Black Power movement in the USA (see page 66), believing they were a divisive force in society. His ideas on revolution were based on class and nation, not race. However, although there was a proportionately higher number of blacks in prison in Cuba – in 1987, 78% of arrests for drug- and alcohol-related crimes were black or mixed-race Cubans – and although black housing conditions were worse than those of whites, these facts do not represent the whole picture.

Chomsky has pointed to the considerable reduction in the gap between black and white Cubans in life expectancy, educational achievement, professional opportunities and access to health care in comparison with both the USA and Brazil. However, the reality is that, since 1989, black Cubans have suffered from having limited access to valuable dollars. Few black Cuban exiles send their families dollar remittances and the tourist industry favours employees with paler skins. They are also not as well represented in positions of authority.

Same-sex relations

In some aspects, revolutionary Cuba was not socially tolerant; most notably, the leadership was at first unsympathetic to same-sex relations. Castro said: 'A deviation of nature clashes with the concept of what a militant communist must be.' Gay men were often taken into camps to be 're-educated' and there was no recognition of gay rights until the 1980s. From 1979, discrimination against same-sex couples officially ended, but in practice there was considerable prejudice. Castro's attitude eventually changed in the late 1990s, when he urged acceptance of same-sex relations.

Religious groups

Like many revolutionaries, Castro associated religion with the old order and corrupt regimes. Officially, his government offered 'freedom of conscience', but Catholic worship was discouraged, Catholic television and radio programmes were ended and Catholic newspapers were suppressed. In September 1961, over 1340 leading clergy members were exiled and Catholic schools were brought under the control of the state. Many Catholics, Baptists and Jehovah's Witnesses found themselves in re-education camps. The CDRs (see page 167) denounced religious practice at a local level. Traditional festivals such as Christmas fell victim to revolutionary zeal from 1969, and in 1976 Cuba was declared an atheist state.

Nuns arrive in Florida, USA, after Castro deported all foreign-born priests and nuns from Cuba in 1961

The movement towards Liberation Theology (the support the Catholic Church gave to social and political reform in South America) brought Castro's regime and the Church closer, and some concessions were made throughout the 1980s and 1990s.

Since 1992, atheism has no longer been 'official' and more religious freedom has been granted. Restrictions on practising religion have eased, but writings by Church leaders are still subject to government control. In addition, churches can only accept funding from the state. Only state-recognised religious groups can operate freely. Discrimination on religious grounds is officially banned, but churches still take care to avoid confrontation with the regime and Cuba remains a deeply secular state. Only around 250,000 of its 11 million people attend church regularly. This is evenly divided between the Catholics and a variety of Protestant churches. There is also Santeria, a popular religion combining some Christian elements with Yoruba beliefs in spirits and ancestors, inherited from West Africa. Its devotees can be seen in distinctive white dress.

What were the successes and failures of Castro's regime?

Activity

Look back at the aims of the 26 July Movement and then copy and complete the table below to show how far they were achieved.

Aim	Political	Economic	Social	Cultural
To give power to the people				
To create a more equal society and create true democracy				
To end the dependence of Cuba on foreign powers				
To diversify the economy and end dominance of sugar				
To create an awareness of Cuba as a nation				

End of chapter activities

Paper 3 exam practice

Question

How successful was Castro's economic policy after 1959?
[20 marks]

Skill focus

Using your own knowledge analytically and combining it with
awareness of historical debate

Examiner's tips

Always remember that historical knowledge and analysis should be the *core*
of your answer – aspects of historical debate are desirable extras. However,
where it is relevant, the integration of relevant knowledge about historical
debates/interpretations, with reference to individual historians, will help
push your answer up into the higher bands.

Assuming that you have read the question carefully, drawn up a
plan, worked out your line of argument/approach, and written your
introductory paragraph, you should be able to avoid both irrelevant
material and simple narrative. Your task now is to follow your plan
by writing a series of linked paragraphs that contain detailed analysis,
precise supporting own knowledge and, where relevant, brief references
to historical interpretations.

For this question, you will need to:

- consider Castro's aims – successes cannot be judged independently
  of what problems were being solved or what ambitions met
- supply a brief explanation of their historical context (i.e. the
  situation in 1959 – the legacy of the Batista years)
- outline what actually happened (i.e. know what the main elements
  of policy were – what measures Castro took to diversify and
  transform the economy)
- provide a consistently analytical examination of the reasons for
  the introduction, success and limitations of these policies.

Such a topic, which has been the subject of much discussion, will give
you the chance to refer to different historians' views.

Common mistakes

Some students, aware of an existing historical debate – and that extra marks can be gained by showing this – sometimes simply write things like: 'Historian X says … , and historian Y says … ' However, they make no attempt to **evaluate** the different views (for example, has one historian had access to more/better information than another, perhaps because he/she was writing at a later date?); nor is this information **integrated** into their answer by being pinned to the question. Another weak use of historical debate is to write things like: 'Historian X is biased because she is American.' Such comments will not be given credit.

Sample paragraphs containing analysis and historical debate

For commentators on the political right, an attempt by Cuba to pursue a command economy based on centralised planning and set targets was bound to fail. By comparing Cuba with Latin American economies such as Chile – which did adapt more to global markets and free the economy from control – they point to a growing gap between free-market economic performance and that of Cuba. For them, Castro followed a model that was likely to fail, and indeed did fail in Eastern Europe.

A more balanced analysis, such as that of Susan Eckstein ('Back from the Future', 2003), still argues that a common feature of socialist models like Cuba is the attempt to rectify inefficient central planning by introducing free-market elements. However, the problems of low productivity and shortages remained unresolved. Such historians also point out the instability in politics, with reversals of policy towards incentives and rewards, and note Cuba's disastrous dependence on the USSR and Eastern Europe, which left it short of food and fuel and with large debts and trade imbalances by the 1990s.

However, other writers take a more balanced view. Aviva Chomsky looks at the resilience of the economy even by the 1990s ('A History of the Cuban Rebellion', 2011) and the social benefits that it managed to deliver, despite all the problems.

Marifeli Pérez-Stable ('The Cuban Revolution', 1993) – before the worst crisis of 1994 – sees rational aims and some successes, for example in 1970-74, but concludes that the long-term dependency on sugar was not overcome. It is difficult to see success in meeting the aims of 1959, but not all commentators argue that Cuba would have been better off by adopting free-market economics. Thus, the issue is whether by its very nature Castro's economic policy was bound to fail, or whether the measures had partial success, achieved a social justice and change, and were adjusted when necessary by a flexible approach to economics, but were simply ruined by the fall of the USSR, over which Castro had no control.

This is a good example of how to use historians' views. The main focus of the answer is properly concerned with using precise own knowledge to address the demands of the question. However, the candidate has also provided some relevant knowledge of historical debate which is smoothly integrated into the answer.

Activity

In this chapter, the focus is on writing an answer that is analytical and well-supported by precise own knowledge, as well as one which – where relevant – refers to historical interpretations/debates. Using the information from this chapter, and any other sources of information available to you, try to answer **one** of the following Paper 3 practice questions using these skills.

Remember to refer to the simplified Paper 3 markscheme on page 223.

Paper 3 practice questions

1 How successful were Castro's social and cultural policies after 1959?

2 To what extent can Castro's regime in Cuba be described as 'socialist'?

3 Account for Castro's survival in power.

4 To what extent did the 'special period' after 1990 change the nature of Castro's regime?

5 How well did the regime in Cuba deal with minorities after 1959?

8 Military regimes in Latin America

Timeline

1947 Colorado Party wins civil war in Paraguay

1954 General Alfredo Stroessner takes power in coup in Paraguay

1955–58 military rule in Argentina

1959 Stroessner closes parliament and purges Colorado Party; revolution in Cuba

1966–73 military rule in Argentina as economic and political turmoil encourages overthrow of Arturo Illia

1969 El Salvador at war with Honduras

1972 General Arturo Molina installed in El Salvador following electoral fraud

1975 anti-guerrilla troops destroy peasant co-operatives, communists arrested and death of leader in Paraguay

1975–83 Dirty War in Argentina

1976–83 military rule in Argentina as Isabel Perón pushed from power

1978 Stroessner re-elected in ballot that excludes nearly all opposition

Key questions

- Why did the military play an increasing role in the politics of so many Latin American states?
- Why and with what consequences did the military dominate El Salvador in the period 1931–79?
- Why and with what consequences did the military dominate Paraguay from 1954?
- How successfully did the military intervene in Argentina in the period 1955–83?
- How similar was the role of the military and its policies in El Salvador, Paraguay and Argentina?

This chapter assesses the reasons for the frequency of military intervention in the politics of Latin America, firstly through an overview of developments and then through a series of case studies. Military rule was a common feature of many states in the region, and this chapter will consider whether there was a general explanation for this. It investigates issues such as economic development, the political situation after the Second World War, and the failure of democracy to establish itself and tackle the problems faced by many of the states in the region. The chapter will also discuss how the military regimes attempted to consolidate their power, and the extent to which they were successful in destroying opposition to remain in control.

Overview

- Military intervention and rule were common features of political life in Latin America; they became more frequent in the 1950s and 1960s as existing regimes proved unable to deal with economic modernisation and the growing communist threat.
- El Salvador was ruled by a range of military regimes throughout the period. Each of these regimes protected its power and that of the traditional coffee-growing élites through repression, and introduced only limited reform.
- The military regime of General Alfredo Stroessner in Paraguay was the longest of all military dictatorships in Latin America, lasting from August 1954 to February 1989. Stroessner won eight consecutive terms in office, largely by repressing any opposition.
- In Argentina, there were three periods of military rule between 1955 and 1983. The military intervened at times of national crisis, when the civilian government was unable to control unrest and the economy was in a precarious position.
- During these periods, military rule in Argentina was characterised by repression, as the regimes attempted to destroy Peronism. The brutality culminated in the Dirty War of 1975–83.

Why did the military play an increasing role in the politics of so many Latin American states?

Military rule – or at least significant military involvement in politics – was a common feature of political life in Latin America throughout the 20th century. To some degree this was due to the strength and organised structure of the military, which in many cases contrasted with the weak institutions of government and the lack of democratic tradition in many countries in the region.

Forms of military rule varied. Sometimes it was characterised by a *junta* – a committee made up of several officers – but on other occasions a military regime might be controlled solely by the senior commander, or *caudillo*. In many instances military power was seized during a coup, but often this was followed by the gradual restoration of some form of civilian power, although not necessarily the reinstatement or establishment of full democratic processes.

The military usually justified its intervention by claiming to be preserving political stability and providing interim leadership at a time of acute crisis – rescuing the state from the threat of dangerous ideologies (which usually meant communism). Many military regimes believed that the civilian government was corrupt, ineffective and unable to maintain law and order in a time of unrest. As such, periods of martial law were not uncommon in Latin America.

Although this chapter focuses on the military regimes of three countries – El Salvador, Paraguay and Argentina – the table below gives a brief overview of military rule in the Americas from 1945 to 1980.

Country	Period(s) of military rule	Number of years military rule 1945–1980
Argentina	1955–58, 1966–73, 1976–83	14
Bolivia	1951–52, 1964–66, 1969–79	13
Brazil	1964–85	16
Chile	1973–90	7
Colombia	1953–58	5
Cuba	1952–59	7
Dominican Republic	1930–61	16
Ecuador	1963–66, 1972–79	10
El Salvador	1931–80	35
Guatemala	1957–58, 1963–66, 1970–86	14
Haiti	1950–56	6
Honduras	1956–57, 1963–71, 1972–82	17
Nicaragua	1936–56, 1967–79	23
Panama	1968–89	11
Paraguay	1954–93	26
Peru	1948–50, 1962–63, 1968–80	15
Uruguay	1973–85	7
Venezuela	1948–58	10

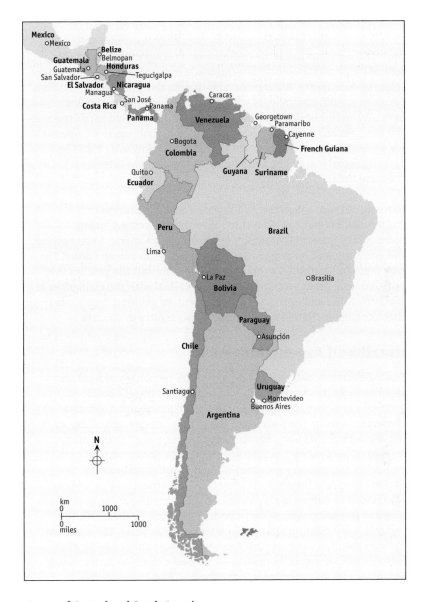

A map of Central and South America

Between 1945 and 1980, only three states – Mexico, Costa Rica and
Suriname – avoided military rule, and in fact Suriname suffered a
military takeover in 1980. The table on page 196 also reveals that the
1960s and 1970s saw an upsurge in military intervention, even in
the more advanced states of Latin America. Previously, one military
regime was simply replaced with another, but during these decades
the pattern changed, as democracy proved unable to cope with the
stresses created by industrial development.

Historian Edwin Williamson states that there were deep social divisions in many of these countries between those who wanted to protect the export industries, often based on agriculture, and those whose focus was on protecting domestic industries in order to reduce reliance on imports. Williamson also argues that there were divisions between wealthy employers who benefited from the export-led agricultural industries, and the workers who were paid very little and did not gain anything from exports. This situation made it impossible for governments to win consent from the population as a whole, causing social instability and forcing the military to intervene to preserve order.

In many of these cases, the military took over the process of modernisation, but carried it through without elections, using technocrats (government-appointed technology experts) to reorganise the economy, and relying on the army to maintain law and order. The new regimes attempted to create a strong state, but the policies they pursued were often erratic, as they tried to deal with the challenges of modernisation and economic development. In addition, responses to these challenges varied dramatically from country to country.

Brazil and Argentina

Such differences can be seen clearly in the responses of military regimes in Brazil, Argentina, Peru and Chile to the economic problems that had brought them to power. Brazil and Argentina chose to continue the policies of the old regimes by upholding state-led import substitution industrialisation (see page 16), by which foreign imports were replaced with domestic production. In both countries, the military government had to arbitrate between the export élites and the élites of protected industries, and as a result was forced to suppress wage demands. The consequence of this was a rise in left-wing radicalism in both states, and by the 1970s the regimes were fighting wars against Marxist guerrillas. The economic policies resulted in severe inflation, which was only halted by the introduction of austerity measures. However, these in turn caused serious social and economic problems and had to be relaxed – which led to high levels of inflation once more. Thus, in the cases of Brazil and Argentina, the military government failed to resolve the problems caused by economic development.

Peru

In contrast, the military government that seized power in Peru in 1962 adopted radical nationalist policies. This approach grew out of demands made by soldiers who had been sent to suppress a guerrilla uprising in the Andes mountains, and who were appalled by the poverty they saw there among the peasantry.

In 1968, the Peruvian government nationalised all major industries, and large estates and plantations were turned into co-operatives for the benefit of the people. Instead of upholding the claims of the élites, therefore, the military sided with peasants and workers, and formed an umbrella movement under government control. This approach was similar to that followed by Perón in Argentina in the 1940s, although the land reforms bore resemblance to those in Castro's Cuba. However, when military rule came to an end in Peru in 1980, the issues that had caused the army to intervene in the first place remained unresolved.

Chile

A third approach to economic problems can be seen in Chile. There, the elected Popular Unity coalition government, headed by the Marxist Salvador Allende, tried to introduce socialist measures. However, when the military under Augusto Pinochet seized power in 1973, it introduced a free-market economy known as economic 'shock therapy' and set out to destroy its left-leaning political opposition. This approach represented the first departure from economic nationalism and state-led ISI in Latin America. It widened the gap between the workers and capitalists, which was worsened by high inflation and savage repression of the unions. By the end of the 1970s, economic productivity in Chile had started to improve, and inflation was coming under control. Although the government therefore had some success in reducing the economic problems, the social costs were immense. Once again, none of the approaches pursued by the military resolved the problems that had initially brought them to power.

Activity

Construct a spider diagram to show the reasons for the establishment of military rule in Latin American states. Which reason do you think was the most important? Write a paragraph to explain your choice.

Why and with what consequences did the military dominate El Salvador in the period 1931–79?

Events in El Salvador are unlike those that took place in any other Latin American country. The military came to power in 1931 and remained in control until 1979. However, during that period there were a number of coups and changes of government, as the military defended the rights of traditional élites and overthrew governments that failed to support its interests. The period from 1932 to 1945 was dominated by a personalist (one-man) rule, but after this time a more institutional form of military rule emerged.

Background

The military intervened in El Salvador due to the deteriorating economic situation in the country caused by the Depression that began in 1929. This resulted in severe economic hardship and a growth in radicalism in the form of demonstrations against falling wages and living standards. Coffee was El Salvador's major industry, so when coffee export prices dropped by 54% in the period 1928–31, it had a significant impact. In addition, El Salvador was a country where wealth lay in the hands of a very small minority. The US military attaché Major Harris said that 'roughly 90% of the wealth … is held by about one-half of one per cent of the population. Thirty or forty families own nearly everything. They live in regal splendour whilst the rest of the country has practically nothing.' In a climate of increasing economic difficulty, there were serious concerns about a possible socialist or communist revolution.

In order to preserve their power, the landed élite turned to the military. General Maximiliano Martínez was installed as leader and almost immediately began brutally suppressing unrest across the country. He also increased the power of the government through financial controls, including the creation of the Central Bank and Mortgage Bank in 1934, and by imposing exchange controls in 1935. Martínez remained in control by ensuring that he was unopposed in elections. There was little pretence that democracy was being maintained.

Military regimes 1944–79

In 1944, the military installed General Andrés Menéndez as leader, but when he offered political liberty and free elections – threatening the influence of the ruling élites – he was swiftly removed and replaced by a more authoritarian leader. The governments of Major Óscar Osorio (1950–56) and Colonel José Lemus (1956–60) further consolidated military power. However, their successes were aided to a great degree by high coffee prices, agricultural diversification and some manufacturing growth. Lemus removed some of the strict controls that were imposed by his predecessor, but a drop in coffee prices and the excitement generated by the Cuban Revolution caused concern among the ruling élites. The army was brought in to crush student protests, and martial law was imposed. Against a background of protest that economic controls were still too tight, Lemus was removed in October 1960.

A further military coup was staged after the new government in El Salvador expressed a willingness to open up elections to leftist groups. Lieutenant Colonel Julio Rivera oversaw the removal of some members of the government, fearing that they were communist sympathisers with links to Cuba. Just as it had in 1944, the military intervened to prevent open elections and the installation of a civilian government.

Although there was vocal opposition to military rule after 1960, manipulation of the electoral process ensured that government remained in military hands under the leadership of Rivera (1962–67), Fidel Hernández (1967–72), Arturo Molina (1972–77) and Carlos Romero (1977–79). This manipulation was most evident in 1972, when the opposition candidate José Duarte was denied victory and Molina was declared the winner by fewer than 10,000 votes.

Repression

The military regimes faced a series of challenges, most of which were brutally suppressed. Such tactics to overcome opposition were used right from the start, when a peasant uprising in 1932 was crushed and an estimated 20,000 people killed. This event, known as La Matanza ('The Massacre'), virtually wiped out the population of native Indians in El Salvador. It sent a clear message that dissent would not be tolerated.

After this, repression of political opposition became a regular feature of life. Following the Cuban Revolution and Castro's rise to power, student unrest grew in El Salvador, but the government responded by banning assemblies and freedom of expression, and allowed dissidents to be rounded up and held without charge.

The government also prevented opponents from taking positions of authority or influence, often finding technical reasons to prevent those who opposed them from standing in elections. This occurred in 1956, when a candidate running against Lemus was disqualified on a technicality and another was barred on the grounds of fiscal impropriety. Even when elections were held, the military often intervened to deny opponents a fair chance. However, in the 1960s, political parties began to emerge that had the strength and support to challenge the military-backed parties at the polls, and this complicated the situation. The military responded by adopting measures such as denying opposition parties access to the media.

In 1969, a war with Honduras resulted in thousands of immigrants returning to El Salvador. This added to the country's social and economic problems, but it temporarily ended the military's difficulties in dealing with the opposition, as the country was united in a common hatred of Honduras. However, in 1972 and 1977, the government was once again forced into massive electoral fraud to guarantee the success of its nominated candidates.

Throughout the 1970s, a world recession encouraged the rise of radicalism and terrorism in many states in the Americas. Inspired by the communist seizure of power in Nicaragua, the People's Revolutionary Army in El Salvador won increasing support, and carried out a series of kidnappings in an effort to secure government support for reform. The military rulers attempted to appease the population by introducing some moderate reforms, but repression remained the most frequent response to social unrest. In 1980, the People's Revolutionary Army was one of several leftist guerrilla groups that joined together to form the Farabundo Martí National Liberation Front (FMLN). With Cuban backing, this organisation began a campaign against the government that only ended in 1992.

Limited reform

During the times of military rule in El Salvador, there were some periods of guided reform in an effort to stop the violence. In the 1950s, Osorio and his successor Lemus attempted to develop the economy, introduce public works programmes and Social Security, diversify agriculture, and improve both sanitation and housing. However, they did not contemplate any reform that threatened the position of the ruling élites. The same was true of Rivera, who – with aid from the USA – brought in limited economic reforms.

When Molina took power, it seemed that at last the most significant social and economic problem – the question of land – would be addressed. By the mid 1970s, 40% of peasants had no land at all, compared with 12% in 1960, and this gave rise to serious unrest in rural areas. Molina introduced laws for the forced rental of insufficiently used land, which allowed it to be brought under government control, but these laws were not enforced. A similar pattern occurred in 1976, when an agricultural transformation zone divided up land to make plots available to peasants; this was abandoned in cases where the land was shown to be used for the benefit of the wider community.

Even in the 1970s, when it seemed that the government was willing to carry out reform, human rights abuses grew. The period witnessed the use of government security forces and right-wing terrorist groups, known as death squads, to deal with opponents. This resulted in the disappearance of many union activists and priests, and a tenfold increase in political assassinations in the period from 1972 to 1979.

The government also pursued an official policy of repression: demonstrators in the capital, San Salvador, were fired on in 1975 and 1977. The government increased its legal powers to deal with disturbances. In 1977, a Law for the Defense and Guarantee of Public Order was enacted, which eliminated nearly all legal restrictions on violence against civilians and resulted in a sharp increase in the number of 'subversives' who were prosecuted.

Against this background of violence and repression, some popular organisations managed to develop – many with the encouragement of the Church, which acknowledged 'the case for insurrection when all recourse to peaceful means have been exhausted'. Although the Church eventually threw its support behind the masses, it did not take action to prevent repression, and in 1980 an archbishop was assassinated in the cathedral of San Salvador. Ultimately, the period ended as it began, with the establishment of a new military government in 1979 and killings reaching an estimated 1000 per month.

Discussion point

Why was the military able to remain in power for so long in El Salvador?

Why and with what consequences did the military dominate Paraguay from 1954?

With the exception of Fidel Castro in Cuba, General **Alfredo Stroessner** held power for longer than any political leader in the western hemisphere. Unlike the military regimes in El Salvador, Paraguay witnessed the continued domination of one man for 35 years. Stroessner became president of Paraguay in 1954, but military influence in the country dates back to 1936.

Alfredo Stroessner (1912–2006) Stroessner was born to a German father and Paraguayan mother, and he joined the army at the age of 16. He fought in the Chaco War and became an officer in 1932. President Federico Chávez appointed Stroessner commander-in-chief of the armed forces in 1951, but Stroessner used this position to divide the government by criticising the policy of economic planning and the close links the country had with Perón's Argentina. As a result, Stroessner was able to assume the presidency himself in 1954. His long dictatorship was characterised by corruption and human rights abuses. He was overthrown in a coup in 1989, shortly after beginning his eighth term in office.

Alfredo Stroessner in 1955, a year after he became president of Paraguay

The Liberal overthrow 1935–47

The Chaco War against Bolivia (1932–35) ended three decades of Liberal rule in Paraguay and triggered a period of social upheaval and political mobilisation. The development of political extremism in the form of communism and fascism, as well as continued liberalism, made governments unstable. As a result, a variety of reforms – including granting workers an eight-hour day and the right to strike – pushed the army into politics.

Although the Liberals briefly returned to power, the period from 1940 to 1948 witnessed a pro-Nazi regime under Higinio Moríñigo, and several wanted Nazi war criminals found refuge in Paraguay after the Second World War. Moríñigo built up army support by increased military spending, but despite his concession in establishing a more liberal coalition government in 1946, a coup led by the right-wing Colorado Party and the military resulted in a civil war in 1947. This conflict was eventually put down by Stroessner.

The establishment of one-party rule

The Colorado Party emerged from the civil war in a strong enough position to depose Moríñigo, but ultimately it failed to achieve stability. This was briefly returned with the appointment of Federico Chávez as president in 1949. Under his rule, political parties were largely eliminated and Paraguay became accustomed to one-party rule, order at the expense of liberty, and the position of the army as the ultimate political decision-maker. However, Chávez was unable to resolve the economic problems caused by political and social unrest, economic depression and civil conflicts. National income fell, inflation rose and the black market flourished.

Despite these problems, in 1953 Chávez decided to run for re-election at the age of 73. This disappointed younger elements within the armed forces, who feared that Chávez would strengthen the police at the expense of the army. However, it was the firing of the director of the Central Bank that ultimately led to Chávez's overthrow. Angered by this move, in May 1954 Stroessner ordered the army into action to depose Chávez.

Stroessner takes power

Stroessner had links with the Colorado Party and, unlike previous military regimes in Paraguay, he won over a base of popular support. The party nominated him for president, although it was assumed that this would be a temporary appointment. After taking power, however, Stroessner succeeded in bringing the party into the fold of his dictatorship. He strengthened his position in 1956 by forcing his main rival in the party, Epifanio Fleitas, into exile.

Stroessner lifted the state of siege (the suspension of normal political powers in a government) and adopted a wage freeze and a reduction in public subsidies. However, this resulted in labour unrest and a general strike in 1958, which was crushed by force. When the government condemned police brutality, the state of siege was swiftly reimposed, the army sent into the suburbs of the capital, Asunción, and politicians opposed to Stroessner were exiled. He quickly established a fascist-style party with a centralised structure. All public employees had to join and members were forced to swear allegiance to Stroessner. He went on to develop a cult of personality, and photographs and busts of him appeared in all public offices and most private companies.

SOURCE A

At the end of the 1960s Stroessner was in a very secure position. He enjoyed a near monopoly of political power; military dissent was dulled by the rich pickings from a massive trade in contraband scotch whisky, cigarettes, drugs and consumer goods; professional groups and trade unions were under government control to varying degrees and he had the peasant 'backing' of the traditional Colorado Party to which he had adroitly hitched his star.

Paraguay: Power Game. 1980. *Latin America Special Bureau, London, UK. p. 46.*

Limited reform

Although Stroessner brought political stability, economic growth did not follow on from this. He maintained the unequal system of land tenure, whereby in 1956 just 106 owners controlled 40% of all land, and developed an alliance between the large landowners and the military. He allowed officers to use their gains from corruption and smuggling to buy estates. Unlike many other regimes, Stroessner's government rejected any move in favour of import substitution as this would limit smuggling activities, which were a valuable source of income for the élites. Instead, Stroessner followed a policy of 'outward-orientated growth' or export-led growth. As a result of these policies, the industrial sector accounted for only 13% of national output, as it could not compete with smuggled imports.

This policy only changed in the 1970s, as Brazil's influence in South America increased. In 1973, work started on the Brazilian-financed Itaipu hydro-electric project on the border between Brazil and Paraguay. Although its development helped to create an economic growth rate of 9% in the period 1977–79, it brought little benefit to the people, as the gains went to the corrupt élites. The minimum wage fell by 30% in real terms between 1972 and 1979, whilst inflation and the cost of services such as electricity and water soared.

The development of the plant provided a major focus for opponents of the regime, and sparked political conflict. They argued that Paraguay had no control over the cost of the project, that it was financed by Brazilian loans (which had to be repaid by selling back electricity at a low price), that Paraguay gained few contracts for the development and that the power was not used to stimulate industry. The development also resulted in much land in the region being bought up by Brazilians, thus removing one of the few areas that were suitable for intensive agricultural development.

The Itaipu Dam, on the border between Brazil and Paraguay

Stroessner was aware that unequal land distribution had been responsible for the rise of communism in the 1950s. However, secure in his power, Stroessner abandoned any consideration of land reform. In 1963, he created the Rural Welfare Institute, which removed squatters and poor farmers from the border region with Brazil to other, less fertile, areas. These dispossessed peasants were provided with a machete, axe and hoe, but no technical help or facilities. Throughout the 1960s, in response to the unequal land distribution, an increasing number of agrarian leagues began to form. By the end of the decade, these largely Church-backed non-violent organisations had a membership of 20,000. Stroessner considered these groups a threat and reacted with typically brutal repression. Around 50 leaders of the agrarian leagues were killed in 1975–76, 5000 were arrested and many more went into exile, driving the movement underground.

Opposition and repression

The Church was a main source of opposition to Stroessner's regime. It supported the agrarian leagues, called for social reform and criticised the government's human-rights record. The Church also took a stand against political prisoners, and supported student protests against attacks by the police. The government responded by violently suppressing a demonstration by priests and nuns. In 1976, a large number of priests were expelled from Paraguay. Similar actions were taken against student protestors, and many leaders of the Independent Student Movement were arrested.

Despite this social opposition, the government faced little in the way of armed challenge. There were attempts at guerrilla invasions in 1959 and 1960, led by members of the Liberal and Communist parties, but these were also brutally repressed. They represented the last significant resistance to Stroessner's regime. The government argued that such repression was essential to combat terrorism, but in reality Stroessner was simply destroying opposition before it gained widespread support. Throughout Stroessner's rule, the government crushed any signs of militancy amongst independent groups through mass arrests to deter other potential opponents.

In order to uphold its power, the regime relied on imprisonment and torture. Most of those detained were held for only a short period, but some political prisoners were detained for more than ten years, and there was a fluctuating long-term prison population of 600 in the period from 1960 to 1977. Very few political prisoners received a trial. When they did take place, signed confessions – extracted under torture – were used to secure a guilty verdict.

Many of Stroessner's political enemies simply disappeared and were never seen again. It is hardly surprising, therefore, that Stroessner was able to create a culture of fear and self-censorship that prevented serious opposition.

Stroessner's overthrow

Stroessner survived for so long because he created a power triangle consisting of the party, the armed forces and the government. Historians Howard Wiarda and Harvey Kline describe this as follows: 'The military serves as the system's guarantor, the party is the primary instrument of patronage and social control, and the government regulates the system in favour of the regime's supporters. The triad's central element was Stroessner himself, the system's architect, who held all the strings, who alone was able to co-opt or repress internal opposition to his rule.'

Despite his power, Stroessner was brought down in 1989 over the issue of succession. The Colorado Party split in the run-up to the 1988 election, as some within the party resented Stroessner promoting his son as the next president. He was overthrown in February 1989 by one of his top aides, General Andrés Rodríguez, who felt that his own promotion was being ignored.

Activity

The extract from the Latin America Special Bureau publication in Source A on page 205 argues that Stroessner was in a very secure position by the end of the 1960s. Using the information in this section, compare his position at the end of the 1960s with the situation by the end of 1988; complete the chart below to help you.

Factor	Position at the end of the 1960s	Position in 1988
Opposition		
Church		
Peasantry		
Economic development		
Trade unions		
Colorado Party		
Other		

How successfully did the military intervene in Argentina in the period 1955–83?

Military rule in Argentina was unlike that in either El Salvador or Paraguay, in that it was not continuous throughout the period. The military assumed power at times of national crisis, when the civilian government was unable to maintain social, economic and political control. However, unlike regimes in other countries, in Argentina there was always an expectation that a democratic process would be returned once the crisis was over – even if the military retained an influence over the civilian government.

The Argentinean military was involved in several coups in the period after 1930, including in 1955, 1963 and 1976. The army claimed that this was on the grounds that military intervention was necessary to save the nation. On all three occasions, political unrest and violence, and social and economic chaos, were used to justify military action.

The fight against Peronism

In 1955, conservative elements within the military intervened as they feared that the violence of the Peronists' attacks on institutions such as the Jockey Club and the Catholic Church, as well as Perón's call to the workers and unions to take revenge on opponents, would cause civil war. In particular, the army was angered by the president's mobilisation of popular support and the desecration of churches. At the same time, the economy was in a state of collapse, and economic nationalism was abandoned as Perón sought foreign investment. The military was unwilling to relinquish its political influence to Perón, and disliked his populist regime – in which the workers and unions seemed to have greater influence than the army.

The fear of Peronism, even after its apparent defeat in 1955, was enough to encourage military action again in 1963. This time the army acted to remove the government of Arturo Illia, which could neither win the support of nor repress the Peronist movement. The army grew concerned that Perón might stage a return to political life, especially after the Peronist Party won 30.3% of the vote in the March 1965 election, compared with the 28.9% of the only other significant party in the country, the Radicals. This period of Peronist agitation coincided with another economic crisis, as inflation and the deficit increased rapidly. The army believed that if Perón was allowed resume power, the economic problems would worsen. Perón's party supported the growth of state industry and ISI, rather than relying on an export-led policy based on agriculture. These factors combined to secure a full military takeover in 1966.

Perón's death in 1974 brought his third wife, Isabel, to power. However, she was unable to prevent a descent into political violence, as guerrilla attacks from both the left and right wings increased. The army believed that such dissent should be met with an all-out offensive, and this culminated in the so-called 'Dirty War', which lasted until 1983 (see page 212). However, during Isabel Perón's rule, the economy was also in chaos, as inflation grew at nearly 1% a day and the value of currency dropped almost hourly. Exports fell and the government adopted a stringent economic policy, as well as seeking help from the International Monetary Fund (IMF).

Juan Perón and his third wife Isabel Martínez de Perón, or Isabelita, who also served as president of Argentina

By 1976, the economic and political situation had deteriorated to such an extent that there appeared to be little choice but for the army to step in and restore order. The coup brought the commander of the armed forces, Jorge Videla, to power, and he implemented the Process of National Reorganization, or *Proceso*. Videla was succeeded in 1981 by Roberto Viola and finally, at the end of 1981, by **Leopoldo Galtieri**, who embarked upon the disastrous Falklands (*Malvinas*) campaign against Britain to try and win popular support. This conflict resulted in the demise of military rule in Argentina.

Leopoldo Galtieri (1926–2003) Galtieri served in the army, and by 1975 he had been appointed commander of the Engineer Corps. He supported the military coup of 1976, was made a major general in 1977 and commander-in-chief in 1980. This military position provided Galtieri with the support he needed to seize power. He became president in 1981 after a coup ousted the former president, General Viola. Whilst in office, Galtieri introduced some limited political reform that allowed the expression of political dissent. However, defeat in the Falklands War resulted in his removal from power in June 1982.

The Peronist threat: an assessment

Peronism provided the greatest and most consistent challenge to Argentina's military regimes. They were never able to rid the country of it, and repression only turned the movement into a major opposition force. The grass-roots support that Perón had built up among the workers remained, despite frequent purges of labour organisations and unions. Concerns about Perón's influence were most clearly demonstrated in March 1956, when the military government declared that Peronism was a crime, banned the party from elections, shut down its organisations and seized its property. Although forbidden from participating in the June 1957 elections, supporters of the Peronist Party returned blank ballot papers as a sign of protest – and these blank ballots proved to be the majority.

The government launched a similar attack on the unions, arresting its leaders and bringing the CGT (see page 112) newspaper under government control. However, the attack on the unions failed. The Peronist and communist-run unions withdrew from the CGT and formed their own group known as the '62 Organisations'. This became the main focus of Peronist support for the next decade. It was followed in 1957 by a series of strikes that damaged the economy. As unions fought to preserve the gains made under Perón, the economy collapsed, making Argentina virtually ungovernable. Despite these problems, there was only one direct attempt to overthrow the military regime in this period, in June 1956, and this was harshly suppressed.

However, the challenges to military rule and its response followed a very different route in the period after 1966. The threat from the unions was reduced as the labour movement grew divided in its attitude. The CGT collaborated with the new government, whilst other labour opposition was crushed. Strikes were put down and the military intervened in the Buenos Aires dock strike, imprisoning its leaders. Towards the end of this period of military rule, in an attempt to shore up his regime, President Alejandro Lanusse withdrew the ban on Peronism and allowed Juan Perón himself to return to Argentina. However, by this point the nature of the threat had changed.

This can be traced back to events in Córdoba in 1969, when student disquiet and union militancy were met by an armed military response that left at least 14 people dead. This was the largest expression of civil unrest the military faced, and its reaction – torture and execution – changed the nature of future opposition. Instead of union militancy, the army faced attacks from terrorist and guerrilla groups at both ends of the political spectrum. There was a growing belief that direct violence was necessary to overthrow the government, and support for revolutionary groups increased. The most notorious of these attacks resulted in the murder of the former president, Pedro Aramburu. High-profile attacks continued, and in August 1972 guerrillas launched an assault on a high-security prison and freed 25 inmates. Sixteen of the prisoners were later caught, but were put to death by the regime as force was met with force.

However, it was during the final phase of military rule that repression reached its peak in Argentina. During the period of the 'Dirty War', thousands of political opponents disappeared. This policy was the direct response to increased guerrilla activity, which included robberies that created a war chest of some $150 million with which to fight the government. The military embarked on the mass arrest of subversives and anyone suspected of sympathising with them. Between 10,000 and 20,000 people simply disappeared after being arrested. The government failed to discriminate between moderates and extremists in this process. No formal legal action was taken against those who were captured, as the military did not trust the judicial process to uphold its aims. Such actions created fear among the population, and helped to keep the military regime in power.

Despite the climate of fear, some protests still took place. One of the most significant was that by the Mothers of Plaza de Mayo, an association formed by mothers whose children had disappeared during the Dirty War. The organisation attracted international attention and made the government's position increasingly difficult.

Theory of knowledge

History and evidence

The records of those who disappeared during the Dirty War are often missing, as the regime destroyed evidence so that the victims could not be traced. How does this help to explain some of the difficulties faced by a historian when carrying out research?

Economic management

Because the military regimes in Argentina came to power at times of economic crises, one of their main aims was to bring about economic stability. However, even if this was achieved in the short term, all the military governments failed in the long term. When democracy returned to Argentina in 1983, the new government faced severe economic problems that arose from years of neglect and the use of the economy to generate political support, rather than to bring about sustainable development.

Earlier military regimes favoured the landowning élites, and encouraged an agricultural and export-led economy that discouraged the development of industry. Although this process was reversed under Perón, the policy of economic nationalism was not sustainable, as Argentina needed to be able to export goods to pay for machinery, whilst also feeding a growing urban population.

The military regime ended Perón's faltering economic programme, shut down ISI, and adopted export and farming-led growth. Although this was a period of inflation, wages were frozen and workers who had both benefited from, and therefore supported, Perón's government saw their economic position decline. The policy was successful at first. Exports created a surplus, but this was impossible to sustain and the economy lurched back into decline as the government tried to deregulate the economy, bring in spending cuts and reduce state intervention.

In 1966, the military stepped in with the intention of maintaining social order whilst allowing the technocrats to deal with the economic problems. Once again, this plan seemed to work to begin with, as economic stability was restored, a wage freeze was introduced in 1967 and successfully enforced, and inflation was brought under control. However, by 1971 inflation had reached 34.7% and continued rising to 58.5% by 1972.

In 1976, the military regime faced similar economic difficulties as it attempted to restore economic stability. The government launched a neo-liberal assault on the industries that had been nationalised under Perón, and brought in a programme of free-market economics. However, this policy proved difficult to implement given the high number of state jobs created by the Peronist regime. The military government did succeed in reducing inflation in the period 1976–79, and created a surplus balance of payments, but by 1981 recession had returned and industry worked at only 50% of its capacity. Even during the early period, real wages for those working in industry fell by 50%, as resources were once again transferred to the agricultural sector. This also caused a rise in unemployment, and welfare subsidies had to be withdrawn, increasing the pressure on the working classes. In an attempt to restore popularity, detract from economic hardships and win prestige for both the country and the regime, the government adopted a nationalist stance that culminated in the disastrous invasion of the Falkland Islands in 1982.

SOURCE B

Whatever the motives, military rule had failed. Economic difficulties mounted: inflation in the 1970s; a build up of debt coupled with recession in the 1980s. Popular pressure, now channelled through new 'social movements' – churches, civic groups, human-rights activists, independent unions, neighbourhood associations – played an important part, seconded by radical Catholic priests and intermittent US pressure. In response, Latin America's armies began a collective retreat to barracks – more precipitate following Argentina's defeat in the Falklands War.

Howard, M. and Louis, W. R. 1998. The Oxford History of the Twentieth Century. Oxford, UK. Oxford University Press. p. 290.

Activity

Read Source B. Howard and Louis suggest that the military defeat of Argentina in the Falklands had an impact on military regimes throughout Latin America and caused their 'retreat'. Find out more about military regimes in Latin America in the 1980s, and then consider how valid this view is. Did the number of military regimes decline after 1982?

Activity

'Military rule in Argentina was not successful.' Complete the following chart to help you reach a judgement about this interpretation. For each regime, decide whether the military governments were successful in dealing with the issues outlined in the first column.

Factor	1955–58	1966–73	1976–83
Economic stability			
Peronism			
Trade unions			
Radicalism/terrorism			
Political stability			
Other			

How similar was the role of the military and its policies in El Salvador, Paraguay and Argentina?

In both El Salvador and Paraguay, the military established long-lasting regimes, whereas in Argentina the direct role of the military was short-lived and was usually a response to a perceived national crisis. However, the similarity between El Salvador and Paraguay goes no further. El Salvador was ruled by a series of military regimes that were often overthrown by another military group. In Paraguay, Stroessner was able to establish a personal regime that maintained his power for a significant period. Stroessner's was the only regime where a cult of personality was developed and encouraged. In this sense, the regimes in Argentina and El Salvador had more in common – a succession of military rulers rather than coming under the control of a military dictator.

In all instances, intervention came at a time of intense social, economic and political difficulty, and with the justification that the existing governments were unable to deal with the challenges. In both Paraguay and Argentina, the country was either on the verge of or had just experienced civil war, and in El Salvador serious conflict soon followed in 1932.

In all three countries the military acted to preserve the powers of the élites, of which they were one. The Depression of the 1930s appeared to threaten the power of the coffee-growing oligarchy in El Salvador, whilst in Paraguay civil war challenged the influence of the landowners. In Argentina, Perón's reforms had given the workers far-reaching gains that undermined the power of the landowners – industry gained at the expense of agriculture. The social and political unrest also caused economic dislocation in all three countries, and reliance upon the traditional agricultural sector began to disappear.

Women working on a coffee plantation in El Salvador in the 1940s

The responses of the regimes to these difficulties had much in common. All three supported the old agricultural-based economies, although Paraguay pursued some industrialisation towards the end of the period. In most instances, pro-agricultural policies were introduced and the policy of ISI was abandoned. Opposition was suppressed, often brutally, as seen in El Salvador in 1932 and Argentina throughout the Dirty War of 1976–83. The challenges posed by guerrilla warfare were probably the greatest threat to the regimes, particularly in El Salvador and Argentina – in Paraguay, the scale of repression meant that after 1959–60 there was little armed resistance.

Political parties and union activity were usually suppressed, particularly parties that had previously held power. This development was most noticeable in Argentina, where the military rulers continued their attempts to destroy Peronism and its legacy throughout the period. The same was true to some extent in Paraguay, where parties other than the Colorado Party were banned.

Perhaps the most difficult element in assessing these regimes relates to their successes. Although they were often quite effective at maintaining power and suppressing opposition, they largely failed to resolve the economic problems they faced. When the regimes did have economic success it was usually short-term, and economic stability was a rare achievement.

Paraguay ended the period with the largest economic growth rate in Latin America, but the benefits of that growth were limited. Economic failings were a major factor in the fall of the military regime in Argentina, whereas in the other states economic problems were only overcome by repression. Many of the crises that justified military intervention were not resolved, and although order was restored, the cost was often high. The regimes survived, but mainly through the use of terror rather than popular support.

Activity

This section has provided a brief comparison of the three military regimes that have been considered in depth. Re-read the sections on each regime and then complete the chart below to enable you to make a detailed comparison of the regimes.

Issue	El Salvador	Paraguay	Argentina
Influence of the military			
Opposition			
Reasons for military involvement			
Influence and power of the landowners			
Influence and power of the Church			
Nature of repression			
Economic development			
Stability of military rule			

End of chapter activities

Paper 3 exam practice

Question

'Terror was the most important reason why military regimes were able to survive in Latin America.' How far do you agree with this view? (You should refer to at least **two** Latin American countries in your answer.)

Skill focus

Writing a conclusion to your essay

Examiner's tips

Provided you have carried out all the steps recommended so far, it should be relatively easy to write one or two concluding paragraphs.

For this question, you will need to cover the following possible factors:

- the direct impact of terror in maintaining at least two regimes in power
- the indirect impact of terror in maintaining at least two regimes in power; this may be linked to issues such as fear of opposing the regime and the lack of unrest
- the economic and social benefits that the policies brought to different groups so that there was genuine support for the regime
- the use of propaganda and the development of the cult of personality in some regimes
- the control over other political parties and whether the people had any choice.

With broad questions like this, you should try and avoid too much generalisation, and support points you make with examples from the different countries. Also, such a question, which is asking for an analysis of several reasons, implicitly expects you to come to some kind of **judgement** about 'how far' you agree. What other factors helped keep the regimes in power and how important were the different elements that you are going to write about?

Common mistakes

Sometimes, candidates simply re-hash in their conclusion what they have written earlier – making the examiner read the same thing twice. Generally, concluding paragraphs should be relatively short: the aim should be to come to a judgement/conclusion that is clearly based on what you have already written. If possible, a short but relevant quotation is a good way to round off an argument.

Sample student conclusion

Terror played a vital role in keeping military regimes in power, but its role varied from country to country. There is little doubt that the 'Dirty War' in Argentina contributed significantly to the survival of the regime from 1976–83. The crushing of peasant unrest in El Salvador in 1932 and that of dissidents in Paraguay in the period from 1955 to 1960 also strengthened the position of the military there. However, after 1932 in El Salvador it was a mixture of terror and electoral fraud, and the banning of opposition leaders for a variety of technical offences, that allowed the military to maintain its hold on power. Death squads were used to deal with the increased terrorist threat in the 1970s, and demonstrators were fired upon in 1975 and 1977. However, in Paraguay, the scale of the terror in the early period had destroyed much of the potential opposition, which meant that after 1960 the population was so cowed that little repression was needed.

Although terror was at the heart of all the regimes for at least some of the period, there were attempts to win support through economic reform, which in El Salvador and Paraguay appeared as if it would bring about some redistribution of land, although in practice little happened. In contrast, Argentina's governments tried to develop a feeling of nationalism, aided in 1976 by victory in the World Cup and then through the invasion of the Falklands in 1982; a policy that ultimately brought about its downfall. With increased threats to military rule as the period ended, the governments frequently resorted to terror to combat terror. Although this helped the regimes survive in the short term, it was not always a long-term solution, as events in Argentina in 1983 revealed.

This is a good conclusion, as it briefly pulls together the main threads of the argument (without simply repeating/summarising them), and then also makes a clear judgement. In addition, there is an intelligent final comment that rounds off the whole conclusion – and no doubt the core of the essay – in a memorable way.

Activity

In this chapter, the focus is on writing a useful conclusion. Using the information from this chapter, and any other sources of information available to you, write concluding paragraphs for **at least two** of the following Paper 3 practice questions. Remember – to do this, you will need to do full plans for the questions you choose.

Remember to refer to the simplified Paper 3 markscheme on page 223.

Paper 3 practice questions

1 Assess the reasons why military regimes were established in Latin American countries in the period after 1945. (You should refer to at least **two** countries in your answer.)

2 How successfully did the military regime in **one** Latin American country deal with the problems it faced?

3 How effective were military regimes in maintaining stability in the countries over which they ruled? (You should refer to at least **two** countries in your answer.)

4 Compare the economic policies of **two** military regimes in Latin America in the period from 1945 to 1979.

5 Assess the reasons why some military regimes were more successful than others in maintaining power in Latin America in the period from 1945 to 1979.

6 'Stroessner was able to consolidate his power in Paraguay because of the support of the Colorado Party.' How far do you agree with this view?

9 Exam practice

Introduction

You have now completed your study of the main events and political developments in the Americas in the period 1945–79. You have also had the chance to examine the various historical debates and differing historical interpretations that surround some of these developments.

In the earlier chapters, you have encountered examples of Paper 3-type essay questions, with examiner's tips. You have also had some basic practice in answering such questions. In this chapter, these tips and skills will be developed in more depth. Longer examples of possible student answers are provided, accompanied by examiner's comments that should increase your understanding of what examiners are looking for when they mark your essays. Following each question and answer, you will find tasks to give you further practice in the skills needed to gain the higher marks in this exam.

IB History Paper 3 exam questions and skills

Those of you following Route 2, HL Option 3 – *Aspects of the History of the Americas* – will have studied in depth **three** of the 12 sections available for this HL Option. *Political Developments in the Americas* is one of those sections. For Paper 3, two questions are set from each of the 12 sections, giving 24 questions in total; and you have to answer **three** of these.

Each question has a specific markscheme. However the 'generic' markscheme in the IB *History Guide* gives you a good general idea of what examiners are looking for in order to be able to put answers into the higher bands. In particular, you will need to acquire reasonably precise historical knowledge so that you can address issues such as cause and effect, and change and continuity, and so that you can explain historical developments in a clear, coherent, well-supported and relevant way. You will also need to understand relevant historical debates and interpretations, and be able to refer to these and critically evaluate them.

Essay planning

Make sure you read each question **carefully**, noting all the important key or 'command' words. You might find it useful to highlight them on your question paper. You can then produce a rough plan (for example, a spider diagram) of **each** of the three essays you intend to attempt, **before** you start to write your answers. That way, you will soon know whether you have enough own knowledge to answer them adequately. Next, refer back to the wording of each question – this will help you see whether or not you are responding to **all** its various demands/aspects. In addition, if you run short of time towards the end of your exam, you will at least be able to write some brief condensed sentences to show the key issues/points and arguments you would have presented. It is therefore far better to do the planning at the **start** of the exam; that is, **before** you panic if you suddenly realise you haven't time to finish your last essay.

Relevance to the question

Remember, too, to keep your answers relevant and focused on the question. Don't go outside the dates mentioned in the question, or write answers on subjects not identified in that question. Also, don't just describe the events or developments. Sometimes students simply focus on one key word, date or individual, and then write down everything they know about it. Instead, select your own knowledge carefully, and pin the relevant information to the key features raised by the question. Finally, if the question asks for 'causes/reasons' and 'results', 'continuity and change', 'successes and failures', or 'nature and development', make sure you deal with **all** the parts of the question. Otherwise, you will limit yourself to half marks at best.

Examiner's tips

For Paper 3 answers, examiners are looking for well-structured arguments that:

- are consistently relevant/linked to the question
- offer clear/precise analysis
- are supported by the use of accurate, precise and relevant own knowledge
- offer a balanced judgement
- refer to different historical debates/interpretations or to relevant historians and, where relevant, offer some critical evaluation of these.

Simplified markscheme

Band		Marks
1	**Consistently analytical/explanatory** in approach, with very explicit focus on all demands of the question. **Understanding and evaluation of different historical interpretations**; good synthesis of **plentiful and precise own knowledge** with different interpretations/approaches. **Argument is clear, well-supported and well-structured** throughout.	17–20
2	**Clear/explicit focus** on all the demands of the question, with **consistently relevant analysis/explanation**. Very **detailed own knowledge**. Argument in the main is **well-structured and supported**. Some **awareness of different historical interpretations**, and **some attempts at evaluation.**	14–16
3	**Some relevant analysis/argument**, mainly linked to the question, with **relevant and precise supporting own knowledge. Reasonable structure, with some explanation** and **some awareness of different historical views** – but not all aspects of the question addressed.	11–13
4	Mainly **narrative in approach**, with **reasonable accurate knowledge**; but **limited focus**, and **no real analysis/explanation. Some structure**, but **links to the question are mainly unclear/implicit.**	8–10
5	**Limited relevant knowledge**, with a **few unsupported comments/assertions. Not well-structured**; and **not linked effectively to the question**, which is not really understood.	0–7

Student answers

The following extracts from student answers include brief examiner's comments, and a longer overall comment at the end. Those parts of student answers that are particularly strong and well focused (such as demonstrations of precise and relevant own knowledge, or examination of historical interpretations) will be highlighted in blue. Errors/confusions/irrelevance/loss of focus will be **highlighted in white**. In this way, you should find it easier to follow why marks were awarded or withheld.

Question 1

How important was Castro's leadership in the success of the Cuban Revolution?
[20 marks]

Skills

- Factual knowledge and understanding
- Structured, analytical and **balanced** argument
- Awareness/understanding/evaluation of historical interpretations
- Clear and balanced judgement.

Examiner's tip

Look carefully at the wording of this question, which asks you to consider **how** important Castro's leadership was. This is different from explaining **why** it was important and requires you to weigh Castro's leadership against other factors that contributed to the success of the revolution.

Student answer

The Cuban Revolution came about in 1959 as a result of the leadership of Castro. He began armed opposition in July 1953 by his raid on the Moncada barracks. The 26 July Movement was named after this, and Castro led the armed revolt that eventually achieved success in 1959. Castro's leadership was therefore at the heart of the revolution. However, this was not the only factor. There had been widespread anger in Cuba over Batista's coup of 1952 as well as resentment about US influence. Also, there were many economic and social problems, which Castro used to win support. Thus, Castro's leadership alone was not the sole explanation for the success of the revolution.

Examiner's comment

This is a clear and well-focused introduction, showing accurate knowledge of the topic and a good understanding of several of the general factors that contributed to the success of the revolution. Much now depends now on how much the answer develops a **judgement** about Castro's importance.

Previous attempts at revolution and change in Cuba had not succeeded. The dictatorship of Machado had ended in 1933 but the problems of corruption and different economic and social problems remained. Castro was determined to address these problems. As a student he had been a member of the reforming party and was influenced by the example of Chibás and before him the great 19th-century reformer Martí.

One of the reasons why Castro succeeded was that he seemed to follow a reforming tradition. He had strong reforming ideas and was a good speaker and an inspiring leader. He also set a heroic example when he attacked the Moncada barracks with a few dedicated followers, and later when he landed in the Granma with a few revolutionaries opposed by the whole of Batista's army. This heroism was very important in winning him popular support.

Fidel had been born in the east of Cuba and his family were sugar planters. Castro was educated in a church school at Havana and then in Havana University. There he read widely and became interested in student politics, especially those of the reforming Ortodoxos established in 1947. He had been appalled at the takeover by Batista and was determined to remove the dictator by force. He was prepared to risk his life by an attack on the Moncada barracks.

Examiner's comment

Although there is some accurate own knowledge, this is mostly **descriptive** material, and so is **not** explicitly linked to the demands of the question. The examiner is left to judge the importance of all this for the success of the revolution and it simply becomes an account of what happened.

Examiner's comment

This paragraph shows awareness of an aspect of historical debate, although these different interpretations are merely mentioned, with no attempt to **evaluate** them. However, the main point is that all this information is largely irrelevant, and so will not score any marks. The candidate is thus wasting time when they should be writing about the importance of military factors, not answering a question about whether Castro was a communist.

There has been some debate about whether these heroic events are part of Castro's commitment to forming a communist society when he got into power, or whether at this stage Castro was more of a nationalist reformer, opposed to the US and wanting to put into practice earlier ideas about reform and nationalism. Some of his biographers stress that he had read and studied Marx, while others use the speeches Castro gave at his trial and when he got into power to show that he was not really a dedicated communist.

Castro's ability to sustain a guerrilla war in the Sierra Maestra and win valuable propaganda, such as through the interview he gave to the reporter Herbert Matthews, not only allowed the revolutionaries to survive but also gave them fame around the world, winning attention for their cause. Castro's policies were also important in gaining the support of the local people in Oriente province.

In 1958, Batista launched a major campaign against the rebels, sending large forces to encircle them. However, this failed and Castro was able to go on the offensive. He sent Che Guevara into central Cuba and he captured a vital armoured train and took the city of Santa Clara.

Castro was a strong leader and his careful treatment of the people and his propaganda ensured local support. Batista's armies were not as strongly motivated as Castro's forces, and lacked US help.

By late 1959 it was clear that Batista was going to lose. He tried to stage elections, but this did not help. He handed over power to the army chief but this could not stop the revolution and Batista fled abroad, taking a large amount of money with him. Castro's forces entered Havana. Castro did not take power as a dictator but appointed a liberal judge as president. However, he wanted to pass reforms to help the people and was determined that his revolution was going to make big changes for ordinary Cubans.

Examiner's comment

Again, there is accurate own knowledge in this section – but this is not what the question requires. Despite an opening paragraph that suggests the correct focus might now be applied, the candidate instead produces more narrative, which is not weighing the importance of Castro's leadership against other explanations for the success of the revolution.

Thus Castro's leadership was very important in the success of the revolution, but other factors were significant, too. The first was Batista. He had a long history of influence in Cuba since leading the Sergeant's Revolt of 1933, which ended Machado's dictatorship. Batista had been influential behind the scenes in the 1930s and brought about some reforms in Cuba. He had stood as president in 1940 under the new constitution he had introduced, and he ruled until 1944. He later returned to power in a coup backed by the army in 1952.

There was also the economic factor of the dependence of Cuba on sugar production. Sugar had been the most important cash crop for Cuba, but many felt that it made Cuba too dependent on the USA. In addition, profits from sugar were falling from their peak during the Second World War, and there were many underemployed Cuban sugar workers.

[There then follow several more paragraphs giving detailed and accurate accounts of different elements, including nationalism and other revolutionary groups in Cuba, such as the student organisations and revolutionaries in the cities.]

Thus many factors brought about the Cuban Revolution. Castro's leadership offered hope and inspiration and also provided a heroic example. He was the revolutionary who gained worldwide publicity and his 'bearded ones' had a distinct identity.

Castro linked with past heroes rather than Marxists, who had relatively little support in Cuba and who had been associated with the Batista regime in the 1940s. Part of Castro's success, therefore, was due to a weak opposition. Batista's regime was corrupt, had connections with US gangsters and was losing US support. This meant that his soldiers were not well-motivated when faced with fighting a difficult guerrilla war in the mountains. People saw in Castro a reformer who would help the unemployed and those who were seriously underemployed because of the dependence on sugar. So it was not just Castro's leadership but his ability to use existing discontents that helped the revolution.

Examiner's comment

There is some relevant focus on the demands of the question, and some relevant discussion of the relative importance of different elements.

So, in conclusion, Castro's leadership is the key to the Cuban Revolution. Other groups helped and Batista's regime was unpopular, but without Castro's heroism and self-confidence, the revolution would not have succeeded.

Examiner's comment

There is then a brief conclusion, which makes a valid judgement. Unfortunately, this is not a **supported** judgement and comes rather suddenly as an assertion – very little information has been given earlier about other groups. There has also been no sustained analysis of the relative importance of different factors in the success of the revolution.

Overall examiner's comments

There is plenty of accurate own knowledge in this answer, but unfortunately it is **not used directly enough**. While there is some analysis, it is mostly descriptive. The bulk of the answer is not really focused on the demands of the question. However, there are brief sections which **are** relevant, so the answer is probably just good enough to be awarded a mark in Band 4 – probably 10 marks. What was needed was an answer that focused more on explaining different factors' links with the success of the revolution, and comparing them with the impact of Castro's leadership.

Activity

Look again at the simplified markscheme, and the student answer on pages 224–28. Now draw up a plan focused on the demands of the question. Then try to write several paragraphs that will be good enough to get into Band 1, and so obtain the full 20 marks. As well as making sure you address **all** aspects of the question, try to integrate into your answer some references **and** evaluation of relevant historians/historical interpretations.

Question 2

Compare the methods by which **two** military regimes in Latin America were able to consolidate their power in the period from 1945 to 1979. [20 marks]

Skills

- Factual knowledge and understanding
- Structured, analytical and **balanced** argument
- Awareness/understanding/evaluation of historical interpretations.

Examiner's tip

Look carefully at the wording of this question, which asks you to compare the methods used by two military regimes to consolidate their power. Questions like this show how important it is to revise **all** the bullet points in the sections you study. If you only select one regime for detailed study, you could seriously limit your options in the exam. To answer questions like this in the most effective way, it is best to structure your answer so that the comparisons/contrasts are brought out **explicitly**. In other words, draw up a rough plan with headings for 'comparisons' and 'contrasts' – then make a note of where aspects of their methods were similar under 'comparisons', and where/how they were different under 'contrasts'. Remember – don't just **describe** what their methods were: what's needed is explicit focus on similarities **and** differences.

Student answer

Although Paraguay and Argentina both witnessed military rule for a significant part of the period, there were considerable differences in the nature of the regimes, as Paraguay was ruled by Stroessner throughout this time, whereas Argentina had periods when the military was not in control and when a junta rather than individuals ruled the country. However, despite these differences, the regimes used similar methods to consolidate their power, relying to a large extent on terror. This took a wide variety of forms, as political parties, unions and terrorist groups were attacked. However, in Paraguay Stroessner used propaganda and also developed the cult of personality to consolidate his position. The regime in Argentina also used economic policies that favoured the élites, particularly landowners, as this encouraged their support for the regime. The final policy used by the military in Argentina was an appeal to patriotism and nationalism in an attempt to unify the country and detract from economic difficulties. However, it was this that finally toppled Galtieri's regime.

Examiner's comment

This introduction starts in a generally promising way. However, the final sentences in this paragraph are worrying, because such an approach will almost certainly result in a narrative of the two sets of policies with, at best, only some kind of implicit comparison/contrast. A narrative account without clear focus on the demands of the question is unlikely to get beyond Band 4.

Throughout the period, the greatest challenge to the consolidation of the military's power in Argentina was the Peronist legacy. Juan Perón had ruled Argentina from 1946 to 1955 and during his time in power he had cultivated the support of the working classes and the unions, bringing the latter firmly under his control. His policy of improving the conditions for workers through increased real wages and improved social conditions ensured their loyalty to the regime. He provided Argentina with a healthcare system and over 4000 new medical units were built. Education was also improved, with over 8000 new schools and 1000 kindergartens.

These developments ensured that the workers remained loyal, as they believed that Perón protected their interests. This meant that it would be very difficult for the military rulers to consolidate their position, as support for Perón remained strong. As a result, the military tried to outlaw Peronism.

Examiner's comment

This paragraph contains a lot of information, which is clearly the result of solid revision. However, it is mainly background material – there is little **on the actual methods used to consolidate power.**

Peronism was particularly strong at grass-roots level. In response, in 1956 the military regime declared Peronism a crime, banned the party from elections, shut down its organisations and seized its property. However, this had limited success, as its supporters returned blank voting papers in the 1956 elections and these represented a majority of the population. Although the policy of repression of the movement continued, the party was later re-legalised during the period 1966–73, as the military regime attempted to shore up its support, *showing that government tactics to consolidate its power had changed.* A similar repressive policy was followed towards the unions in Argentina. The military crushed the Buenos Aires dock strike with force, but most notoriously it opened fire on a student union demonstration in Córdoba in 1969, killing 14 people. There were also some attempts to get the unions to collaborate with the regimes. CGT, a former bastion of Peronist support, was won over.

Examiner's comment

Again, there is a lot of accurate own knowledge – this time, a little of it is relevant, as it deals with the methods used to consolidate power. However, so far this answer has been largely a descriptive account – there has been no attempt to address the key issue of similarities/differences. This is the danger with taking such a 'one by one' approach to questions like this that ask for comparison.

The policy of terror to consolidate power reached its peak in the last period of military rule in Argentina. The military had been responsible for the murder of the former president Aramburu, and had also carried out a high-profile attack on a high-security jail, during which 25 prisoners were released. Faced with this well-financed challenge of guerrillas and terrorists from both ends of the political spectrum, the government met terror with terror. The period from 1976 to 1983 has become known as the 'Dirty War', as the government arrested opponents and suspected opponents of the regime. This policy was so extensive that the government was responsible for the disappearance of some 10,000 to 20,000 people. This policy served to create fear among many of the population and severely limited criticism of the regime, although it did not prevent the protests of the Mothers of Plaza de Mayo, which brought the regime international discredit.

Examiner's comment

Again, there is plenty of accurate own knowledge and explanation, some of which supports the argument as to the methods used to consolidate power. However – as in the previous paragraphs – no comparisons/contrasts with the style and policies of Stroessner have been made.

[There then follow several paragraphs on the way that economic policies and the appeal to nationalism were used to consolidate power. However, no information is given about Paraguay.]

Both regimes used terror to consolidate their power, but in Paraguay terror was more extensive at the start of the period, whereas in Argentina it was at the end, during the period of the Dirty War. In Paraguay, terror prevented the development of opposition, whereas in Argentina it was used more as a weapon to destroy the opposition. Imprisonment and torture were regular features of both regimes, as they intimidated the population and prevented opposition from developing. However, the regimes did not rely solely on repression to consolidate their power.

Both regimes also attempted to win support from the landowning élites by policies that favoured agriculture and preserved the large estates at the expense of the peasantry.

Where the regimes did differ was that in Paraguay, where Stroessner dominated the period of military rule, he was able to develop a cult of personality. This was not possible in Argentina, as military rule was not dominated by a single individual.

Examiner's comment

This is a good conclusion – brief and to the point. However, it is not a supported judgement or conclusion as there is nothing about Stroessner's policies in the main body of the essay. The only real reference to him comes here in the conclusion.

Overall examiner's comments

Although there is precise and accurate own knowledge, the essay is basically about Argentina and the military regimes after the fall of Perón. If the candidate had written about Paraguay in the same way, then the answer would have been awarded 10 marks, even though it has not really addressed the demands of the question. To achieve higher marks, the answer would have had to sustain a comparison and contrast based not on one 'story' after another, but on themes of consolidation.

Because this answer deals almost exclusively with Argentina, it can only be awarded a mark in Band 5 – probably 7 marks at most. To reach Band 3 or higher, the answer would need some **explicit and well-structured treatment of comparisons and contrasts, with consistent analysis of both similarities and differences.**

Activity

Look again at the simplified markscheme, and the student answer on pages 230–33. Now try to draw up a plan, with a structure focused on the demands of the question. Then try to write your own answer, making sure you consistently make comparisons and contrasts – so that the answer can get into Band 1 and obtain the full 20 marks.

Further information

Sources and quotations in this book have been taken from the following publications.

Bethell, Leslie. 1993. *Argentina Since Independence*. Cambridge, UK. Cambridge University Press.

Bryant, Nick. 2006. *The Bystander: John F. Kennedy and the Struggle for Black Equality*. New York, USA. Basic Books.

Camarcho, George. 1973. *Latin America*. London, UK. Allen Lane.

Cannon, Terrance. 1981. *Revolutionary Cuba*. New York, USA. Thomas Y. Cromwell.

Chomsky, Aviva. 2011. *A History of the Cuban Revolution*. London, UK. Blackwell.

Creighton, Donald. 1970. *Canada's First Century*. Basingstoke, UK. Macmillan.

Dallek, Robert. 2003. *John F. Kennedy: An Unfinished Life*. London, UK. Penguin.

Farber, Samuel. 2006. *The Origins of the Cuban Revolution Reconsidered*. Chapel Hill, USA. University of North Carolina Press.

Ferrell, Robert. 1984. *Truman*. London, UK. Thames and Hudson.

Fuento, Alejandro de la. 2001. *A Nation for All*. Chapel Hill, USA. University of North Carolina Press.

Genovese, Michael. 1990. *The Nixon Presidency*. Westport, USA. Greenwood Press.

Giglio, James M. 1991. *The Presidency of John F. Kennedy*. Kansas, USA. Kansas University Press.

Gonzalez, Edward. 1974. *Cuba Under Castro: the Limits of Charisma*. London, UK. Houghton Mifflin.

Hedges, Jill. 2011. *Argentina: A Modern History*. London, UK. I.B. Tauris.

Heywood, Andrew. 2000. *Key Concepts in Politics*. Basingstoke, UK. Palgrave Macmillan.

Howard, Michael and Louis, William. 1998. *Oxford History of the Twentieth Century*. Oxford, UK. Oxford University Press.

Kapcia, Antoni. 2000. *Cuba: Island of Dreams*. Oxford, UK. Berg.

Mooney, P. and Brown, C. 1979. *Truman to Carter: Post-war History of the United States of America*. London, UK. Arnold.

Moore, Carlos. 1998. *Castro, the Blacks and Africa*. Los Angeles, USA. UCLA.

Morgan, Iwan. 2002. *Nixon*. London, UK. Hodder Arnold.

Patterson, James T. 1984. *Oxford History of the USA 1945–1974*. Oxford, UK. Oxford University Press.

Patterson, James T. 1998. *Grand Expectations: The United States 1945–1974*. Oxford, UK. Oxford University Press.

Pérez-Stable, Marifeli. 1993. *The Cuban Revolution*. Oxford, UK. Oxford University Press.

Schlesinger, Arthur Jr. 1965. *A Thousand Days*. London, UK. Andre Deutsch.

Schweikart, Larry and Allen, Michael. 2004. *A Patriot's History of the United States*. New York, USA. Sentinel.

Smith, Lois and Padula, Alfred. 1993. *Sex and Revolution: Women in Socialist Cuba*. Oxford, UK. Oxford University Press.

Sorensen, Theodore. 1965. *Kennedy*. New York, USA. Harper & Row.

Williamson, Edwin. 1992. *The Penguin History of Latin America*. London, UK. Penguin.

Zinn, Howard. 2010. *A People's History of the United States*. New York, USA. Harper Perennial.

Further reading

Anderson, Jon Lee. 1997. *Che Guevara: A Revolutionary Life*. London, UK. Bantam.

Bethell, Leslie. 1993. *Argentina Since Independence*. Cambridge, UK. Cambridge University Press.

Bethell, Leslie. 1994. *The Cambridge History of Latin America, Volume 6, Part 1: Latin America Since 1930: Economy, Society and Politics*. Cambridge, UK. Cambridge University Press.

Blanksten, George. 1974. *Perón's Argentina*. Chicago, USA. University of Chicago.

Bothwell, Robert. 2006. *The Penguin History of Canada*. London, UK. Penguin.

Bothwell, Robert, Drummond, Ian and English, John 1990. *Canada, 1900–1945*. Toronto, Canada. University of Toronto Press.

Dallek, Robert. 2003. *Kennedy: An Unfinished Life*. London, UK. Penguin.

Gott, Richard. 2005. *Cuba: A New History*. New Haven, USA. Yale University Press.

Griffith, Robert and Baker, Paula. 2001. *Major Problems in American History Since 1945*. London, UK. Houghton Mifflin.

Hedges, Jill. 2011. *Argentina: A Modern History*. London, UK. I.B. Tauris.

Kapcia, Antoni. 2008. *Cuba in Revolution*. London, UK. Reaktion Books.

Kearns Goodwin, Doris. 1991. *Lyndon Johnson and the American Dream*. New York, USA. St Martin's Press.

Lewis, Daniel. 2001. *The History of Argentina*. New York, USA. Greenwood Press.

Lewis, Paul. 1980. *Paraguay Under Stroessner*. North California, USA. University of North Carolina Press.

McCullough, David. 1993. *Truman*. New York, USA. Simon & Schuster.

McNaught, Kenneth. 1973. *The Pelican History of Canada*. London, UK. Penguin Books.

Paolera, Gerardo della. and Taylor, Alan M. 2003. *A New Economic History of Argentina*. Cambridge, UK. Cambridge University Press.

Patterson, James T. 1998. *Grand Expectations: The United States 1945–1974*. Oxford, UK. Oxford University Press.

Pérez-Stable, Marifeli. 1993. *The Cuban Revolution*. Oxford, UK. Oxford University Press.

Reeves, Richard. 2002. *President Nixon: Alone in the White House*. New York, USA. Simon & Schuster.

Skidmore, Thomas. and Smith, Peter. 2005. *Modern Latin America*. Oxford, UK. Oxford University Press.

White, Christopher. 2008. *The History of El Salvador*. New York, USA. Greenwood Press.

Williamson, Edwin. 2009. *The Penguin History of Latin America*. London, UK. Penguin.

Wright, Esmond. 1996. *The American Dream: From Reconstruction to Reagan*. London, UK. Blackwell.

Index

Acknowledgements

The volume editor and publishers acknowledge the following sources of copyright material and are grateful for the permissions granted. While every effort has been made, it has not always been possible to trace all copyright holders. If any omissions are brought to our notice we will be happy to include the appropriate acknowledgement on reprinting.

Picture credits

Cover Interfoto/Pulfer/akg-images; p. 10 Getty Images; p. 21 Getty Images; p. 27 Library of Congress; p. 28 Time & Life Pictures/Getty Images; p. 31 Bettmann/Corbis; p. 35 David J. & Janice L. Frent Collection/Corbis; p. 36 Library of Congress; p. 40 Bettmann/Corbis; p. 43 AGIP/Epic; p. 51 AF Archive/Alamy; p. 56 ZUMA Wire Service/Alamy; p. 59 Flip Schulke/Corbis; p. 59 Cecil W. Stoughton/White House Press Office; p. 65 Getty Images; p. 70 Bettmann/Corbis; p. 73 Getty Images; p. 81 Time & Life Pictures/Getty Images; p. 87 Bettmann/Corbis; p. 90 AP/Press Association Images; p. 96 Bettmann/Corbis; p. 100 Bettmann/Corbis; p. 111 Keystone Pictures USA/Alamy; p. 115 AP/Press Association Images; p. 124 Getty Images; p. 128 Bettmann/Corbis; pp. 130–131 Bettmann/Corbis; p. 139 SZ Photo/Scherl/Mary Evans Picture Library; p. 144 Sales Archive Photos/Alamy; p. 146 Gamma-Keystone/Getty Images; p. 147 NY Daily News/Getty Images; p. 148 Getty Images; p. 168 The Granger Collection/Topfoto; p. 170 Gamma-Keystone/Getty Images; p. 179 Getty Images; p. 183 AFP/Getty Images; p. 185 Fabian Bimmer/Alamy; p. 187 AP/Press Association Images; p. 189 Bettmann/Corbis; p. 203 Bettmann/Corbis; p. 206 Bettmann/Corbis; p. 210 Getty Images; p. 216 Bettmann/Corbis.

 Produced for Cambridge University Press by
White-Thomson Publishing
+44 (0)843 208 7460
www.wtpub.co.uk

Series editor: Allan Todd
Development editor: Chris McNab
Reviewer: Alastair Dunn
Editor: Sonya Newland
Designer: Clare Nicholas
Picture researcher: Sonya Newland
Illustrator: Stefan Chabluk